The Use and Abuse of History

'Marc Ferro is remarkable in writing history enjoyed both by scholars and by people curious about the world in which they live and its past. He has explored everything from high politics to popular culture. His interests have taken him across narrow national boundaries and won him enthusiastic readers in many lands.'

Natalie Zemon Davis

'*The Use and Abuse of History* . . . has the singular effect of bringing into focus a dimension of historical awareness which is much more integral to the understanding of the contemporary world than we might have thought.'

The Times Literary Supplement

'Part of the necessary function of history is that, in advancing understanding of the past, it challenges and deflates myths, while at the same time explaining their origins and significance. This is conclusively demonstrated in Marc Ferro's study of the way in which history is taught around the world.'

Arthur Marwick, author of The New Nature of History

Marc
Ferro

The Use and Abuse of History

Or how the past is taught to children

Revised edition, with a new preface by the author

Translated by Norman Stone and Andrew Brown

 London and New York

Comment on raconte l'histoire aux enfants published 1981 by
Payot, Paris

English edition published 1984
by Routledge & Kegan Paul

First published in Routledge Classics 2003
by Routledge
11 New Fetter Lane, London EC4P 4EE
29 West 35th Street, New York, NY 10001

Routledge is an imprint of the Taylor & Francis Group

© 1981 Editions Payot & Rivages, Paris

Translation © 1984, 2003 Routledge

Translation of revisions and Preface to Routledge Classics
edition © 2003 Andrew Brown

Typeset in Joanna by RefineCatch Limited, Bungay, Suffolk
Printed and bound in Great Britain by
TJ International Ltd, Padstow, Cornwall

British Library Cataloguing in Publication Data
A catalogue record for this book is available from the British Library

Library of Congress Cataloging in Publication Data
A catalog record for this book has been requested

ISBN 0–415–28592–5

CONTENTS

PREFACE TO THE ROUTLEDGE CLASSICS EDITION

This work was written before the great events which left their mark on the last quarter of the twentieth century: the fall of communism in the East, the end of apartheid in South Africa, the confrontation with Islam – the challenge posed by Islam to the West, or more generally speaking the return of Islam.

And yet it seemed to me essential not to modify the 1980 text by a single comma – at the most, simply to add a couple of extra points – because the historical memory of societies resists political change and the progress of historical knowledge more than is usually imagined. On this last point, surveys show, for example, that the French continue to lay the blame for the 1940 defeat on the Popular Front, whereas many researchers both in France and abroad have proved that this was not at all the case. Another sign: it can be verified that since the crises which the different worlds of Islam have experienced over these last decades, the view of the history of the Arabs, Egyptians, Persians and Turks has barely changed since the first edition of this book, whose text has remained unchanged.

However, several modifications have been deemed necessary.

The French edition of 1992 included a few addenda on the USSR and Russia, Poland, South Africa, and Australia; likewise, I added a comparative study of the history of the Second World War.

In this new edition, aimed at an English-speaking public, these modifications have been preserved, and I will here add a few changes observed in France affecting history as it is taught to children.

First, as regards content.

Faced with the critique of the excesses of the nation-state – whether it was brown in Nazi Germany, red in the USSR, or 'red-white-and-blue' in French or British colonies – a powerful reaction of 'repentance' has found expression first and foremost in a condemnation of the behaviour of the Vichy government and the fate the Pétain regime reserved to the Jews living in France. Then this 'repentance' has been extended to the presentation of colonization, whose black pages have taken over from the rosy-spectacled and imperialist view of an earlier age. The ideology of human rights has replaced that of the nation-state.

Second, as regards method.

History is no longer simply narrated, but rather analysed through documents, engravings, drawings, etc., as if their selection were any less arbitrary than the telling of a certain story. In school textbooks, lay-out started to seem more important than text. It was up to the teachers and the children to reconstruct this history, rather than getting to know, and correct, the story of the nation, which however remains the historical memory of society, and gave it a meaning.

The excesses of this pedagogy have been amply demonstrated: 'children and teenagers don't know anything any more'. So we have returned to a more balanced conception, in which both narrative and analysis play a part. For History is as much a matter of passion as of reason.

PREFACE

Our image of other peoples, or of ourselves for that matter, reflects the history we are taught as children. This history marks us for life. Its representation, which is for each one of us a discovery of the world, of the past of societies, embraces all our passing or permanent opinions, so that the traces of our first questioning, our first emotions, remain indelible.

It is these traces which we must know or rediscover, both our own and those of other peoples, in Trinidad as in Moscow or Yokohama. It is a journey through both time and space. It has the quality of reflecting moving images from the past, for it is not simply that this past is different for everyone, but that everybody's memory changes with time, and that these images alter as knowledge and ideologies develop and as the function of history changes within society.

It is high time to confront these differing presentations of the past, for with the widening of the world's horizons, with its economic unification but continuing political disunity, our differing views of the past have, more than ever, become one of

the factors in conflict between states, nations, cultures and ethnic groups. To control the past is to master the present, to
legitimize dominion and justify legal claims. It is the dominant
powers – states, churches, political parties, private interests –
which own or finance the media or means of reproduction,
whether it be school-books or strip-cartoons, films or television
programmes. Increasingly, they are abandoning us all to a uniform past. Revolt comes from those to whom history is
'forbidden'.

And then, tomorrow, which nation, which human group will
still be able to control its own history?

Already, in the older countries, ancient communities or states,
like the Khazars of the Volga or the Kingdom of Arles, have seen
their identity dissolve in an anonymous past. Only recently,
opposing each other as if at a new Treaty of Versailles, historians
from France and Germany met to correct some frontier: what to
the one side was a massacre, appeared to the other a violation of
territory. In the East, from Prague to Ulan-Bator, every variety of
ethnic and national grouping finds its history explained by the
same model, that supposedly conceived by Marx, but revised by
Moscow. Seen from this capital, what difference really exists
henceforth between the history of Georgia and that of Armenia,
even if their separate national identity is recognized – not that
that, necessarily, is the case. Finally, in the rest of the world – the
'south' – societies are decolonizing their history, yet often with
the same instruments as the colonizer, constructing a history
which is the obverse of that which, not so long ago, had been
imposed upon them.

Thus today, in nearly every country, histories superimpose
themselves upon, or confront, each other: in Poland, for
example, what is presented in schools differs appreciably from
the history told at home. The Russians do not exactly play the
same role. Collective memory and official history thus confront
each other in a real test of force which shows, probably better

than the work of historians themselves, the problems which are
posed by history.

Provided we do not limit ourselves to the study of school
textbooks or strip-cartoons, nor to the present-day constitution
of the historical science, the history which is taught to children,
to adults, will also be able to tell us something about the identity
of a given society and its status across time. For example, the
history of the Armenian people which is taught in Soviet
Armenia, that which is learnt by the children of the Armenian
diaspora (and by many of the children of Armenia, though at
home, after supper), and the picture which is painted in the
universal historical 'vulgate', constitute three different versions.
It is by no means certain that the last-named has more reality or
legitimacy than the others.

Independently of its scientific vocation, history effectively
exercises a double function, both therapeutic and militant. At
different times the 'cause' of this mission has changed, but not
its significance: in Franco's Spain it was to glorify Christ the
King; during the Republics in France, the nation and the state; in
the USSR or in China it is no less missionary as regards the
communist party; the talk of science and methodology are no
more than fig-leaves covering the nakedness of ideology. Bene-
detto Croce wrote, at the beginning of the century, that history
pinpoints the problems of its own times more fully even than
those of the era about which it is supposed to be concerned.
Thus, both alluding to the Russian Middle Ages, Eisenstein's
Alexander Nevsky and Tarkovski's *Andrei Rublev* tell us, in the one case
about Stalinist Russia and its fear of Germany, and in the other
about Brezhnev's USSR, its fight for liberty and its hatred of the
Chinese. The history which is taught today to young Africans
teaches us as much about contemporary problems of the black
continent as it does about its past. Children's history books are
written to glorify the great empires of the African past, whose
splendour is contrasted with the decadence and decline of feudal

Europe during the same era: the therapeutic function is clearly expressed. Or else, also for topical reasons, the difficult question of the conflict with Islam is deleted, mitigated or even placed in doubt altogether by the use of the conditional.

In the Caribbean, where one sees a population cut off from its roots (blacks, Chinese, Indians, etc.), the history taught to children transforms the descendants of former slaves or coolies into citizens of the world who have the unique advantage of partaking in all the cultures of humanity. The history of slavery is presented in such a fashion that the black child of Jamaica pities less the fate of his ancestors than that of the poor English who, in the history books, were the first slaves sent off to Italy at the time of Caesar.

As for 'militant' party history, one naturally thinks above all of the sort of manipulation practised in the USSR: for a long time Trotsky had been thrown into oblivion and there was mention only of Stalin; then for ten years Stalin had disappeared, or almost, and Trotsky was cited frequently, though only to condemn him. But in the USA the evolution of history teaching is even more radical: it expresses an ideological transfer from 'melting-pot' to mixed 'salad-bowl', where different cultures keep their identity.

In spite of these changes, there remains a matrix of history within each country: it is the dominant element that distinguishes the collective consciousness of each society. It is therefore important to know the elements of this matrix. The stories and beliefs which constitute it – whether we talk of the fighting hero Shivaji in India, or the misfortunes of Yoshitsun in Japan, or the adventures of Chaka, king of the Zulus, or of Joan of Arc in France – contain a 'myth' more powerful than any analysis: this is to the benefit of the historian as much as the reader.

Thus I am not trying to express a universally valid historical truth, which would be absurd and imaginary; I am trying only to put together the diverse images of the past, as it is seen in various countries of the world. It might, of course, be that these images represent the exact opposite of others and are even factually wrong: in this case I hope I shall be allowed, when necessary, to restore the truth, as a humble professional exercise.

No doubt my survey of the first images of history will not always tell the whole story of the history taught to Soviet children or the children of Trinidad. I shall nevertheless try, in each case, to give an overall representation that is as faithful as possible, for it is this overall vision which is at the origin of our image of others and ourselves. If need be, I shall juxtapose conflicting interpretations of a particular problem, but I observe some limits in this, for what interests me here is the identity of each national history, the vision of the past which is proper to each.*

My aim is to question the traditional conception of a 'universal history'. I do not begin with the Pharaoh and end with Khomeini, or the vicissitudes of Poland. For such a methodology would automatically commit itself to a teleological vision of history, whether it be Christian, Marxist, or simply associated with the idea of progress. This way of writing was, though tacitly, narrowly Eurocentric, since other peoples only 'entered' the history books with their 'discovery' by the Europeans. In this book I have avoided such methods. My general approach will, I hope, have a readily comprehensible logic; I shall not fatigue the reader with efforts to justify it and only hope that the reader will follow my lay-out.

We shall encounter history as seen from Europe several times, but only in its relationship with the rest of the world. As regards other aspects of this history which we all know, it would be impossible, in the present context, to deal with more than one feature or other.

* So in this new edition I add a comparison between the different versions of the Second World War – that developed by the Anglo-Americans and that developed by the Germans (in West and East Germany), and by the Soviets and the Spanish (who were, in their own way, neutral between 1939 and 1945).

As far as the substance and content of history seen from Europe are concerned, let me only say that they are the same, or much the same, whether you are in Paris, or Milan, or Berlin, or Barcelona, or Lisbon, or even Zagreb. History is seen as the history of the West, and you encounter the same kind of ethnocentricity, though at various levels; there is a European level, taking Europe, as against the peoples of Asia or Africa, but also there is a level of ethnocentricity inside the European continent itself, in that, for instance, Russian history is particularly studied after Peter the Great, that is, from the time when Russia was 'Europeanized'. In this way Europe is identified, in the main, both with Christianity and with technical progress. The second level of ethnocentricity is shown for every nation in its relationship with its neighbours. In France, for instance, once Charlemagne's name has been mentioned, that is about all we hear of the Holy Roman Empire, even though it went on for nine centuries – mention is rather made of its end in 1806, the better to illustrate the share which Napoleon took in it. In the same way, the French underrate the importance of the Romantic movement which flourished in Germany and influenced all of Europe; in France the stress is, rather, on the effects, within Germany, of the 1789 revolution. This ethnocentricity of the second type has been developed particularly in France, Spain, Germany and England, though less so in Italy, where the nation-state was a latterday creation. On the other hand, history in Italy has an ethnocentricity of a third type (as in France), by which northern Italy (or northern France) is emphasized at the expense of the southern provinces. In Great Britain this feature has been corrected for many years, in that the individual histories of Wales, Scotland and Ireland have been analysed in their own terms, and not simply in their relationship with London and the British government.

The aim of this book is so truly vast and megalomaniacal, that I must confess and justify its inadequacies.

Selecting the fifteen or twenty societies which figure in this book would imply research on a still larger corpus of material than textbooks, films, cartoons, historical novels, etc., in count-less foreign languages, not to speak of the study which is needed on each separate culture, on the historical record of each coun-try, and on the changes in its historiography. I have not aban-doned any of this, but what I have abandoned is the idea that each chapter can be a doctoral thesis. A whole life would not be sufficient for this; and even then it would be in vain, in that once I had finished my reading it would be necessary to go back to the books, films or other products which would have been produced in the mean time.

There is thus a serious inequality of treatment between the chapters, and I am well aware that certain analyses are more lightweight than others, certain sections only descriptive, and the pedagogical problems not approached as often as would be desirable;* but at least I have managed to tie this panorama together without any serious gaps (I hope) and in future edi-tions I will be able to turn into whole chapters matters only put forward here in the form of modest 'notes'.

* The Index will serve to show in which countries these problems have been approached (Nazi Germany, France, USSR, Poland, USA, etc.).

FOREWORD TO THE 1992 EDITION

This new edition preserves intact the original text, which thus still bears the traces of its growth – and also expresses the time it was written in. Any modification would constitute a mere face-lift.

Nonetheless, as History has continued to develop, it has transformed the situation of history as it was being taught in 1981, especially in the East. So I have added a supplementary discussion to the chapter on the USSR, dealing with 'History in the USSR since perestroika', and I have included a few additional lines to the chapter on Poland.

ACKNOWLEDGMENTS

This book, which I have enjoyed, has also been enjoyed by those who have lent me their help; and so it pleases me all the more to thank them, and none more so than P. Sorlin who knows that, in his own way, he has been at the roots of this book.

Then I must also thank friends and students who have been kind enough both to obtain books and to translate them for me: Magda Wassef for Iraq and Egypt; Mahyar Djahaderian for Persian; Eliane Blondel for Polish; M. Blaise and Michel Cartier for Chinese; Klaus Wenger and M.-J. Patrix for some of the German works; Olga de Orellana for Mexico; Ch. Lemercier for Turkish. Others have introduced me to new cultural worlds and acted as guides: the help of Pierre-François Souyri in matters Japanese has been incomparably valuable.

In addition, Michel Cartier and J. L. Domenach for China, Catherine Coquery-Vidrovitch for Black Africa, Lucette Valensi for the Islamic world and Krzysztof Pomian for Poland (who also kindly agreed to read the relevant chapter). Claire Mouradian for Armenia, Gilles Veinstein for Turkey, J. P. Berthe for Mexico all pointed me towards useful reading.

For France, I would have been lost without the enlightening and friendly help of Alice Gérard, and I am also grateful to Christian Amalvi who allowed me to read the unpublished manuscript of his thesis.

I have certainly not used as much as I had hoped of the various works I have received on Indonesia, Israel, Switzerland or Croatia, but I am grateful to all who sent them to me, particularly F. Garçon, M. Friedmann, and M. Pouchepadass, who obtained for me the essential books on the history of India and corrected the Indian chapter, a service that H. Moniot also kindly did for my chapter on Black Africa.

As always, my debt to the Bibliothèque de Documentation Internationale Contemporaine cannot ever be paid. This time, however, I have had other creditors, particularly the Bibliothèque de la Maison des Sciences de l'Homme; I also owe much to the Franklin Library and the University Libraries of Stanford, Yale, Manoa (Hawaii) and Columbia, at New York, the Bibliothèque du Centre Russe de l'Ecole des Hautes Etudes, and the Centre Africain; and finally to J.-L. Charmet, whose knowledge of iconography is incomparable.

Finally, my thanks to Marylène Daudier, of Editions Payot, who has painstakingly edited the manuscript.

'Tell me, mother, why do people hate the Jews so much?'
'Because they killed the infant Jesus and poisoned the wells. That is what I learnt when I was small, in the catechism.'

Heydrich: 'I know all this is a pack of lies, but who cares; the tradition can be useful.'

Holocaust

Brussels, during the Occupation

The Helper. So why don't you want to go on hiding this child any more?

The Citizen. Because he's a thief.

Helper. A thief . . . but he's not even four years old.

Citizen. All the same, he's still a thief.

Helper. How can that be? Tell me what he's stolen.

Citizen. He stole the Infant Jesus.

Helper. He stole the Infant Jesus?

Citizen. Yes, my wife and I were preparing the crib for Christmas and surreptitiously he stole the Infant Jesus.

Helper to the Jewish child. Is this true, did you steal the Infant Jesus?

The Child, obstinately. It's not true, I didn't steal it, I didn't steal it.

Helper. Come on Samuel, tell us the truth; these people don't want to do you any harm; you know very well that they are sheltering you from the Germans.

The Child, in tears. I didn't steal him, I didn't steal him; but the little baby Jesus, he is Jewish, and I hid him; I sheltered him from the Germans.

From the film by E. Hoffenberg and M. Abramovitch,
As if it were yesterday, 1980

1

'WHITE HISTORY', A VESTIGE: JOHANNESBURG

CHRONOLOGY

1488	Bartholomew Diaz rounds the Cape of Good Hope.
6 April 1652	Jan Van Riebeeck lands near the Cape. He represents the Dutch East India Company.
1658	First arrival of slaves from Angola.
1685	Revocation of the Edict of Nantes: immigration of French Huguenots.
18th C.	Beginning of the struggle between the Boers and the Xhosa, the Zulus and ultimately the other Bantu peoples.
1795	End of the East India Company. Establishment of the Batavian Republic. The British occupy the Cape.
1806–14	South Africa becomes British.
1833	The British abolish slavery.

1837–54	The Boers' Great Trek under the leadership of A. Pretorius. Boer victory over the Zulus at the Battle of Blood River.
1839	Proclamation of the Republic of Natal.
1843	The British annex the Republic of Natal.
1852	Foundation of the Republic of Transvaal.
1877	First annexation of Transvaal by the British.
1879	End of the Zulu kingdom.
c.1880	Discovery of diamonds in Kimberley and gold in Johannesburg.
1881	First War of Independence in Transvaal: Kruger defeats the British at Majuba Hill.
1885	Discovery of gold in Witwatersrand; massive influx of British immigrants, the Uitlanders. Cecil Rhodes, Prime Minister of the Cape and President of the De Beers Company, apologist of British imperialism, seeks to dominate Kruger's Transvaal.
1887	Cecil Rhodes annexes Zululand.
1899–1902	Second Boer War. Lord Kitchener and Lord Roberts victorious after three years of fighting.
1910	Birth of the Union of South Africa, a British dominion.
1913–26	The Native Land Act forbids blacks from acquiring land outside the Reserves. The Colour Bar Act excludes them from qualified employment.
1925	The Dutch (Afrikaaner) language becomes the official language next to English.
1931	South Africa becomes independent.
1948	Dr Malan's apartheid programme: separate development of races.
1959	Establishment of the nine autonomous Bantu regions.

1960	First major black riots in Johannesburg; sixty-nine are killed in the repression.
1975	Soweto riots, harshly repressed.
	Intervention of the UN, which condemns apartheid.
1990	First of the measures which will lead progressively to the abolition of apartheid.

'White' history is moribund; but the 'whites'' history is not.

Selecting systematically the school textbooks of several European nations, Roy Preiswerk and Dominique Perrot have made up a record of the stereotypes underlying this 'white' history, the principles behind its periodization, the principal values stressed by the whites in comparison with the rest of the world – respect for law and order, national unity, sense of organization, monotheism, democracy, settlement, industrialization, the march of progress, etc. Much of the same can be found in every European country.

However, during the last half-century this type of history has been under scrutiny. True, the very attack on it has, in a sense, been 'white', but, nevertheless, it is clear that the struggle for independence from the colonizing world has been the principal agent of a far-reaching revision. Against the overwhelming pressure of History in process, 'white' history has conceded ground; but only step by step, and in proportion to the process of decolonization.

During the 1950s, for example, as Denise Bouche notes for the history of Black Africa, some minor concessions were made in the school textbooks: the Toucouleurs of El Hadj Omar, who had resisted the French conquest in 1870, are no longer called 'fanatical Moslems'; while Omar no longer 'pillages' the Bambouk, he 'conquers' it. Even in the former colonial powers, diplomatic expediency and prevailing fashions required a more considerate policy. For example, in 1980 there disappeared from the French third-form textbook, Hatier, an illustration from 1907 showing some Moroccan corpses in Casablanca: it had as its caption, 'A street after the passage of the French.'

However, if in the West this sort of history is disappearing in the textbooks, it remains alive and well in the collective consciousness. There will be many opportunities to demonstrate this.

Yet, apart from South Africa, there no longer exists, as such, a 'whites'' history, whether in Europe or, obviously, still less intact, outside it; it is disappearing by itself. In the extra-European world seeking to bring its cultural past back to life, there survives hardly more than a single 'whites'' history in its pristine conditions: only that which is taught in the country of apartheid, to the little white children of Johannesburg.

In the Africa of the Afrikaaner, history is not only a matter of 'white' origins which, in the words of Frantz Fanon means 'the history of the white man and not those whom he oppresses, rapes, plunders and murders.' History also draws equally upon the 'Christian' tradition: the Bible and the rifle have always been, for the Boer, in those huge open spaces of the country, the companions of his fear and solitude.

A statement by the 'Institut vuur Christelijke-nasionale Onderwijs' (ICNO) epitomizes both the Christian and racist objectives of history teaching: it dates from 1948 and reiterates formulae or themes which had already been launched in the aftermath of the French Revolution, when J. A. de Mist, having attempted, vainly, in 1804, to laicize education, found his reforms attacked and then annulled.

> The instruction and education of white children must be based upon the conceptions of their parents, hence it must be

founded upon the Holy Scriptures ... love of what is our country, its language and its history.

History must be taught in the light of revelation and must be seen as the accomplishment of God's will (Raadsplan) for the world and humanity. We believe that the Creation, the Fall and the Resurrection of Jesus Christ are historical facts of capital importance and that the life of Jesus Christ is the great turning-point in the history of the world.

We believe that God willed separate nations, separate peoples, and gave to each its vocation, its tasks and its gifts. Our youth can only continue, in faith, the tasks of its elders if it has a knowledge of history, that is to say, a clear vision of the nation and its heritage. We believe that after our maternal language, a patriotic history of the nation is the only means by which we can love one another.

FROM THE GREAT TREK TO MARCO POLO

The fundamental event in Afrikaaner history, apart from the arrival of the first colonists, is the Great Trek of 1838. The Great Trek was the decision of an entire people to migrate across the country, in search of a land of refuge from the English, who had been masters of the Cape since 1815.

The Boers therefore wanted to maintain their beliefs, keep Afrikaans as the official language, maintain their traditional way of life and their 'traditional' modes of relations with the blacks, which the English intended to reform by giving to the Hottentots an equal status to those of the whites:

That was contrary to the law of God and opposed to the natural differences of race and religion. For every good Christian such a humiliation was intolerable: that is why we have preferred to separate ourselves in order to preserve our doctrines in all their purity.

This conception of the relations between blacks and whites was written in the constitution of the first Afrikaaner Republic of Transvaal, founded in 1858: 'There will be no question of equality between Whites and non-Whites, whether in the Church or within the State.'

For the Boers, the Great Trek, this Anabasis of several years, was, in the words of Marianne Cornevin, the precise equivalent of the Exodus of Moses, the search for the Promised Land. Its route is sacred and so are the dates and places through which it passed, such as the day on which Andries Pretorius made his call to the Almighty, the *Geloftedag*, when the Boer people contracted their pact with God. Inspired by this oath, they carried off a brilliant victory against the Zulus, at Blood River, and thirty years later the Boers restored the camp (*laager*) which had sheltered them during the battle. Later on they also restored the place where, in 1880, they fought their first war of independence against the English, who wanted to lay their hands on Transvaal: the late Lord Milner, who appreciated the symbolic significance of such objects, had had most of the place thrown into the Indian Ocean.

Thus these places, these stones and objects made up the triumphal stages of Afrikaaner history; in the children's history books there is a whole chapter given over to cataloguing them. This is a unique example. History in South Africa is as much a pilgrimage as an understanding of the past.

The voluntary decision to depart, the Great Trek, bore witness to the will of the Boers not to be oppressed by laws and customs contrary to their convictions. This symbolism imbues the spirit of their entire history.

Thus, the very choice for the opening chapter of the history book used in the fourth form: astonishingly, it concerns none other than . . . Marco Polo. The apparent function of this chapter is to place South Africa on the great routes of the voyages of discovery. But the facts which precede this show exactly why

Marco Polo turns up in this way in Johannesburg, and we become able to read this chapter in a different way, to see it as a sort of premeditation on the events that will follow.

How would you like to leave your country at the age of 19 to go on a journey that will last 24 years?

How would you like to visit an exotic country and become very rich?

How would you like to see strange things that you'd never seen before?

Our story begins a very, very long time ago, more than a thousand years before your great-grandfather was born. At that time people did not go far from the village of their birth, for it was very burdensome and very dangerous to travel.

There were some people, however, who went on distant journeys, pilgrimages; they returned to the Sacred Places, the most popular of which, although it was also the most difficult of pilgrimages, was the Holy Land, Palestine. There, the pilgrims met Arabs who slept on mattresses, and not on straw; who had spiced foodstuffs and all sorts of luxurious objects, such as silk, velvet, carpets and perfumes. Imagine what stories these pilgrims could tell when they returned to their country. In 1071, Jerusalem, the Holy Land, was captured from the Arabs by a people of warriors called the Turks. A large number of soldiers took part in these Holy Wars, or Crusades, against the Turks, before the Crusaders, in their turn, came to know the riches of the Orient.

The merchants of Europe, and above all the Italian towns of Genoa and Venice, predicted a huge demand in Europe for luxury goods, especially spices and silks. These were expensive products, for the merchants had to take great risks to get them and were often attacked by wild beasts or else by ferocious tribes, such as the Tartars.

It was at this time that Marco Polo left for his great voyage.

Marco Polo came from Venice, which was a very strange place to live in, for it had canals in place of streets. We would find the world a very odd place at this time for there were neither cars, nor planes, or even steam-ships then and nobody had even yet heard of South Africa. Even if we found ourselves in England, we would find it very hard to understand their language.

One day, Marco Polo's father and uncle, who were both merchants, left on a long business journey. As the years went by, and they failed to return, people began to believe that they had died. Nine years later, however, they suddenly reappeared in Venice and told of how they had discovered a marvellous country, called Cathay. Imagine how Marco must have marvelled when they told him of the wonders they had seen. He must have become even more excited when he learnt that Kublai Khan, the king of Cathay, had invited his father and uncle to return. Perhaps they would allow him to go with them.

And Marco Polo did go with them, two years later.

A whole host of surprises awaited Marco Polo on his arrival in the capital of Cathay. The first was the fact that they used paper for money. Nobody had ever heard of such a use for paper in Europe, for at that time printing had still not been invented, while the Chinese had practised it for centuries. Another strange custom was the nightly curfews. Nothing was spared to make Kublai Khan's palace the most beautiful in the world. And what wonders there were . . . ferocious animals and stables packed with thousands of white horses. Everywhere craftsmen were busy making silks and carpets; and here and there one might see an alchemist changing metal into gold or finding the elixir of life. Banquets and celebrations were continually taking place.

After he had been some time in the capital, Khanbalik, Marco Polo was asked what he found most surprising about China. Do you know what he replied?

His reply was astonishing.

To Marco, who came from a country, Venice, where only one religion was practised, it was amazing to see a king who allowed his subjects to practise different religions. Amongst Kublai Khan's subjects, there were Christians, Buddhists, Jews, Hindus and Mahommedans . . .

VIRTUES AND COURAGE OF THE BOERS

South Africa, land of liberty and religious *tolerance*: such is the first impression young children are given of this country. This introduction to history, with that reply by Marco Polo, is reinforced by other factors – the arrival of the Huguenot refugees, who escaped from Louis XIV, and of other countries' citizens, to find liberty in South Africa. It was these free citizens who made up the nation and who, later, in their struggles against the English came to attach less importance to gold and riches, than to the more noble values of the faith. . . . South Africa was a land of tolerance and welcome, but she was also a daughter of necessity.

> Since the Turks were barring all routes to the Orient, western merchants had to look for alternative routes to Asia. Sailing down the African coast, the Portuguese became the first to reach India by the south and the west: 'This is why our country has many ports with Portuguese names.' But they did not stay long 'for, conflict having broken out with the Hottentots, the king of Almeida and sixty-nine of his men were killed during a struggle to regain their ships anchored off the coast.' From that time on, the power of the Portuguese began to decline, while the English and Dutch were beginning to exploit the same route.
>
> Up until that time, the Portuguese, who had become extremely wealthy through their trade with India, kept all its benefits to themselves, and the route to India was a closely

guarded secret. The Dutch had to content themselves with retail trade. When in 1580, Philip II, King of Spain and Portugal, closed Lisbon to the Dutch, it was a devastating blow to them, for the Dutch depended upon this commerce. They were forced to seek the route to India by themselves. Hardy sailors, they thus came by our country.

After the death of Almeida, the Portuguese were too frightened to remain in South Africa, because of the Hottentots, and so the place became free; the Dutch thought the Hottentots might well be disposed to do a deal with them, particularly in the exchange of cattle. In spite of the mistrust of the Hottentots, they established themselves here. Some fifteen years later, in 1652, 200 Dutchmen, led by Jan Van Riebeeck, founded the first permanent establishment of South Africa. This is why 6 April is a national holiday.

ON THE HARDSHIP OF BEING A COLONIST

Van Riebeeck was eager to establish relations with the Hottentots, who had at their disposal a large number of cattle. At the beginning only a few berry-gatherers came to visit the colonists. One of them was called Herry, and it was through him that barter was established with the Hottentot tribes.

13 April. A cow and a plate are swopped for three copper plates, and a copper chain.

6 June. Disease is becoming rampant. Out of 113 men, only sixty are capable of work.

4 September. The first peas and carrots come through.

Van Riebeeck's men were discontented; they had been working hard and did not have enough to eat. One night, four of them tried to escape. But they came back and were punished with two years' work in the mines.

Unfortunately, the Hottentots were becoming equally mistrustful. They were giving cattle in exchange for various objects, and then coming back to steal back the cattle. Herry was no longer reliable. And then one day, all the cattle were found missing. There was so little food that the colonists were forced to eat monkeys.

The Hottentots stole cows and sheep. They reclaimed the areas which the Company had reserved and burnt all the pasture lands in protest. In order to solve the problem, Van Riebeeck built a wooden fence as a border; just as the Dutch had taken their cattle, the Hottentots now complained that they had taken their land. The quarrels did not stop. And finally a war broke out; the Hottentots lost the land which they had occupied near the Cape. As for the colonists, they now complained at no longer being able to do business with the Hottentots.

In order to provide the colonists with workers, after the Hottentots, Van Riebeeck decided to introduce slavery.

28 March 1658. One hundred and seventy slaves arrive from Angola. Most of them are ill and die en route. The remainder are girls or young boys who would be useless for the next four or five years.

17 April. The Company buys a building from a Portuguese merchant in order to establish a school for the young slaves. To encourage the slaves to become Christians, they are given a little glass of brandy and two pinches of tobacco after every sermon.

Introducing these slaves to the Cape colony was a great mistake. The colonists tended to leave them with the most difficult tasks.

The young colonists were no longer able to carry out the craftsmen's skills since there were slaves to do this work. But the importation of slaves helped towards the development of the colony. It was the labour of slaves which built most of the beautiful farms of our country. . . .

Mentzel, who visited South Africa at the beginning of the eighteenth century, described the mores of the period. The

Colonists and the administrators of the Company would call upon each other, to be offered wine or tea, a slave would offer round a pipe with a spill to light it. There was no social barrier preventing a colonist from marrying a member of the Company, no more than there was one between the most humble soldier and a girl of the highest birth.

Besides private slaves, who tended the fields and carried the produce to market, there were hundreds of slaves belonging to the Company, who were boarded in a special building. Unfortunately, these slaves were not very well treated; the law was strict and punishments harsh. Slaves would be hanged in public if they stole. Governor Tulbagh mitigated the laws concerning slaves; nevertheless they remained harsh. He showed his humanitarian sentiments by the way in which he treated his own slaves who were liberated on his death.

This 'idyllic' era came to an end with the Batavian Republic, which, being a 'fraternal republic' in the French system, sought to secularize institutions; the land was changed completely with the annexation of South Africa by Great Britain after the Congress of Vienna (1815).

The Boer colonist was now colonized by England.

Measures taken by the crown as regards the blacks caused, as noted above, the Great Trek of 1838, the establishment of the Boers beyond the Orange River, and then the foundation of the Republic of Transvaal in 1852. These events went together with the destruction of the Xhosa and of the Zulu kingdom.

Twenty years later, the discovery of diamonds and gold in the Transvaal asserted an irresistible pull upon fortune-hunters, and one of them, Cecil Rhodes, was able to associate the government of Queen Victoria with his conquering endeavours. Attempts by the English to appropriate Transvaal caused several wars between the Boers and the British, who finally won in 1902. South Africa became a dominion whose independence was recognized in 1947.

The Boers, henceforth called Afrikaaners, were once more dominant and once more asserted their idea of apartheid. The Bantus were settled in the 'Homelands' or territorial units with frontiers defined by Pretoria.

THE PROBLEM OF THE BLACK HOMELANDS AND THE JUSTIFICATION FOR APARTHEID

In history as taught to children, just as in 'white' memory itself, the Bantus are supposed to have left the Great Lakes and Central Africa for South Africa while the whites were moving north. The blacks were crushed as the Boers moved northwards so that the Voortrekkers are made out to have taken empty and owner-less lands after the massacres inflicted by the Zulus and the Matabele.

> The Trek Commissioners, sent out as scouts in 1834 to gather information on the region beyond the Orange River, sent back altogether favourable reports about the fertility of the soil and the quality of the pasture-land. It also appeared that the lands were *practically* void of inhabitants, since the natives had been massacred by the Zulus and the Matabele while all the survivors had hidden themselves.

Thus, in a sense, the whites' arrival saved the blacks from extermination. . . .

> The Trekkers managed to destroy the power of the Zulus and the Matabele. This resulted not only in the opening out of terri-tory to white people, but also in the end of the terrible wars which had devastated the country and destroyed all the smaller tribes. Thus, *without realizing it*, the Trekkers had saved the small tribes from annihilation by suppressing the power of those who had hitherto persecuted them.

The italics are mine and show how school-books are more subtle than politicians' speeches. The peremptory claim is that whites and blacks arrived at the same time over the Orange, for this gives them the rights of co-occupation. Marianne Cornevin has no prejudice as regards the legitimacy or effectiveness of this statement, but she has shown that, in fact, it is mythological. She refutes these assertions one by one, drawing upon the anthropological and archaeological works of the last fifteen years. These give evidence of the original occupation of the Transvaal area by the Bantus and their dispersal after the civil wars and the wars with the Anglo-Boers. They show that the present distribution of the Black Homelands is a result of the political force which expelled the blacks from the best land. It is thus wholly false to suggest, as the white version has it, that they now live within their original tribal territories.

A GOOD RACIST CONSCIENCE

How would you like to live with people who never wash themselves?

How would you like to wear nothing more than a loin cloth?

How would you like to spend your life in the desert and never go to school?

Do you know why foreign scholars and students are more interested in Bushmen than they are in the other white people who inhabit this country? Because the Bushmen of today are at the same stage of development as the Europeans were thousands of years ago. Studying the Bushmen helps us to discover how our ancestors lived when they were still in the Stone Age. . . .

Master hunters, disguising themselves as ostriches, imitating the cry of birds, tirelessly chasing hares across the fields, they end up by crushing the animal that falls into their hands. They also use poisoned arrows, following the tracks of an animal, stocking water in ostrich eggs, and sucking the liquid from vegetable plants with little pipes. An arrow stuck into the ground marks a Bushman's supply of water and it is forbidden for others to tamper with it.

One day a Bushman was invited to visit the Cape; he was shown all the wonderful inventions of the city. When he was asked what had impressed him most, he pointed to a tap. That one might turn water on at will seemed to him the most extra-ordinary thing of all. . . .

The Bushmen have strange ideas about religion. They have a number of gods, among them the moon, the rain and even the praying mantis.

They do not raise cattle as they have not yet reached this stage of development. When they see cattle belonging to white people or the Bantus, they hunt them as though they were wild animals. The owners naturally want to protect their cattle and therefore many Bushmen get killed. At one stage they were becoming so destructive that they had to be chased out like vermin. They were simply unable to understand that the ani-mals belonged to other people, and because of this they were almost totally eliminated as a race.

And here are the questions asked in the exercises at the end of the chapter:

What stage of evolution have the Hottentots reached?
(Answer: the stage of development)
In what way do they resemble the Bushmen?
(in their methods of hunting)
Which animals do they farm today?
(sheep and goats)
Why do they throw their witch-doctors into cold water?
(to exorcize them when they have cast an evil spell)
What does the word Hottentot mean?

(it comes from the Dutch *Huttentut*, meaning stammerer)
Name four tribal groups who share Hottentot blood.
(the Korana, Griquas, Orlam and Cape-Coloured).

These questions typify both the biological and racist vision of a white history, that only South Africa perpetuates openly. But it was a history that was glorified, not so long ago, in the works of the great 'colonizing nations'. Dominique Maingueneau has examined the school-books of the Third Republic, showing, through a strictly linguistic analysis, that hierarchical gradation of races and peoples is one of the founding principles of these textbooks, whether Le Tour de France par deux enfants (published for the first time in 1877, frequently republished up to 1914, and successfully reprinted very recently), or in geography and history books. P. Foncin's geography book, for instance, says in the chapter on African races that Bushmen were 'undeveloped beyond a pre-tribal stage . . . given over to a gross fetishism . . . and are small and uglier than monkeys. . . .' Using a wide variety of criteria, such works can be seen to have drawn up a hierarchy of peoples – depending on activity, habitat, social organization, etc. The Arabs, Berbers and Moors are placed at the top of the hierarchy.

Unconnected to the history of South Africa, but immediately following, come several chapters on general history which complete the third-form work. These chapters concern the progress of civilization and technology from ancient Egypt to the jet-engine. To place South Africa within the context of the broad history of the West is vital, for the general approach, as we have seen, is the vision of the colonists, the history of the colonists by those who experienced it, and shaped it. This is a long way from the same history seen from Europe, that is to say, a manifestation of the expansion of Europe and the early phase of imperialism.

On this point, as will be shown later, the Africans adopt the traditional perspective of history seen from Europe – though, as it were, in the reverse. The same problem recurs, even if the facts are not exactly comparable, with the Arabs' and the Israelis' versions of the Palestine conflict.

But it is the last chapter of the South African work that, for us, is most strange. It gives a detailed list of the historical sites of the Afrikaaner's Africa, the fifty places upon which the citizen must walk in order to base his roots more firmly in a country whose ownership might be challenged.

A comparable phenomenon can only be found in the USA and in Canada, although no real threat exists there, the Indians having been either penned into reservations or annihilated. Pilgrimages will impregnate citizens with a country in which they have only existed for a few generations. The experience of 'history with the feet' is an exercise in symbolic exorcism.

CREDO MUTWA: BLACK COUNTER-HISTORY

The Bantu tradition offers a radically different version. A witch-doctor, Credo Mutwa, gathered together several strands of history from his grandfather and from more distant relatives. 'These are the stories that the Elders tell to boys and girls, sitting open-mouthed around the fire at night – children whose faces are not yet marked by the life to come.'

Credo knows the white history. He contests not so much its accuracy, as its blind shamelessness.

> The 'superstitions' which are supposed to be so strange, are mentioned to show the Africans as inferiors. But suppose that a pig were let into a mosque at Dar-es-Salaam or that the effigy of the Virgin in a Sicilian procession were defiled?

For want of education, Credo argues, Bantus are still quite often ignorant of the kind of technical discoveries that have been made: they tend not to live near telegraph poles for fear that they might transmit conversations to the police; and the mechanics of photography or of finger-printing seem to hide the secrets of strange procedures, known only to the white man. But the Bantus and Bushmen also have a knowledge that the white man could never possess.

> Long before the Europeans, they knew how the solar system worked, and they knew nature better than the whites who had lost contact with it. They also had an elaborate code of laws, of which the Portuguese and Dutch not only did not even know the existence, but could not even have imagined.

From this point of view, the Kaffir wars have a quite different explanation from the white one. The most difficult to defeat had been the Xhosas, a fine nation which existed long before the Zulus, which had emigrated southwards after the destruction of the Munumutaba empire. They had mixed with the Hottentots and the Bechuanas. Unlike the Zulus, they fought from close range, not from a distance, as they had failed to devise proper javelins; they made mass use of knobkerries, eschewing shields altogether and they had developed the art of using a sling.

> Their speciality was cattle-thieving, for which they made use of ancestral talents and practises; but, like the Masai of Kenya, they did this more out of pleasure than need, and decorated the beast afterwards until it was hardly recognizable. However, in Xhosa law, it is just as legitimate for the thief to be robbed, as it is for he himself to rob. The Xhosas were perfectionists and stole in ever more refined ways, it being understood that his victim might do the same back to him.

In bartering, the Xhosa and the Portuguese or Dutch did not follow the same customs. For example, they accused the Xhosa of stealing when the latter, succumbing to temptation, were merely taking a gift on their departure, according to the Xhosa custom; 'had the Europeans not taken food when they came to feast with them?'

Above all, the English and Dutch did not know, on the eve of the Kaffir wars, that a cow cannot be bartered for material objects, even large quantities of metal or tobacco. The accepted practice in bartering was to give back one of a cow's offspring. In this way the whites were surprised that they had managed to dupe the Xhosa so easily that he had given away his cow, whereas the beast was only a sort of pledge in exchange for another deal at the same time, by which, several months later, the calf could be given back in the form of one or two other beasts. The colonists, not understanding the terms of the exchange, were more than a little surprised then, when, having dealt in hundreds of beasts, they found them disappearing after the supposed exchange.

Credo Mutwa blames the authors of these white textbooks, such as J. C. Johns, for not taking the trouble to analyse the different conceptions of law held by the Dutch on the one hand and the Xhosa on the other, treating the latter as 'superstitious people who did not understand the meaning of a treaty.'

True, a knowledge of the mores and customs of the Xhosa may not always be to their advantage. George Grey learnt this in the nineteenth century. Knowing their beliefs as to the need for 'respite' between two wars, he appreciated that the Xhosa would not attack the European settlements in the seven years following their defeat, unless a particular revelation incited them to. He managed to trick them into thinking there was such a revelation and that their gods were inciting them into a sort of collective suicide. In this way, without having to run the risk of renewed war, a part of the Xhosa community disappeared, by suicide.

The testimony of Credo Mutwa is not unique. There are efforts to create a 'black history' in South Africa, especially since the rest of Africa has become independent and the Soweto massacres have stirred international opinion against the racist practices of the Pretoria government.

This 'black history' contests the explanation of the past that (as Marianne Cornevin showed) legitimized the tribalization of natives and their dispersal to the arbitrarily-defined 'Home-lands', creating a moral and historical base for apartheid, while justifying the limited extent of the black 'Homeland' areas. As we know, in spite of their increasingly pressing and confident demands for the future, the blacks themselves have little opportunity, at least within the territory of South Africa itself, to affect the whites' history, and to change its contents.

Black history can only be written outside South Africa.*

* For fifteen years or so, white South African historians have attempted to correct the excesses of the historical tradition. The same phenomenon can be observed in Australia.

2

'DECOLONIZED HISTORY': BLACK AFRICA

THE STRATIFICATION OF HISTORY IN BLACK AFRICA

In Black Africa, knowledge of history is the outcome of a three-fold stratification. The oldest, oral tradition, works not only at the level of fact but also on that of myth – the legend of a Chaka, or of a Soundiata has as much reality as their real exploits, while a Torodo could identify with both the acts and the legend of El Hadj Omar. The second stratum is the history taught by the colonists. Finally, since independence, the work of African historians and today's Africanists has resulted in a general, and still evolving, reevaluation of African history: their conclusions are expressed, for instance, in the journal *Afrika Zamani* and its results may be seen in the various new school-books of French-speaking Africa. They offer a 'decolonized history'.

FROM HISTORY TO LEGEND: CHAKA, KING OF THE ZULUS

In African memory, the adventures of the Zulu kingdom, strengthened by Chaka (1816–28) are today a mixture of legend and historical fact. Black African literature, particularly in its French variant, has taken up this theme and given it a new function.

Chaka was a warrior of astonishing bravery, and he betrayed the king who would not install him as successor: he told the enemy where the king meant to fight a battle. Once his king had been captured, Chaka took his title and guaranteed Zulu supremacy over the Mtehtwas (1816). Almost immediately, he began to modernize military methods and reorganized the army, to which he gave Spartan training. Firstly, he changed the shape of the throwing spears which the Zulus traditionally made long so that they would travel further; he replaced them with shorter assegais, which could be used only in hand-to-hand combat. To train the Zulus, he developed physical exercises to strengthen the muscles of fighters whom he put upon an increased meat diet. He encouraged their training by introducing tests where he allowed the competitive spirit full sway.

Those successful in battle were offered nubile young women, the most beautiful at the king's disposal. The women, too, had been initiated to the ways of combat; and Chaka had them train where his bright-eyed warriors might see them. However, until the tests they were forbidden to have the slightest contact with the women, or even to touch them, on pain of death.

Circumcision ceremonies had already been abolished amongst the Zulus, and so enemies no longer benefited from the collective convalescence periods, when they could attack a tribe deprived of the support of its youngest men. With Chaka 'sexual energies were diverted from their reproductive functions and turned into a motor for war.' (Randles)

After twelve years of Chaka's rule, in 1828, a section of the army became tired of the military and administrative tyranny (which made the Zulu kingdom a great military empire which even the whites did not dare to challenge), rose in rebellion and assassinated Chaka.

Whether through impotence, homosexuality or morbid fear of ageing, Chaka left no descendants. His successors dismantled his military empire, whose power, nevertheless, continued to worry the Dutch and the English. During the Great Trek, the Boers pushed the Zulus back towards Natal after the victory at Blood River. Fifty years later, the English decided to subdue them further. Having suffered a severe defeat at the hands of the Zulus, during which the prince imperial, son of Napoleon III, was killed, they finally destroyed the Zulu army on 4 July 1879; thus ended the empire of the Men from the Sky.

This is a historical reconstruction. In the Zulu memory and, above all, beyond the frontiers of 'South Africa', Chaka's life represents another reality, half-way between myth and legend. This has more reality than History.

Chaka was, for some, black Jesus Christ, and for others the symbol of negritude; his adventurous life has clearly been transfigured by the oral and written tradition. To begin with, there is the *Chaka* of Thomas Mofolo, a black epic written by a religious Bantu, the Sesotho original of which remained for many years buried in a cupboard of the Missionaries of the Evangelical Society of Paris. His hero triumphs with the assistance of the Devil, and there are a thousand crimes, extortions and similar cruelties, before Chaka dies in a plot hatched by his brothers. In other versions, Chaka kills a leopard at nineteen, defeats the witch-doctors, locks an enemy queen alone into a hut with a ravenous hyena. From a hard core of 500 men, he builds an invincible army which, according to another tradition, soon swells to 400,000 and is destined to govern the world.

But the myth was soon strengthened as against Mofolo's

version. Praise replaces blame in Izibongo; with Nenekhaly-Camare's *Amazoulou*, Chaka becomes a collector of land, and so the symbol for African unity.

In the poems of L. S. Senghor, and the plays of Badian and A. A. Ka, Chaka was soon to be an object of increasing honour; he lived beyond death, or, rather, submitted to death, which would be a liberation, provided his work of resurrecting African power were understood by the Africans whose history he had begun. If for the Christian Mafolo, Chaka's death symbolized the defeat of evil, now it meant the heroic sacrifice of a man who was the founding-father of a true African state. Once he was dead, the whites were free to enslave Africa and so his death meant the End.

> We'll be turned into the slaves of the white man. The empire of the Men from the Sky will go under another name, South Africa. And our Gods will allow this to happen. Our intellectuals will whistle in the wind. Our priests will turn a blind eye. And so our brothers will beat us to death for a fistful of rice. Treated worse than dogs, we will even be barred from walking in the streets. Any foreign tear for our misery will soon be dried by the lure of diamonds. All protestation will be powerless. We will become the greatest martyrs of history.
>
> (*Amazoulou*, Act III)

THE ROLE OF THE EARLIER PAST

As regards the more distant past, for instance amongst the Agni of the Ivory Coast, African historical learning 'does not occupy, as it tends to do in Europe, a role of its own'. It is not a particular branch of knowledge, but is intimately linked to social con-science and is recalled at ceremonies such as the wakes and yam-feasts, etc. History thus comes to life in such vital moments of social existence, although access to it is governed by strict rules, and since it is an ancestral matter, only specific holy men may touch it, and even then only at specific times, such as these ceremonies. Since history involves transfer of political power, its content is 'shaped according to power' and is thus presented in a bowdlerized version. It is no easier to talk of ancestors' lives and achievements than to name them. Their virtues and exploits can be celebrated. But defeats and errors are concealed; wars are always won and sovereigns are always exemplary. In a general sense, 'this past is a model and the present only a pale reflection of it.' The memory of history is kept alive as a sort of reservoir, in which the Agni people can find inspiration and precedents: at the coronation of the king the list of his ancestors is read out and 'he is given good advice', according to a precise ritual, accompanied by a model reading that might show no weakness or hesitation.

This past goes back to the time of the exodus, that is, the period when the Agni settled in their present-day lands. It ends with the colonial conquest, while the period of colonial rule is given little emphasis – individuals are free to remember as they like and memories are not codified.

Claude Perrot relates one of these historical narratives of the precolonial period, which she learned from Nana Alou Mea, chief of the Kouadiokouro. It concerns the origins of the system of chiefs in Indiéné and demonstrates how far the desire to glorify the system's origins can be a matter of vital concern for the present-day power.

In Indiéné three men count as safohènes (military chiefs). In the political hierarchy they came immediately below the king. The origins of two of these chiefships conform to the official version, for in all the variants of the exodus-story, their ancestors played a great part, equal to the king's, or his ancestors'. But the third of these chiefships is another matter – the official story conforms to the original model, but the spoken tradition varies from village to village. The founding ancestor of the third of these chiefs was not from the exodus, but from the succeeding generation, becoming rich through trade, with Gwa and the Cape Coast, and gold-mining. Money gave him a hereditary kingship, whereas usually the contrary occurred, in that royal promotion gave wealth. That is 'how the world was given to him', i.e. how he became a safohène.

The office of the third military chief was not earned through bravery in war, according to custom, but by services rendered. However, that ran contrary to custom and the ancient values; the Agni could not admit such origins, which did not figure in the official tradition.

The origins of power is therefore a story which admits variations and this is also true of the dynastic tables. Those of Indiéné have ten names after Ahi Baye, who was king at the time of the exodus; and yet Claude Perrot notes that with new discoveries the non-official list amounts to seventeen kings, in the right order of succession. The names of at least four kings are unsung – some of them, unlucky heroes of the wars with European conquerors, others, victims of fate or an accident. 'A true king can be neither beaten, nor taken prisoner.'

THE SECOND LEVEL: 'OUR ANCESTORS, THE GAULS'

This phrase figures among the best-known ludicrous stereotypes of French colonization in Black Africa. It may be a legend. Literally speaking it certainly is, to judge from the careful work of Denise Bouche on education in Senegal from 1817 to 1960. In the early days only European children went to school, particularly at St Louis, where the teachers were brothers of Ploermel or sisters of the Immaculate Conception. Now, whether white or among the first blacks admitted to the schools, the children of the early nineteenth century did not run the risk of hearing about Gallic crudities, for at this time the French nation had not really discovered the Gauls as ancestors. Notions of history came from various lessons concerning church history and the first kings. French history was cut into centuries and reigns and began with Pharamond, whom we now know to be an invention, and ended with Charles the Bald or Saint Louis. Teachers seldom reached the Bourbons.

But the Bourbons were there in spirit. By 1898, the Director, Garrigues, was accusing the Senegalese public schools of teaching exactly the same subjects as in France. 'We could surely at least omit the murder of Clotaire and the baptism of Clovis.' He also thought 'that there is something objectionable about revealing, through history, the mistakes we made before arriving at the stage of civilization we have attained.' There were some efforts to include a little African geography and history, but they had only a very limited role and even that was reluctantly concerned. The colonists did not like the natives to have an education. However, George Hardy, the inspector-general of French West Africa, was an advocate of universal education, and he stressed the beneficial effects that such schooling might provide.

> It is not so much a history of France that we are proposing, as an historical view of French power to counteract the tendentious and all too often, anti-French history of the *marabouts* and above all the *griots* which presents the French victory as temporary and owing to accidental causes.

The history that was taught to children was not just communicated in history lessons but affected the whole of school work. In his book, *Le Chant à l'école indigène* – (Hymn to the Native School) George Hardy extolled industriousness, thrift and the other French virtues:

> Pour que notre Afrique soit riche,
> Ami, mettons-nous au travail, au travail . . .

Au lieu de dormir ou causer, allons,
Allons débroussailler la terre.
Avant d'inviter parents et voisins,
Payons nos impôts, acquittons nos dettes,
Mettons de côté quelques sacs de grains,
Nous pourrons alors chanter à tue-tête . . .
Salut, France, et gloire à ton nom,
Nous t'aimons comme notre mère,
Car c'est à toi que nous devons,
La fin de toutes nos misères. . . .*

It was natural, especially given the origins of primary and secondary teaching staff, that, as schools spread, instruction of the metropolitan type should accompany it, even though there were several books written for the schools on the history and geography of Senegal. 'In Senegal', wrote the Englishman, Mumford, 'apart from the colour of his skin, the Negro of French culture is French in every respect.' The definition of the 'Union Française' in 1946 implied assimilation and the turning of Africans into Frenchmen. The spirit of equality which prevailed, at least in the administration which, from the rue Oudinot in Paris dealt with Africa, led to the introduction of the metropolitan curriculum for schools at all levels and in all subjects. In history, it was only then that the Gauls really turned up. From now on history meant, for all in primary education, the history of France; in secondary schools it was history from classical times to the European era.

'The colonist makes history', wrote Franz Fanon, 'and he knows that he is doing so because here he is the agent of the

* For an Africa to be rich/Let us get to work my friends/Enough of sleep and gossip/Let us start to clear the land/Before giving parties for family and friends/We'll pay our taxes and our debts/Let us put aside some sacks of grain/ And then we can go and sing/'Hail France and glory to you/We love you as our mother/For to you we owe so much/The end of our poverty.'

mothercountry; the history which he writes is not that of the plundered country, but the history of his nation as it loots, rapes and famishes.' Senegal does not figure, except in its submission, and then its regeneration through French colonialism. This was true everywhere in the French empire, for it incarnated the progress of history and civilization. When, in 1948, in a junior class at Oran, I began my lesson with a general view of the course, and told forty *Pieds-Noirs* children that after the fall of the Roman empire and the barbarian kingdoms Arab civilization took over, the whole class burst out laughing. 'Arab' and 'civilization' did not go together. . . .

THE TESTIMONY OF A YOUNG SENEGALESE WOMAN, SOW NDEYE

What has Sow Ndeye retained of this history? She was twelve years old when Senegal gained its independence, and was in the first form of a school catering mostly for white children.

History, for her, was essentially the Romans, the life of those Roman children whom she imagined, bathing and going to the theatre or the circus. She also remembered the Gauls, their green and leafy country, with four well demarcated seasons, so different from Senegal. She could picture this refreshing and wonderful past under the sun of Provence: *Au Pays bleu* was her first reader, with pictures relating to Greece and Rome. And then there was Charlemagne, who founded his school, Louis XIV who built those extraordinary gardens and those palaces. Such is the area within which her idea of the past operates: neither her native country nor Africa interferes with it. It is only much later that they come on the scene for, as her teacher says, their history was not 'interesting'.

There is no embarrassment or shame, but the history of Africa left only two faint traces. Firstly, she remembers Moussa, wife of Kankan, king of Mali, who went on a pilgrimage to Mecca and, while crossing the desert, she felt a sudden desire to bathe. Her servants soon dug out a basin in the sand. Her other memory is of the bloodthirsty Samory; he had the foetus of his servants pounded in a mortar specially made for this end. No, African history was not likely to nourish Sow Ndeye's imagination. History and her dreams were elsewhere.

The first wound, hardly healed twenty years later, came one day in the fifth form, during a lesson on the great invasions.

> After the Goths [said the teacher] the Ostrogoths and then the Franks flooded into Gaul; then came Islam, the Moslem invaders, who were from Africa and passed from Spain into Gaul; but luckily they did not succeed in conquering it and Charles Martel stopped them; they had to retreat and then were chased, first from Gaul, and then later from Spain.

That 'luckily' pierced Sow Ndeye's heart like a dagger. She whispered her anguish to her neighbour who, like her, was black and Moslem. The wound healed slowly. She revived later when the French teacher had her read a poem by Bernard Dadié, 'Je vous remercie, mon Dieu, de m'avoir créé noir.' – A tear ran down her cheek.

And from that point on the tie was established within her between the fight for independence, the struggles of Abd El Krim and the effort to re-evaluate African culture. 'Black is beautiful,' sang Sow Ndeye's girl-friends; she tried out the dresses and hair-styles of the past and looked at history for the sources of her identity.

In Black Africa today, this search tends to exclude even those historians or film-makers who are well disposed towards the African past. 'A stay of twenty years is not enough to know us,' says Sow Ndeye. Behind her secretive smile, I sensed that ultimately she thought that the foreigner, having conquered, plundered, exploited, still wanted to deprive her of the pitiable remains of her secret identity, and to lay her open.

Only the ancient past cannot be talked of, for it has been codified. The more recent past, still fresh in the memory, does not have the same status, and may be freely discussed. So it is the colonial conquest which African memory still recalls, a memory which Jean Rouch has beautifully restored in his *Babatou and the Three Counsels*.

THE PROGRAMME FOR DECOLONIZATION

It has become increasingly accepted since the sixth Pan-African Congress at Dakar in 1967, and the recent works of Dart, Leakey and countless other scholars, that tropical Africa is the cradle of humanity.

This is the first observation made by Oumar Kane, one of the founders of *Afrika Zamani*, the African historical review whose self-declared aim is to 'decolonise History'. And this does not mean simply correcting its European 'viewpoint'. . . .

Thus we must stress the priority of the prehistoric African people; nearly every step forward taken by prehistoric man was first registered on African soil, particularly on the high plains of eastern and southern Africa.

In the study of prehistoric Africa, particular stress must be given to the Neolithic Revolution, based, as it was, upon agriculture and the domestication of animals. Up till now the theory of external property has prevailed in relation to the invention of agriculture and its introduction into Africa. But if the role of ancient Mesopotamia, the Fertile Crescent and the Nile cannot be denied, then why can't we envisage the birth of agriculture in Africa independently of property?. . . .

It appears from all the works on the subject that agriculture was adopted throughout Africa between the fourth and second millennium BC, while other areas were not affected until the second half of the first millennium BC. The most important plants for our nutrition had already been selected: millet, sorghum, yam.

Particular stress must also be given to the increasing desertification of the Sahara and its consequences. This process allows us to explain the location of African peoples through history and the great migrations of shepherds, who, in search for pasture, were forced to uproot other settlers. Are the people of our savannahs anything more than the population of the Sahara during the neolithic period? Aren't the peulh or touareg shepherds simply descendants of the Saharan shepherds?

Such dislocation of the plan of 'Universal History' implies a new periodization.

For the historic period Oumar Kane suggests adopting the chronology of Hrbek who 'left the beaten track of western chronology and the Marxist plan for history, which completely failed to serve the evolution of African societies.' Hrbek proposes a chronology based upon the dynamic of African societies themselves. Its periodization would be as follows, in reverse chronological order:

The 1950s: twentieth-century independence movements.

1890–1910: end of the period of independence that began about 1830.

1805–20: corresponding to the 'profound reversals in the zones of contact and the isolated zones: *jihad* of Ousman-dan-Fodio in western Sudan; formation of Chak's Zulu state; the rise of Buganda; foundation of modern Egypt by Mehmet-Ali; unification of Madagascar; beginnings of the Omani hegemony on the eastern coast. Generally, a tendency towards unification and monarchical absolutism; this also coincides with the abolition of the slave trade.'

End of 15th/beginning of 16th century: 'Arrival of Europeans and introduction of American tobacco plants. Invasion of eastern Africa by Nilotic tribes (Gallas). Foundation of Kuba, Luba, Lunda; decline of Songhai and disappearance of the city-states of Haoussa, Kanem – Bornu, Wadai and the Fundj sultanate. Southern migration of the Bantu. Mediterranean Africa comes under Ottoman domination.'

Bantu diaspora in central and southern Africa during the iron age in Black Africa (third century BC to fifth century AD): 'The iron age began with the movement of Bantus from the upper Congo basin towards the southern savannahs. This development would have been connected with the introduction of vegetable plants from south-east Asia.'

The spread of Islam and the foundation of the central empires are thus relegated to a secondary level.

The originality of this outline lies, as we can see, not only in its disassociation of African history from that of the Orient or Europe, but in its elimination from African history of all that might cast shadows over the present, stir up arguments, or endanger African unity and Africanism. In point of fact, the textbooks that are written for children manage to keep a relatively independent stance from these 'recommendations'. For instance, far from relegating to a secondary level the foundation of the central empires, the extremely innovative work of M'Bow and Devisse places them right at the centre of things. To anyone brought up on history from a European perspective, this outline cannot fail to be revealing, even if, at times, it stresses, to excess, the state of Africa before Europe.

ACHIEVEMENTS AND OMISSIONS OF THE NEW AFRICAN HISTORY

To young Africans, the history of their continent appears as an endless procession of kingdoms and empires, each more glamorous or perfect than the last. First there is the Ghana empire, ruled by Sissé, the golden king; then there is the Mali empire, which had its greatest period of development under Mansa Moussa who

> gave noble and generous charity. Having started out with a hundred packs of gold, he spent them all during his pilgrimage to Makkah (Mecca), first amongst the tribes which he encountered between Mali and Cairo, then in Cairo itself, and finally between Cairo and the noble Hedjaj; he spent so generously that, penniless on his return, he had to borrow from merchants under jurisdiction.

Then comes the Songhai empire of Gao, 'a centralized state, with advisers and ministers of protocol, justice, finance, police, navy, army and cavalry.' The Aksia dynasty developed its culture and, in particular, founded the university of Timbuktoo 'whose reputation went beyond the empires's borders' (fifteenth century). Further south the Mossi kingdoms distinguished themselves 'by flexible precision in political organization, extraordinary social stability, and an almost total refusal of contact with the outside world.' The Houssa cities were also stable, and yet fought amongst themselves, though it was just this democratic character which made them original. Further south, 'the countries of the coast' were just as famous, with the Yoruba cities and the kingdom of Benin. As for the Bantu kingdoms, which came into existence much later, they were 'rich and peaceful'; but, apart from the Congo, they soon became victims of colonial expansion. More glorious was the fate of the Monomotapa in eastern

Africa. Its wealth explains the prosperity of all that coastal region, which, through its links with India, the Arabs and China, produced a dazzling civilization, the civilization called 'Swahili' after the language used throughout the region. The arrival of the Portuguese ended this Swahili civilization at its apogee.

At the same time, the Christian West was afflicted by endless woes – the 'insecurity' which destroyed the Carolingian order, the break-up of states, and war. 'Men travelled little and knew themselves less'. The renaissance came only much later, with the rise of the Dutch and the Italian cities. But as soon as Europe recovered its wealth and population, it was driven to diverse forms of expansion, the crusades and colonial conquests.

Thus a striking parallel can be drawn between this brilliant African world and the West. This can be shown in terms suitable for the kingdom of Ghana and for the Christian West:

Kingdom of Ghana	Christian West
Powerful empire	Feudal labour controlled by the lord.
Profitable commercial relations	Famine.
A *simple* law of succession of *remarkable* precision.	Lack of surplus to sell. Poor state of population.
The remarkable site of Tegdaoust.	Disease and epidemic.
Light taxation.	Restraints on liberty.
Extremely *valuable* imperial treasures.	Peasants are victims of social organization.
Richness of the countryside.	
An *active* commercial centre.	Worsening conditions of the serfs.

Another characteristic is that the relations maintained by many black kings with Islam are rarely made explicit. If mention is made of those kings converting to Islam, and the resistance of the jungle countries, it is only in passing. Curiously enough, this is the only area where historians admit difficulties in the problems they are tackling and their own inability to resolve them, or to agree as to a satisfactory interpretation. The conditional tense and the use of 'perhaps' makes a sudden and singular appearance.

> One tradition which many historians consider as uncertain concerns the occupation of Ghana by the Almoravids in 1075. They are said to have forced the king to convert and massacred all those who still believed in spirits. Abou-Bakr gave the last years of his life to the fight against these pagans. He met his death in battle in an unidentified place.
>
> *Perhaps* the pressure of the Almoravids forced the animist leaders of Ghana to retreat southwards and to choose a new capital less vulnerable than Koumbi-Saleh. All these questions are very tricky and are still a subject of research and discussion amongst historians.

No sooner is he forced to write about Islam, than the hand of the historian begins to tremble.

THE CEDDO AND ISLAM

How did this omission of Islam and the memory of its conquests come about? A film by Sembène Ousmane, *Ceddo*, explains the tragic context.

From his own researches and the use of the oral tradition, Sembène Ousmane has brought the resistance of the Ceddo during the distant seventeenth century back to life. The Ceddo were men who disobeyed, both in the Ouolof and in the Pular states. They hankered after absolute freedom and yet corresponded neither with a particular ethnic group nor with a religion. In the film, the Ceddo have kidnapped the king's daughter and are holding her prisoner. The Ceddo people continue to recognize the king's authority, but demand simply that he should disband the Council of the Imams which, in the name of the Koran, was gradually taking power. Aware of his own diminishing power, but too weak to do anything about it, the king did not really condemn the kidnapping of his daughter, for he understood its significance. But he was a prisoner of the power-system which the Imams had instituted with his tacit consent, for Islam appeared to him a superior wisdom and knowledge, affirming that His Reign was above and beyond the normal reign of kings.

The princess, a prisoner of the Ceddo, waits for deliverance. She too is Moslem and the failure of her two brothers, killed in succession by the Ceddo, has strengthened her pride. But to her despair, her father is killed in the campaign against the insurgents, who are finally defeated. They lack weapons and have had to approach the White Man to obtain them.

Once the Ceddo are defeated, the Princess's hand in marriage is promised to the Imam. But during the wedding ceremony she seizes a weapon and kills him in front of a crowd of forced converts, who rally to her. . . .

In this marvellous and moving drama, the Muslim leaders felt themselves attacked; so is the white man who appears, yet again, in the figure of a priest; his only care is the ideal of a black church for all and, chasing this chimera, he is absolutely indifferent to the fate of the Ceddo, their destruction, and their will to survival.

THE ANTI-CHRISTIAN TRADITION IN SWAHILI POETRY

What is true in Senegal is not necessarily true for the rest of Africa; there were no 'wars of religion' in eastern Africa and the collective memory retains a completely different image of Islamization. Jan Knappert has shown this in his studies of the various styles of Swahili literature, and particularly the local poems transmitted by popular tradition. In the *Herekeli*, the oldest of these poems, there is constant mention of the conversion of Christians and pagans. The poem began with the death of Jaafar, the cousin of Mahomet, killed by the Christians whom he was trying to convert. The Archangel Gabriel then presented himself to Mahomet, ordering him to make war on the Emperor Herekeli. 'If you become a Moslem', Mahomet said, 'we'll make a nation out of you'; which was, indeed, the specific quality of the animists' conversion in Africa.

In the Herekeli, when the bishop received a letter, he would stamp with rage, the usual Christian reaction to the Swahili people; they were always impatient, irritable and brutal. 'The Christians, greedy and irascible, behave like children; they don't have the dignity or the eminence of the Moslems.' – 'Nonsense', replied the bishop, 'we worship the Little Jesus who could be the favoured child among our children.'

The reply had a surprising effect on the blacks who, if absolutely necessary, might accept the worship of a fully grown man, but certainly not a child. The Christians show other ridiculous eccentricities in these poems; their armies are preceded by crosses and by ornamented scrolls, which they gaze upon at the most dangerous moments of battle. The success of the Moslem cavalry over the Christian cavalry shows the will of God who gave victory to the Moslem warriors; even if they die they will still receive riches and glory. The battles of Ajnayin and Yarmouk are still celebrated by the Swahili oral tradition. Thus conversion by faith is the most usual form of conversion, even if a few have to be converted by force. It is the old method of carrot and stick. Other characteristics of the epic tradition can also be used to explain the conversions to Islam, e.g. the miracles which Mahomet accomplished and which complement practices that fill a magical universe. The cult of virility was equally important in seducing the blacks: Mahomet had nine wives and Moslem boys claimed to know the names of all of them. He had nine because, exceptional as he was, he could satisfy all of them in one night.

Thus while Christianity preaches abstention and chastity, Islam teaches 'better one wife than many, but you may have four, to forestall sin.' The need for polygamy is thus catered for, which also, in turn, guarantees male supremacy.

ONE-WAY SLAVE-TRADE

As regards Islam, the same hesitancy emerges in the chapters on the slave-trade, although it is used as title for the junior textbook.

> We call 'slave-trade' the commerce which tore black men from their families, sold them as slaves and transported them away, principally to America, from the end of the fifteenth century. This trade, practised by the majority of European nations, by the Americans and the Arabs, with the complicity of the African chiefs themselves, lasted until the end of the nineteenth century, and has strongly marked the history of Black Africa.

This would be a perfectly good account if the Arab slave-trade had not started seven centuries earlier and if there had been any mention of slavery in Islamic countries (there is only a 'reading' taken from Louis Frank). The hand of the historian has clearly trembled yet again, once it had to write about the crimes committed by the Arabs who castrated thousands of men and deprived them of any progeny, and yet the record of crimes committed by the Europeans occupies, quite justly, whole pages.

Let us now follow these slaves, or their descendants, on the other side of the Atlantic in the West Indies, where the blacks, transplanted like the 'Hindus' who came from Asia in the nineteenth century, live together with Asians in Trinidad, Tobago or Jamaica, where they replaced the Caribs and Indians whom the first Spanish, Portuguese or Dutch colonists massacred.

What vision of their past is offered to the descendants of these forced migrants?

3

SOME REMARKS ON A VARIANT: TRINIDAD AND THE EXORCIST REACTION

When we walk down the street of a West Indian town, we meet people who seem to come from nearly every country of the world. There are Chinese, Jews and Syrians; there are negroes and Asian Indians; there are Portuguese and Spaniards; and there are others who might come from France or England, Holland or Germany. In British Honduras there are Maya and Carib Indians, while there are Arawaks on the little island of Dominica.

There are millions of children in Europe who have never seen anybody from China, India or Africa. There are millions of children in China who have seen only Chinese. But in our schools, there are often boys and girls of different races in the very same class; there are Indians and Chinese who have Lebanese and blacks as their best friends. Truly, there is no country quite like ours.

We must not forget that in many parts of the world people fight each other for no other reason than that they have not yet learnt to live with people of a different religion or even a different colour skin. Here (Trinidad and Tobago, Barbados, Jamaica) in the West Indies we know how to manage and have known for many years. This is a great achievement. If only we could teach the rest of the world, we might be very proud.

Such is the beginning of Our Heritage, the first history book picked up by the black or Indian children, who together make up 95 per cent of the population of the islands. In Trinidad and Tobago their parents dispute the power and money in the two islands: the blacks control political power, the press and television, and the economic infrastructure dominated by the State – in particular oil; the Indians (Asiatic) have gradually become masters of the market economy and also the landowners. Two proletariats, black or Indian, live separately, dependent on the leadership of their own communities. The Indian community is more homogenous, as though transplanted whole from the east, and it forms a huge cultural enclave. Its members, having gained economic power, would like to gain a more consistent position in political terms.

Despite its political divisions, the black community is still in the dominant position. It is a good deal more westernized and looks east or west according to its ideology. In the Caribbean, class struggles and racial rivalries are intricately interwoven. However, thanks to President Eric Williams, 'Father of the Nation', who was constantly reelected with very respectable majorities from 1962, these conflicts have kept the forms of representative democracy, in the English mould. The powerful and active unions function freely, numerous political parties live together and the opposition is as firmly rooted amongst the black community as it is amongst the Indians. The country remains tied to the West, more than Guyana or Jamaica, though less so than Barbados or Haiti. Thanks to the oil, the country is enjoying a period of gradual growth; it is still poor, but it is no longer poverty-stricken.

The land which Christopher Columbus discovered offers an interesting opportunity to find out just what sort of history is taught to children. Today it is multi-racial, while Europe has also been present under the flags of its colonizing countries: the Spanish and Dutch were there first (Tobago was, for a time, Nieuw Walcheren); the French also arrived in the era of Toussaint-Louverture (both as refugees and as conquerors); and finally the English, who took over the two islands in the Treaty of Amiens (1802), have left a powerful imprint upon the island. It was they who imported the first Indian workers, and recognized the independence of the islands in 1962.

This introduction will explain why 'exorcism' is the first concern of classroom historical discussion. The racial conflict, the living reality of the islands, is denied and nullified from the very first paragraphs of the book. But it is clearly present in all the following chapters; the problem of racial or national identity forms the theme of seven of the twelve chapters, which go from the cave-men to today. The most striking example is the chapter on the history of slavery. It should, however, be placed in the context of what is first taught, as 'historical knowledge', to the young Caribbean child, whether black, Indian or white.

In the distant past, after the age of the cave-men, it is China, India, Babylon and Egypt which 'constitute the first landmarks of culture'. Europe makes its first appearance with the Greeks under the sign of a warship. 'The Romans were conquerors and built an empire, a little like the British empire.' Then came the Middle Ages, the spread of Christianity, the beginnings of the modern world. 'The western world, particularly Europe, has been the master of industrial civilization. One might say that western civilization is a civilization of the machine.'

The remaining chapters concern the great civilizations which constitute the heritage of the people of the Caribbean – China, India, Africa.

China, 'peaceful people', to whom Confucius taught the principle 'do unto others as you would have done unto you', a civilized people 'appreciating fine art', who invented such useful objects as paper and medical science. Sun Yat-Sen modernized the country, which developed further under the communist regime, established just after the Second World War.

India. This country was civilized at 'a time when Whites, Europeans and Englishmen were still living in caves.' The Indians already knew how to write and chart the movement of the stars: there were great doctors in India from very early on, and there were even hospitals for animals. It was the Indians who invented 'zero' and first used our system of counting in tens. The country was divided into a caste-system.

Many great men have been Indians, such as Buddha, who taught that the great woes affecting humanity were the result of egoism and ignorance; whoever overcomes these reaches Nirvana. 'Ninety million Indians are Moslem, which means that they believe in a religion taught by Mahomet. Mahomet was not an Indian but an Arab who lived thirteen hundred years ago.' . . . 'As a young man he saw the Archangel Gabriel who told him he was the prophet of Allah, which is the Arab name for God.'

Many other great men have been Indians besides Buddha. During our own period, for example, there is Gandhi. All his life he spent fighting for Indian independence. Gandhi wore Indian clothes and fed himself as the very poorest Indians did, on goat's milk and vegetables. Although he was rich, he lived very modestly and 'to help his neighbour' gave all his goods away to the poor. He suffered a great deal for his country. Millions of Indians, in India and elsewhere, respected and sought his opinions. 'He preached peace to all Indians.'

Peace for all Indians: that is the only reference to non-violence, the partition of India, the war between Hindus and Moslems and the division with Pakistan.

Africa and the Africans. Eight out of ten inhabitants here have African blood in their veins. There are also large numbers of Africans in the USA, Brazil, Cuba and South America. It is said that the Africans who live here are negroes, but the negroes are only one of the races of Africa and, besides, the negroes are not the only people with black skin: the inhabitants of southern India are also black.

In some countries there are people who would be glad to rid themselves of foreigners. – The Jews, for instance, have been chased from country to country for centuries. During Hitler's time, the Jews were hunted out of Germany and Poland; millions of them were killed or made into slaves. Ever since, an independent Jewish state, Israel, has existed, but the old conflicts with the Arabs still go on.

To take another example, in South Africa, Africans and Indians still suffer all sorts of hardships, simply because they are not Europeans. The same used to be true in the USA 'but recently a law brought segregation in the schools to an end' – blacks and whites are no longer separated . . . all this might seem strange to us here, where what matters is not the colour of one's skin, but honesty and good citizenship. Every man can be proud of his race. All races have had their famous men.

Under the title 'Two famous negroes', the following chapter recounts the lives of Booker T. Washington and George W. Carver – the first, 'a former slave who managed to become Principal of a school, Tuskegee College in Alabama', the second, 'an engineer and botanist who managed to find 300 uses for the peanut, and 118 for the potato. He was universally admired, in

America and Russia, and was even personally invited there by Stalin.'

Then comes the chapter on slavery.

SLAVERY THROUGH THE AGES

Freedom is to do what one pleases, provided it does not harm other people. When a man becomes a slave he loses this freedom and belongs to another man as though he were an animal or an object. If a slave runs away from his master, if he is 'stolen' the law returns him to his owner. He is the property of his master.

We do not know who was the first man to have a slave. Whoever he was, we can be sure he desired someone to serve him who needed neither payment nor thanks. We can also be sure that this custom of keeping slaves is very old, very old indeed. Some people think that only negroes have ever been slaves. They could not be more mistaken. Men, women and children from all nations have been slaves at some time in their history: India, China, Egypt, Persia, England, France, Spain. White men have also, sometimes, been the slaves of black men, as we will see in the chapter on Turks and Moslems.

Not long ago, a man might be made a slave for having committed a crime, or else all his family might be sold if he should run into debt. When one tribe defeated another in war, the vanquished were often sold as slaves; otherwise they were killed. We read in the Bible how the whole tribe of Israel was sold as slaves in Egypt.

In Greece slaves were left in charge of commerce and also became schoolteachers. They were much better treated than the slaves of later periods.

There is a famous story concerning the English boys who were sold at a slave market in Rome. This was during the Roman empire. So handsome were the boys with their long blond hair and pretty faces that a Christian priest asked them where they came from. They said they were Angli, which is the Latin word for English. The priest did not call them Angli, but Angeli (angels) and sent them on a mission back to his country.

The spread of Christianity resulted in the disappearance of slavery in Europe and the slaves became serfs. These were tied to the land and could not leave it without the authority of their landlord. When the land was sold the serfs were sold with it. Only 300 years ago Scottish serfs wore metal chains around their necks. But in England there have been no serfs for the last 500 years. In Russia, there were still serfs only eighty years ago.

One particularly terrible form of slavery existed around the Mediterranean for hundreds of years. Turkish Moslems used to sell captive Christians as slaves because they refused to reject their religion and become Moslems. Moslems were forbidden to take their brethren as slaves. This was a crime condemned in their Bible, which is called the Koran. For many years, the Moors of Algeria and North Africa filled the Mediterranean with their vessels, so that it became dangerous for Europeans to go there. In this way, Europeans from all countries became slaves and spent their lives as rowers in the galleys, chained to the deck and submitted to all sorts of cruelties, the whip the most terrible of all. When one of the galleys was sunk in battle, the whole crew would sink with it. During a later period, the Turks manned their armies with captives who, as children, had been kidnapped from their parents, who were Christian. They were then trained for battle and made into fearful warriors.

You will learn about slavery in West Africa in the next chapter.

But our story is not finished, for there are still cases of this old and shameful practice in modern times.

This context takes the drama out of the slave-trade, so that children, in a year or two, will no longer attach specific importance to it. Nothing is said of its scale, longevity or magnitude.

We are not even told that all blacks living on the American continent were originally taken there as slaves.

And soon, for the young people of African origin living in Central America, the sole image of slavery which will remain will be that unique picture 'of the young Englishmen, taken off to Rome as slaves'.

4

INDIA: HISTORY WITHOUT IDENTITY

INDIAN CHRONOLOGY*

c.2500 BC	The Aryans start arriving in India
c.623 BC	Birth of Gautama Buddha
273 BC	Beginning of Ashoka's reign
beginning of Christian era	Birth of Jesus Christ
AD 320	Accession of Samudragupta
643	Harshavardana meets Yuan Chuang
c. 642	Beginning of the great constructions of the Pallava dynasty
1296	Ala-ud-Din Khalji becomes Sultan of Delhi
c. 1488	Birth of Kabir
1498	Vasco da Gama lands at Calicut

* This chronology is based on the one that appears in the textbook published in New Delhi.

1509	Accession of Krishnadeva Raya
1532	Birth of Tulsidas
1582	Akbar founds a new religion, Din-i-Ilahi
1611	Jahangir marries Nurjahan
1615	Sir Thomas Roe visits Jahangir
1627	Birth of Shivaji
1632	Work starts on the Taj Mahal
1757	Battle of Plassey
1799	Last of Tipu's battles (against the British)
1833	Raja Ram Mohun Roy dies in England
1857	The Great Mutiny
1920	Gandhi begins his non-cooperation movement
1947	Proclamation of independence
1950	India becomes a republic

Have you ever counted up the colours of a rainbow? There are so many colours in a rainbow that it is often difficult to distinguish between them. In a sense, our country is just like a rainbow. People of many races have come to India at different periods of history. After the Aryans there were the people of Central Asia and Mongolia, and many other countries still. Others have only passed through the country, or studied in the great Indian universities. But many of them ended up by staying here and making this country their own. Like people in other countries they had to adapt themselves to their new homeland. The outcome of this is that today there are many different elements making up India, just like the rainbow.

Ours is a wonderful history of which we can be proud. True, there are periods we can not be quite so proud of . . . but it is important to know the good as well as the bad from our past.

From the beginning, two themes appear in history as taught to Indian children: that before borrowing, India both gave to,

and taught, others; and that the invaders of India were soon
assimilated within it, so that, like ancient Greece, 'she conquered
her fierce conquerors'. Amongst these, no mention is made of
either Arabs or Turks, Persians or Afghans, all of whom were
constant predators upon Indian territory.

As with Black Africa, reevaluation of the past makes for a
closer consideration of today's debility.

THE ANTIQUITY AND EXCEPTIONAL WISDOM
OF INDIA

> Our scientists have discovered an ancient city of the Sind,
> called Mohenjo Daro. Buried under the ground, this city is
> 6000 years old. Its people had built it out of brick and even
> installed a sewage system to keep it clean. There were baths
> and broad avenues. They must have been very skilled crafts-
> men, for there were also pieces of fine clay pottery and
> weapons made out of copper and bronze. The country, then,
> was green and fertile, which is even more surprising, for today
> it is a desert.
>
> We can take pride in the fact that the people of our country
> were so clever all those years ago.

The wisdom of the Indians comes to them from 'their knowledge of the *vedas*, which teach them to control both woe and
happiness, anger and desire, and to search for the Truth.' These
vedas also teach them that 'the soul is born several times, that God
is One.'

In this way, the beliefs of the Hindu faith slip into history,
which does not distinguish value-judgements and factual
statements.

> The Aryans came from Europe or Central Asia in search of
> a home. They fought several battles against the original

inhabitants of India, but then settled down in amity. . . . The
Aryans taught them the *Vedas* and caused them to adopt the
caste-system. . . . It was an obstacle to the unity of the Indian
people in time of danger, as will be seen.

In fact one never does see it. Throughout this book for Indian
children, there is not a single reference to the caste system except
to condemn it: 'this was a great misfortune for India.' 'But let us
rather tell the story of Rama and Sita.'

THE WONDERFUL HISTORY OF RAMA AND SITA

You must all have heard of Rama and Sita and know about the
huge effigy of Ravana which we burn every year: processions
and fires celebrate the great victory of Rama, the good king of
Ayodhya who defeated and killed Ravana, the wicked leader of
Lanka who had kidnapped his wife, Sita. Here is the story.

In the kingdom of Ayodhya, there was once a king called
Dasharata. Rama was the name of his eldest son. Everybody
loved him and hoped that he, too, in turn would be king. But
his stepmother, Kaikeyi, wanted the throne for her eldest son,
Bharata. She forced her husband to banish Rama for fourteen
years to the forests. Out of obedience to his father, Rama left
with his much-loved wife, Sita, and his brother, Lakshmana.
The king was so stricken with grief that he died. And the young
Bharata was so fond of Rama that he refused the throne.

In the forests, Rama, Sita and Lakshmana were forced to lead
a life full of danger, without any of the comforts of the palace.
But they were happy living by nature, close to the trees and the
animals. But they also had to fight the demons in the forest.

Surpanakha, sister of a demon-king, Ravana of Lanka, caught
sight of Lakshmana one day and thought him so handsome
that she demanded him for a husband. He refused. But she
was so stubborn in leaving him, that Rama finally lost his

temper and hit her on the nose. Ravana was so angry when he heard this that he decided to take his revenge and sent his uncle, Mareecha, after Rama, who promptly turned himself into a doe. Sita was so delighted by this pretty little animal that she asked her husband to capture it for her. Rama agreed to do it, but asked his brother to look after Sita during his absence. It was not long before he heard Rama call for help; what should he do, go to the aid of his brother, or stay and look after Sita, as he had been told? Finally he departed; but it was all a trap by Mareecha who was only imitating Rama's voice. Ravana took advantage of the situation and, disguised as a Sunnyasee, crept into Sita's hut to kidnap her.

Rama naturally came back empty-handed for there was no doe to catch. Sita had disappeared and he was heartbroken. Together with his good brother, he went off to look for her. They were helped by Sugriva and his minister Hanuman, whose army used thousands of boulders to fill up the sea and build an underground passage to get them to Lanka. There, Rama fought Ravana and killed him. Sita was saved, and, the years of exile completed, they now could return to Ayodhya. There was great joy on Rama's return. Bharata had kept the throne open for him and Rama was now able to be crowned at last. His reign was a just and good one, since which people talk of the Ramayana as the ideal of government.

PURIFICATION AND SECULARIZATION OF HISTORY

This history of origins, where myth and history go hand in hand, is all shiningly positive. Legend is purged of everything that might pollute the sources of the past. The *Ramayana* becomes a form of ideal government from which subsequent princes were supposed to have found inspiration. In the same way, the 'faults' which Rama might have committed are well-hidden. His most shameful crime is probably his offence against the laws of war when he treacherously murdered Valin, who could not see his assailant approaching from behind as he was fighting another. It was again a crime that he repudiated Sita, his loved and faithful bride, whom he rejected after his victory because she had lived in another's household. In the legend, Sita goes to the stake, but the flames spare her and she is allowed to return to the throne.

In this way, the reputation of Rama has been saved by silently ignoring these episodes and others like them. Indian historians know these episodes well, but are also afraid of them, since they traditionally try to 'justify' Rama and to explain 'Rama's conduct'.

In the debate over origins – historical this time – there is a tendency to pass silently over the ethnic conflict between the Aryan invaders of the north, who were lighter in colour and openly racialist, and the Indians of the south, whose skin was markedly darker. All we hear is that they 'became friends'. Similarly, there is a noticeable silence over the *Darmashastra*, the fundamental laws which determine and define the ways of life for the head of the Hindu family, a collection of prescriptions and manly duties, of rites and modes of conduct to be observed, from birth to death. Now it is exactly these domestic rites which form the Hindu, not 'the Indian', and this is an essential aspect of the life and the history of India.

This regard for rites is not mentioned, as though the teaching of history is intended to purge India of its Hindu identity. This can be seen in other contexts.

The record of the virtues of Buddha and the princes who governed India forms the chief element in India's glittering history during the following centuries.

> Buddha had possessed the most wonderful objects, tasted the finest fruits, worn the most sumptuous clothes, married the most beautiful of princesses. . . . Then one day his life was

changed by a beggar who told him that he wanted to renounce life. Shattered by this encounter, he decided to give up everything. From now on, his unchanging aim was to rid the world of sadness and misfortune. . . . He cut his hair, refused to eat and consulted the Sages of India, but nothing came of this great fast, this pilgrimage. . . . However, one day as he sat under a huge tree, the answer suddenly came to him. It was greed and the desire to possess which brought so much conflict to the world. To end it, one must follow the eight paths of Wisdom and seek after 'the golden mean'. He brought good to everyone, refusing to distinguish between the castes.

As for the princes, pride was, with mercy, the virtue which distinguished them most:

How am I to treat you?, asked Alexander the Great when he came to India and captured King Porus. 'Like a king', replied Porus. Alexander was deeply impressed by this answer and left Porus his kingdom. His soldiers were tired and refused to go on. He returned to Greece.

One young Indian prince, fascinated and excited by Alexander's exploits, wanted to imitate him and dominate India. This was Chandragupta Maurya. He came to found an empire which covered nearly all of India. He governed the country well and even wrote a book explaining how to do it: this book was called the *Artha-Shastra*.

A recurrent theme was India's need to remain one, and it came up in the allegory of Ashoka's bouquet of flowers.

ASHOKA'S BOUQUET OF FLOWERS

Ashoka was a descendant of King Porus, who had met Alexander the Great. He succeeded in unifying all of India, from the Himalayas to the Kayseri. His defeat of the Kalinga brought the

Mauryan empire to its height of greatness. However, this did not make him any happier. Sickened by the sight of battlefields piled high with the corpses of men and animals, he became a disciple of Buddha and resolved never to kill again. He also decided not to eat meat and to try and stop the slaughtering of animals. To make his laws known in such a vast empire, he had them engraved on stone columns which were erected in all four corners of the country.

And what did these laws say?

They asked the people to be kind, to tell the truth and not to kill. They also told of Ashoka's greatness and his love for his people.

On the columns were drawn four lions and a wheel, now the crest and seal of our government.

If you have ever had a bunch of flowers, you'll know how tightly one has to hold them to stop them being blown away. The Emperor was a man who held on tightly to Indian unity, the flowers of which were those little kingdoms of India that grew up when his grandfather became emperor. When Ashoka died, the flowers blew away.

Under his descendants 'India taught the world'; distant countries came to buy her rubies and textiles. China 'herself' wanted to become enlightened and sent Yuan Chuang 'to find out what was Buddhism'. Harshavardana came to meet him, leading a magnificent procession, dominated by a huge golden Buddha. After a stay of fifteen years in India, during which time he became a Buddhist, Yuan Chuang returned to his country.

While northern India was being governed by the Guptas, and then by Harshavardana, two great dynasties fought for preeminence in the south: the Pallavas and the Chalukyas. This was 'the era of Mahabalipuram's cultural splendour, and of Kanchipuram, the great university'.

Many years ago, an Indian prince left from these states with five thousand men: they arrived in Bali and made this island into their homeland. This is why Bali has the Ramayana dance as in India. Java also became an Indian island ... as well as other countries which have learnt the Indian ways of life: they found that there were many beautiful and noble things about Indian culture; so thought Cambodia, Thailand, Malaysia.

WHAT IS NOT SAID TO YOUNG INDIANS

The era of the great empires, the Mauryans, the Guptas, the Harsha, shines brightly in the Indian memory as the longest period of splendour which India has ever known. It stretches over more than a millennium, from the fourth century BC to the seventh century AD. The mark of this era's greatness is that India should have been a teacher to China. Even the Huns' invasion was only a brief, though tragic, episode.

What is not told to young Indians is that the laws of the Mauryan empire were not just principles and precepts of virtue. This empire was a police-state, or rather a spy-state, the only one in history. It instituted spying as a principle of government, a practice which lasted through several empires and was carried on during the Islamic period up to the arrival of the English.

Spies have always played a vital role in Indian public life; even in the *Ramayana* a spy denounces the pollution to which Sita had been exposed. During India's great historic period, a sort of spy book established some kind of code and practice for the profession. The *Artha-Shastra*, written by one of Chandragupta's ministers, put spies into five categories: idle lay-abouts who did not appear at all alarming; astrologers and palmists, who looked reliable; ascetics, who had access to all the social classes; and finally the farmers and merchants. There were also spies to be found amongst nurses, cooks and prostitutes.

Moreover, the morals of this era hardly seemed inspired by the precepts of saintliness. In the *Gouhya Samadja*, one of the books of the Secret Congregation, Buddha is seen to be continually giving way to debauchery with the angels. On earth, it does not seem that this was an era of melancholy: nuns and priests had ways which at best may be described as easy-going. One particular holy book by Kchemendra, one of the great educators of the time, was, in a way, the autobiography of a prostitute recounting her exotic adventures, sometimes as mistress of a nobleman, sometimes as a spurious nun, and at other times as a visitor of sanctuaries, or even as an initiator of the young to the refinements of debauchery.

Such characteristics naturally gave rise to a reaction, the Hindu reformation. The need for it is ignored by these schoolbooks, where only the teachings of the *Ghita* are cited.

'When religion declines', said Krishna, 'and the Forces of Evil will have to be destroyed, then I shall be born again.' This task of reincarnation, or of the Avatar, is stated in the *Ghita*. In contrast to Buddhism, it condemns all pretensions by man to reach a level of personal divinity. Its great priest was Sankara. 'His teaching was a great help to the Hindu religion. Many Buddhists became Hindus. Gradually, you could no longer tell the difference between a Hindu and a Buddhist. Hinduism became the main belief in India.'

Thus the fundamental event of the disappearance of Buddhism, the return to a more religious source of faith which was more mystical and less connected to morality and social behaviour, is concealed: for it is not easy to square the history of India's resplendent past with the eclipsing of the saints at its foundation.

The most highly-elaborated historical episode, the cultural expansion of India overseas, was in some respects a shameful business. In Cambodia, for instance, in Funan, formerly, the country had been governed by a queen; she, seeing a man from Ki arrive by sea, tried to stop him from disembarking. But the foreigner shot at one of the queen's ships with his longbow, killing an oarsman. The queen took fright, threw off her veil and surrendered. Hoeun-Tien married her, and, as she was entirely naked, covered her with a piece of cloth.

It is clear that in Cambodia, Java and Sumatra, the influence of India was victorious only by force, a fact which is never specified by the histories taught to children, where Indianization always appears as spontaneous adoption of the Indian way of life.

What is also not stated is that in 484 AD the king of Cambodia, an Indian by culture, sent an ambassador to China to seek help and protection against the increasing power of his dangerous neighbour, the kingdom of Champa (Vietnam). For the emperor of China, this simple request meant that Cambodia was declaring allegiance to him. His reply reflected this: it took the form of an edict. The king of Funan, Kaoundinya Djayavarman, lived at the furthest ends of the ocean. From generation to generation, he and his ancestors governed distant southern territories, and, in spite of the distances, their loyalty was unquestioning. It was therefore just in return for China to give him the benefits of royal favour and to confer on him the glorious title of 'general of the pacified south and king of Funan.'

Thus, the Chinese since the sixth century, then the French from the nineteenth century and then the Chinese again during the second half of the twentieth century took over from India, as that had failed in its 'natural task', the safeguarding and defence of Cambodia, an abandonment which history does not teach to young Indians.

THE DEFEAT OF ISLAM

'India was divided into a great many kingdoms which spent their energies in internecine war. Where an attack came from without, they were too weak to resist.'

The Arabs, who first arrived as traders, were stupefied at the wealth of India, and sought to conquer it. The Rajput princes resisted them for 300 years; but later on Mahmud of Gazni invaded India seventeen times, carrying off rubies and jewels on each raid, and destroying what he could not carry, such as the temple of Somnath, guarded by 700 Brahmins. 'Despite this lesson, the Indian kings continued fighting each other until finally Mohammed Ghori took Delhi.'

The Moslem occupation was an era of ordeal and humiliation; the sultan wanted humility and obedience from the Indians.

> When the tax-official asked for money from the *Khiraj Guzar* (the name given to Indians by Moslems – it meant 'paying swine') they had at once to hand over the gold. If the collector decided to spit in the tax-payer's mouth, the payer had to open his mouth at once. This meant that the Hindus, in behaving so abjectly, were showing gentleness, humility and respect.

The *Children's History of India* dwells little on these difficult centuries. What is stressed is that 'the Moslem conquerors made India their home, intermingled with Hindus and adopted their customs. There was a kind of synthesis in art, religion and daily life.'

Islam's success is therefore veiled.

> The caste-system had become very strict amongst the Hindus and the people from the lower castes were being very harshly treated. This produced, amazingly, a new conception of God and religion. When you are older you will understand how ideas can be a powerful force in changing peoples' lives. It was this new vision which the Saints made popular: Ramanuja, who freed Hinduism from its complicated ritual. Man had to lose himself to find God, said the preachers of the Bhakti, the most famous of whom was Kahir . . . a Moslem. He taught that 'God is One' and that 'we worship him under the name of Rama or Allah.' Thousands of Indians, Hindus and Moslems became

his disciples. When he died, there were disputes over the body; the Hindus wanted to burn it, the Moslems to bury it. Legend tells us that when they lifted the veil covering his body, a pile of rose petals lay beside him which blew away in the wind.

This pretty story also veils the Bhakti movement, even though its atrocities seem to have surpassed anything India has ever known. The lower castes were exploited by the occupying forces and were also victims of Brahmin reaction. The increasing inequality was sorely felt by the oppressed; did they perhaps see in Islam an egalitarian religion which knew neither riches nor poverty? Islam signalled a fearful defeat for Hinduism which in turn reacted by sanctioning a more personal religion, no longer steeped in ritual and aspiring to the sublimation of the individual before God as a way of avoiding the harsh realities of life.

Up to then mysticism had been reserved for the Brahmins, i.e., the élite. From now on, in consequence of the miseries of the times, the popular classes took refuge in contemplation. They had lost everything, and all that remained to them was the faith that the Bhakti saints regenerated, such that Tulsidas wrote the *Ramayana* in popular Hindi. The Saints taught that both the poor and rich alike could communicate with God. Their religion was thus a form of liberation, for henceforth new believers could forget inequalities both in wealth and religion. This syncretism was thus an Indian response to oppression and inequality. Its effect was to reduce the number of conversions to and the appeal of Islam.

THE GRANDEUR AND DECADENCE OF THE GREAT MOGHULS

With the occupation of Delhi by Babur the Lion, descendant of Tamerlane and first of the great moghuls to reign over India of the Ganges (1526), The *Children's History of India* becomes more edifying in tone and cannot conceal a certain sympathy with the regime in power. There is firstly Babur the Old, who sacrifices himself at the bed of his dying son, who can thus recover; then there is Akbar, who restored the 'unity of India from Kabul to Bengal and as far as Godavery'; and finally there is Shah Jehan, 'the greatest builder in history', who constructed the Jama Masjid and the famous mausoleum called the Taj Mahal.

But the tone changes with Aurangzeb who had triumphed over his brothers 'and thrown his father into prison'. He could not gain the Rajput alliance; he also had the Sikhs executed. He had to fight the Marathas, bold horsemen who practised guerilla warfare.

> These were bloody wars, after the splendours of Shah Jehan. The Indian peasants became increasingly impoverished by war taxation. There was increasing instability. Aurangzeb's austerity added to the general feeling of discontent; he had banned music at court and dismissed poets and writers. A strict Moslem, he recited the Koran. He destroyed the Hindu temples, imposed extra taxes upon the Hindu merchants and brought back the *djizya* for non-Moslems. This made the Hindus into his enemies.
>
> He undid all that Akbar had managed to achieve.

The Moghul state stood like an old oak tree, with totally worm-eaten roots. While the empire was collapsing from within, Nadir-Shah invaded India with the aim of realigning it with Persia. This was closer to pillage than to conquest, for the magnificent palaces of Channi Chowk were wholly put to fire and sacked. Finally Nadir-Shah retreated, carrying off enormous treasures from India, including the famous golden throne of Delhi and the most famous diamond in the world, the Koh-i-Noor. The Moghul empire never recovered from this blow.

It also fell prey to the attacks of the Hindu Marathas, disciples of the Bhaktis, of Kabir and Nanak. The most famous of them was Shivaji.

THE EXPLOITS OF SHIVAJI

Shivaji's father was an officer in the sultan's army. Thus Shivaji was brought up by his mother, a very religious woman who told him stories of the Pandavas and noble Rama; she sang old songs to him of heroes from India's past. He lived in the conviction that he also would achieve great things. He lived among shepherds, and loved to ride around the jungle, unheeding of its dangers. One day he attacked and seized forts belonging to the sultan of Bijapur. Shivaji's father, summoned to see the sultan, replied that he no longer had control over his son.

As Shivaji refused to give in, the Sultan sent his best general, Afzal Khan, against him, who boasted that he would bring back Shivaji in chains without having even dismounted from his horse. What happened in reality was totally different. Unable to overcome the fort of Pratapgarh, where Shivaji was established, Afzal Khan gave up siege and called for negotiations with Shivaji. They met, but not in amity. Afzal Khan came with a stiletto hidden in his sleeve. But Shivaji was wearing a coat of mail and a steel helmet under his turban. He was also wearing steel thimbles spiked with studs. As they met, it appeared as though both men were greeting each other, but in fact they were fighting. In the struggle, Afzal Khan was killed. A signal was given and it was not long before the Marathas were attacking Bijapur's army.

Shivaji laid the blame directly on the great moghul. It was then that Aurangzeb called him the Rat of the Mountains. But his guerilla tactics made him invincible. The emperor was so disgusted with his failure to defeat him that he invited him to court. It was a trap. Other war-lords had been invited to Agra that day. To trap his guest, the emperor made him sit at a table of inferior officers. Shivaji took the insult, as planned, and lost his temper. Thus, as had been planned, the imperial guard was able to arrest him. Then, in front of all these people, Shivaji feigned a sudden mysterious illness and fainted. He was carried out to receive attention; then, nobody knows how, he managed to escape his guards and leave the Agra Palace concealed in an enormous bread-basket.

He returned to the Marathas in triumph and was crowned king of the Marathas.

Worthy and courageous, Shivaji was a loved and just sovereign. He made sure the peasants paid taxes in relation to their means. He was very pious and worshipped the Ramdas Saints and his Guru.

Two hundred and fifty years later, the Marathas still recall and honour the name of Shivaji.

Shivaji's successors did not have his qualities, even if the Peshwa, the descendants of his ministers, unceasingly fought the great moghul. They were eventually strong enough to take Delhi, but were stopped in their expansion northwards by Ahmad Shah Abdali who was installed in Kabul. He crushed the Maratha army at Panipat (1761), with the loss of 200,000 men.

At this point the Marathas appealed to the English for help.

THE ENGLISH, OR THE STORY OF THE MONKEY AND THE TWO CATS

The opulence of India had attracted both merchants and conquerors. When the Moghul empire weakened, the Portuguese gave way to the Dutch, the Danes and finally the English and French.

The English were the shrewdest of all of them, and it was they who stayed. Do you know how they did it? Robert Clive, for example, of the East India Company. He noticed that the Indian princes were always fighting each other. So, like the cunning monkey in the story who arbitrates between two cats fighting over a piece of bread, he offers his services. And on each occasion, he managed to take some kind of advantage for Great Britain. In the story, the monkey pretends to divide the bread into exactly two pieces; so he endlessly weighs them out, taking a bite out of one piece to make it equal with the other, and vice versa, until he has eaten them both and there is nothing left for the cats. This is how Clive operated. . . . Another time, when he was fighting the nawab of Bengal, he made a secret pact with his general whereby he would become the next nawab if he lost the battle. And so this is how the English won the battle of Plassey (1757).

From then on, the Bengal nawab and the English merely collected the taxes in the great moghul's stead. The English government was delighted. However, when Clive returned to England in his old age, although he had done everything possible to build the British empire in India, he found people in England who were eager to blame him for his methods. He was accused of dishonesty and cruelty. The accusation hit him hard and, having lost his money, he committed suicide.

On Clive's role, Panikkar's judgement gives a better account of Indians' attitudes to this.

Clive was a gangster who won honours, a counterfeiter, a liar and a shark, as he himself admitted. His so-called military operations appear ridiculous when compared with the campaigns of other generals of his day. The State which he created and administered for seven years was nothing but a system of daylight robbery, the sole aim of which was to take the maximum profit from the lands which he was supposed to govern. English historians prefer to throw a veil over the whole period from 1757 to 1774, but they still agree on this one point; at no other time in the long history of India, not even under the reign of the Turamana and Mohammed Tughlak, did the people have to suffer, in any province, such misery as they did in Bengal at the time of Clive.

INDIANS AND ENGLISH: UNINTERRUPTED RESISTANCE

From the European historical viewpoint, India appears as the mere pawn in the power game and ceases to exist as a nation once the English have expelled the French from her borders. Young Indians themselves are being taught that Indian resistance survived right through the period of English rule until independence, without a break in continuity.

They are told of the exploits of heroic Indian freedom-fighters against the English, Hyder Ali and his son Tipu Sultan, real soldiers who were defeated only by a far superior military force. During the time of Warren Hastings and Wellington, English power grew 'inexorably', while India, after the annexation of Mysore, no longer had the means of raising a great army. But at least their 'heroic' actions prevented a part of the country, the India of the princes, from falling under the direct domination of the British.

Within 'occupied India', the exactions of the Company were becoming increasingly hard-felt; the greed of its agents, the ruin of handicraftsmen caused by the Lancashire cotton industry, the exclusion of Indians from political administration and the general impoverishment of the population, all served as gunpowder which found its detonator in the Cartridge Affair that sparked the Great Mutiny of 1857.

> The English did not even try to understand our mores and customs. Their new cartridges were coated with pig or cow

grease and you had to pull them with your teeth. Their officers did not know or did not want to know that they were commanding Indian soldiers to violate the law of both Hindu and Moslem religion. The soldiers refused to obey and fired on their officers. This was the revolt.

The whole army was filled with hatred at such contemptuous treatment and was won over to the rebellion, as was the population itself. The revolt spread like wildfire. The rebels appealed to the old Moghul emperor, who for many years had lost all power and in character 'was more inclined to write poems than to wield weapons'. His participation in the revolt was nonetheless symbolic. 'Heroes, both men and women, such as the Rani Lakshmibai of Jansi, rose up everywhere and died in battle.' However, 'at a decisive battle there was treachery and the revolt was put down.'

The English learnt their lesson from these events and withdrew the Company's rights to administer India, which henceforth was placed directly under the crown.

From then on, the nationalist movement made unceasing progress, inspired by the 'example of the American and French Revolutions' and 'of the teaching of two men, the Irishman Burke and the Frenchman Jean-Jacques Rousseau'.

Modern India thus came from a grafting of Indian tradition onto the West. Several men embodied this transformation, such as Ram Mohum Roy, one of the first Indians to study in England, Tilak, Gokhale, Rabindranath Tagore, and finally Gandhi: 'they shook society in the depths, whereas the surface appeared calm and even very calm.'

Gandhi, 'father of our country' whom

you children have not known but of whom you must know that though he did not wear clothes, he had more strength and power than the greatest of emperors. . . . His strength was that of goodness, and Einstein, the famous scientist, said of him that in ten centuries the existence of such a paragon would seem impossible.

The Indians have made Gandhi into a hero of strip-cartoons and films.

As a young lad, Gandhi was already as proud as Artabanus. At school, he refused when his teacher asked him to spell the word 'kettle'. As his older brother was hard up, he pilfered money from his parents to give to his brother, but then he confessed everything to the whole family as he burst into sobs. His mother sent him to England to complete his studies: but first he had to promise to respect three abstentions: alcohol, women and meat.

In London he dressed like an English gentleman and took part in the vegetarian movement. He took a degree in law.

When he returned to his country, he left for South Africa to plead his brother's case. It was his first case and when he was ordered to take off his turban, he refused and left the court-room. On the train from Pretoria, he was thrown out of a first-class carriage on the complaint of a white Englishman, even though he had paid the correct fare. Deeply humiliated by these harassments, he dedicated the rest of his life to the defence of Indian rights. At first, he told Indians to learn English, abandon the caste-system and forget about religious discrimination between Indians. Having read Ruskin, he became the apostle of non-violence, broadly in the manner of Tolstoy. But when he met General Smuts, Pathan extremists accused him of treachery and attacked him for having supported the British during the Boer War. But his tactic of non-violence, *satyagraha*, eventually brought about the right of Indians to marry according to their customs, and the legal recognition of these marriages.

When he returned to India, to be named Mahatma by Tagore, he began, from 1917, to organise a protest movement among the peasants. Then he went on hunger-strike in support of the textile workers who received a pitiful salary. In 1914 he exhorted his compatriots to join the English army: for later this would reap dividends. However, on 13 April 1919, a riot against the expulsion of the nationalist leaders from Amritsar, gave rise to terrible repression, killing 379 Indians.

At that time Moslems were angered by the deposition of the sultan of Turkey. Gandhi joined forces with them to present a common Hindu-Moslem front against the English. The boycotting of English goods was such a success that Gandhi encouraged its extension and sanctioned the development of craft-weaving by hand. But when violence was committed against an English officer, he immediately abandoned the non-cooperation movement and concentrated on a hunger-strike. When he was arrested, he asked for the longest possible sentence. He was condemned to six years in prison.

THE VICTIM'S VIEW

Naturally, English children know little of this long history, the children of today even less than those of yesterday. On Robert Clive, for instance, the *Kingsway Histories for Juniors*, which is still widely used in schools, is extremely elliptical. It even presents old 'John Company' as something of an innocent, only pushed to bloodshed by the efforts of the Portuguese and Dutch to stop its trade. Furthermore,

Indian leaders at that time had not appeared very friendly. However, a young man, Clive, proved to be a skilful warrior against the French, who were made to give up plans to found an empire in India. For a century, it was the Company that was the real ruler of the country.

On the later period, the *Kingsway Histories for Juniors* (15th edition, 1967) is even more discreet. Did England ever have an empire? We might seriously wonder about this, were it not for the existence of a complete para-historical literature in England, trying to make good for the deficiencies of history. It remains very popular. In essence it boasts of the English qualities and uses India as demonstration-ground.

This literature, whether in the style of Thackeray or Lord Curzon, talks of the suffering of British sons:

> For me, there is a strange pathos in our history in India. Besides the official history of the periodicals which waves the flags of victory and gives hostile moralists cause to denounce English plundering, or little patriots the chance to boast English invincibility, besides the splendour of conquest, wealth and glory, the achievement of all our aims and the noble blood willingly given to gain all that, should not we also recall the suffering of it all? Shouldn't we spare a thought for those women who had to make the greatest of all sacrifices for such victories? Yes, this sacrifice has been made for two centuries, for above the viceroy's throne there is not only a canopy embellished in gold, but a veil of human tears. The majority of those who suffered must have done so in silence. But let their fellow-countrymen hear their sorrow; let them know that the stones upon which this Indian empire stands, have been cemented with the blood that flows from the hearts of murdered women and men. For the government of India is not an amusement but a trial, and more often a form of suffering than a ball.

Indeed, in *Plain Tales from the Hills* there are more balls and picnics than suffering and bloodshed. For Kipling, as for Annie Steel and Perrin, India is divided into 'equal portions between tigers, jungle, balls, cholera and sepoys'. But apart from this division, Indians appear in Kipling only as stable-boys, or rather, the Indian comes on to represent the exact opposite of what may be defined as the true Englishman; with his stiff upper-lip, sense of humour, honour and sportsmanship. War is seen as a game, and so is the mutiny. The Indians are shot calmly, as at the fair: 'Well done, Harry, well shot.' And Harry must respect the rules of the game, i.e. fair play. 'He could have used his pistol to shoot the fakir defending the temple, but the Indian had only a sword and so Harry killed him with a sword.' It is this kind of virtue which gives the Englishman the right and the duty to teach these people how to live. Any interchange or mixing with the Indians can only weaken this spirit: the worst of all shame that can be placed upon the heroine of Crooker's novel is that, during the Sepoy revolt, she gave herself to an Indian to escape massacre. She has thus lost both dignity and identity, for in all ways the 'British way of life' is quite the opposite of the 'passivity' of India, which must always be led and protected: wars, in the literary and cinematic tradition, have always occurred on the borders and margins of the country, for its safety.

To enter the Indian world is dangerous, almost obscene and even comical. When Strickland, the police officer, becomes a *sais* so as to get closer to his beloved, Miss Youghal, he makes himself look perfectly 'ridiculous'. This true eccentric, Strickland, is generally avoided.

> he put forward this ridiculous theory about how in India a policeman must know the natives as well as he knows his own people. Sticking to this absurd theory, he would flounder about in the most unwholesome places where no self-respecting man would dream of carrying on any sort of investigation, let alone before the whole Indian rabble. He educated himself in this way for seven long years, without the slightest benefit to anyone. He was soon introduced to the Sat Bhai, at Allahabad, after which he learnt the Sansis' lizard song and then the Halli-Huk dance, a kind of religious cancan of the most astonishing variety. But

people often said, and not without cause: 'Why doesn't Strickland stay in his office and edit his newspaper, or do some recruiting, or at least stay put instead of demonstrating the incapacity of his superiors?'

In any case, it is not the done thing to try and understand India. India is like a woman: she does not ask to be understood but to be held.

Held firmly, but not in McLachlan's way, for the task tormented him and he could not receive an order without trying to improve it. He thought that some thirty pages of reflections on business not worth thirty rupees would advance the cause of humanity. The doctor told him he was taking too much trouble.

His doctrine 'made people too responsible'. But 'this is not England, it is India', a country in its infancy. 'You may sometimes mount an old horse with only a leading-rein, but not a young colt.'

In English eyes, what the Indians lack is just the three qualities which make up the true Englishman – physical strength, discipline and sense of organization. As long as these qualities are lacking Indians have to be treated like children. Harshness is necessary for justice; strength must be shown as Lord Curzon did long after the mutiny. From then on, the India of box-wallahs and 'factories' gave way to the India of military parades and of the *Bengal Lancers*.

The more India sought liberty through the unity brought by the English, the more carefully the English distinguished between Bengali and Mahratta, Moslem and Hindu, Sikh and Rajput. Probably they showed a certain preference for the Moslems, since their ancestors had also once dominated India, and they behaved, still, as superiors. 'They rode horses and were excellent polo players.'

In the stories of Annie Steel, there is blatant sympathy for the conquering Moslem emperor Bahur. More significantly, though the Great Mutiny had been inspired by Hindus, in the English accounts it was always the Moslems who were seen as the true men of action. Clearly, the English imagined the Indian to be passive and unreliable – especially the Bengali. In a short story by Kipling, a Bengali, who had been given a position of great responsibility, runs away from his duty at the first danger; he shows a complete incapacity to control himself.

In these conditions, the existence of a nationalist movement was beyond imagination; and indeed, the history which is taught to children (and adults) totally ignores the rise of the *Swaraj* movement; it recognizes only some mysterious and inexplicable explosion. The mutiny is reduced to a history of cartridge grease. Later on, the English came to realize that this was their mistake: 'they did not know how to educate the Indians.' Later, Indians showed only 'ingratitude' towards the English who had done so much for them: railways, hospitals, dams, etc.

One final question: does India 'deserve to be forgiven her ingratitude'? Annie Steel puts this question. As a child, she had lived through the mutiny; she retells it in *On the Face of the Waters*. What filled her with joy was not that her book sold like hot cakes; it was a letter she received. One reader, having finished the book, wrote that he now felt ready to pardon India for the death of his wife who had been killed during the revolt; for Annie Steel's short story had shown that not all Indians had been responsible for violence. Many of them had remained loyal, faithful, obedient and grateful.

THE INDIAN VIEW

The Indian representation of the nationalist movement passes over one of its most important aspects, the conflict between

Hindus and Moslems. It does not state clearly that the unification of India by the English, which instituted the principle of equality between all citizens, liberated the Hindus from the inferior status they had suffered for centuries. The history does note that the English paid attention to India's past, but that was to flatter vanity, given that this past was a Hindu one, and its revival was an advantage for the Hindus, and not for the Moslems.

Tilak understood instantly how the Hindus could turn the situation to their advantage in creating 'Societies for the Protection of the Cow', and in glorifying Shiva. For, under the cover of reverence for the past and its culture, they could revive Hindu India, and not the part of India that had joined Islam. Even Gandhi, later on, appealed to the practices of non-violence as a means to combat the foreigner, the English; but these means were also drawn from the Hindu tradition, and not the Indian one.

Above all, while the English occupation shook the Moslems from their 'position of power and wealth', the money of Hindu businessmen, which until now had been constantly threatened, became in its turn a powerful force under the regime of Capital. This transformation hit the Moslems doubly hard, and lifted the Hindus equally high. Such a process cannot be fully expounded in history as taught to children, for it would show that, under the cover of independence, the main leaders were really seeking to restore the Hindus to their dominant position through an apparently innocent rallying of people behind the democratic methods instituted by the English; such that, given the numerical superiority of the Hindus in India, it would ensure the superiority of non-Moslems in an independent and unified India. With independence, the formerly dominant minority would find itself in a hopelessly subordinate position, even if the leaders of the Congress Party took precautions to help the Moslems save face, and in particular accept the principle of separate electoral colleges.

There is no explanation of the Moslem view. Indian children are not even allowed to imagine that there might even be one such, even if that means ignoring the fact that the British, having leant upon the Hindus to smash the old Mongol state, later leant upon the Moslems to stop India's march towards independence.

The conflicts between Moslems and Hindus are only mentioned as a 'great misfortune'. They are never analysed, and nor is the 'Partition' of 1947, which is also seen as a 'regrettable' event.

Another problem to be skipped over concerns the caste-system and its effects on the history of India. True, it is often said that in the past it caused harm in Indian society, the suggestion being that any division mattered in this context. Of the Moghul and British periods, it is only said that the Saints and then Gandhi wanted to end the condition of the Untouchables. In fact when Gandhi was forced to accept a separate electoral college for the Moslems, he went on hunger-strike against the Untouchables' gaining the same privilege or being able to send their own representatives to the Round Table Conference.

History as taught to the Indians tends to ignore this event because it shows that the caste-system was a reflection of Hinduism; 'official' history neutralizes the problem by presenting it as a sort of given social fact rather than a phenomenon religious in origin, or connected to Hinduism.

The truth of the matter, as Louis Dumont has shown, is that the three principles in the caste-system – separation, hierarchy, and independence of hereditary groups – only amount to one: the religious contrast between pure and impure. The nationalist movement tried to reform the caste-system to save Hinduism. But open mention of this would only revivify memories of the Hindu bias of the nationalist movement, which could only increase opposition to Hinduism as well as to a Brahmin-dominated government.

In this way, relationships of repression and exploitation, the huge problem of debt, and vital aspects of the hierarchical society – all of them being linked with the problem of colonialism – are expunged from a history which leaves out the Untouchables, the workers' movement and even the movement of Internationalism, whereas one of the founding fathers of 'third-worldism' was an Indian, N. Roy – though it is also true that in India itself communism had no great role before independence.

Silence also reigns over the overpopulation problem, the problem of *sati*, or widows' suicide, and the conflict of nationalities – which continually comes up, and where there is clear resistance to the Indian will to dominate minorities, such as the Nagas or the Mizos, or to control even further Bhutan and Assam. Thus history in India, through its desire to legitimize the country's unity and – as we know – the dream of reunification, finally deprives history of much of its substance. India and its people lose, thereby, a part of their identity.

5

THE HISTORY OF ISLAM OR THE HISTORY OF THE ARABS

If today there is a community of nations in which history has a prominent place, it is certainly in the Islamic countries. It is quite a recent phenomenon, hardly a century old, which arose as a reaction to increasing contact with industrial and colonial Europe, which caused the past to come alive again. Until then, history had not counted for much in the Islamic countries. It was always in the shadow of theology which saw it as a possible competitor and debased it. But contact with foreign conquerors revitalized history which now went through a renaissance, first of all in Egypt. It is true that the Islamic countries were pre-disposed to give history a high place, for Islam is a religion founded not only upon a holy book, the Koran, but also on the great deeds and historic acts of the Prophet. To know these is an essential part of the duties of a believer. Besides, Mahomet ascribed a historic role to himself and, from the lessons of the past, placed his own doings midway between Creation and Last Judgement. The doctrine *Ijma* makes the whole community, after the Prophets, responsible for achieving his tasks. History is the realization of this mission: it is 'God's plan to save humanity'.

In Islamic countries, the conviction is that man's wilfulness and compulsion to sin have led to the repetition of historical processes, and to the same tragedies. But, fortunately, throughout history men have been inspired who have given man the chance of salvation. More often than not, man has rejected these opportunities. For example, Jesus offered the Christians a unique opportunity; from then on, the possibility of salvation existed only after life, in heaven. As far as the Jews are concerned, their sufferings will be permanent until the Messiah arrives.

Only Moslems can be said to have an optimistic vision of existence, thanks to the revelation of Mahomet. Every incident in the life of the Prophet, and then the victories of Islam bear out such a view.

In this sense, history is only history if it contributes to the victory of Islam. History is not seen merely as a continual succession of events, the roots of our own times, or a chronology. It has an inner logic and meaning which are based on the principle of selecting facts and events. It does not begin with Mahomet but with the failure of earlier prophets; history is the story of an Islamic community, a civilization surrounded by barbarians, or people without history – rather like the West's way of saying that some people 'had no history' because they had not been integrated into western civilization. History came to life again when the Islamic countries, under the imperialist yoke, rediscovered a consciousness of their identity and started to struggle for freedom. Emancipation is the vital reference-point which gives meaning to each problem and places it in context.

These principles appear strikingly, as though in relief, in those parts of history which are devoted to the problems not specifically Moslem. The Middle Ages in the West are defined only in their relation to the East and are seen as obscurantist, compared with Arab brilliance. The history of the great discoveries, which in the western tradition is associated with the voyages of Magellan and Christopher Colombus, is seen by Arab-Islamic historiography as a continuum from the explorations of the Phoenicians to the voyages of the Arabs in the Indian Ocean, since their geographical and scientific discoveries prepared for the later ventures of the Germans and Venetians. The history of the emancipation of peoples begins with American Independence and the French Revolution of 1789; it continues with Italian and German unification, and culminates in the liberation of all colonized peoples and the unity of the Islamic-Arab world.

Though owing much to western historiography, the history which is taught to children has also inherited qualities from the Arabic-Moslem historiographical tradition, whose nature is inextricably connected to the functions which it occupies.

Ever since the time of the caliphs, Moslem leaders have wanted to know of their predecessors' great deeds, so as to equal or outdo them. In this sense it is easy to understand the importance of history in Islamic countries – why, for example, Ibn Al-Athir, a historian of the twelfth century, should say that 'we must set sovereigns both good and bad examples.' Biography necessarily occupies pride of place; the scribes and functionaries of Arabic, Persian or Turkish states gathered together all sorts of information in their efforts, for history had a precise utilitarian function and did not have to contain judgements of philosophical significance.

But, if the historiography of Islam inherits this biographical tradition as a genre, it also descends from the tribes of the Arabic peninsula and is affected by their territorial base. This identification of Islam with the Arabs is the central issue in the greatest conflicts among Islamic peoples. In historiography at least, it seems that it was in eighteenth-century Egypt that territorial and national identity began to become synonymous with Islamic identity, as against the domination of the Turks. The concept of the *watan*, or the fatherland, henceforth defeated the ideal of fidelity to a particular dynasty, however strong its links with the Prophet. The pre-Islamic past of Egypt was soon reconsidered, just as happened in Iran with old Persia. Soon it was not so much the land of Egypt or of Iran which became the object of veneration and history, as the nation itself, the Egyptian people, which became identified with the Arab nation.

In the present century, the will to 'Arabize' the history of Islam was publicly shown at the fifth cultural Arabic Conference when a decision, ratified by the Council of the Arab League, prescribed 'unification of historical textbooks and uniformity of teaching to stress the Arabs' role in the development of civilization and the struggle against imperialism.' This is also applied to literature. In 1964, the Arab Memorandum of the High Committee for Poetry of the United Arab Republic attacked writers who 'on pretence of overthrowing the outdated and of changing the metre of poetry, wish to betray what is Arabic'. In fact, the 'new poets' wanted to overthrow the rules of classical Arab poetry so as to rediscover its local and popular sources, though these were not necessarily Arab. This poetic movement has found little echo. On the contrary, in each country and in spite of the instructions of the Arab League, history has kept an identity, which, for Egypt at least, goes back to the nineteenth century. The movement, under western influence, started with Shaykh Rifa'a Rafi Al Tabawi, pioneer of a history of Egypt that was Egyptian, not Arabic. Elsewhere the discovery of a pre-Islamic and pre-Arabic past went more slowly: especially in Iraq, where Babylon has had attention only since Saddam Hussein. But in Iran (of which only the southern part speaks Arabic), and even in Algeria, history takes little, as we shall see, from the norm, the purest expression of which may be found in the textbooks for Iraqi children. In Egypt, 'pharaohism' can be seen right from the Introduction of the first history book.

> In this book, past truths are presented not so as to serve reactionary causes, but for you, in the schools, to stop and

consider them. Just what factors brought your ancestors to their high level of civilization and enabled them to rely upon themselves, to face the problems of life, with reflection, work, perseverance and cooperation?

There is no doubt that the factors which helped our fore-fathers of ancient Egypt to lead the countries of the world are still there today; that the path mapped out by our ancestors must also be the best example for us to follow.

THE ROLE OF GEOGRAPHY

This vision of history is completed by the Arabic-Moslem world's idea of its own geography, and the geography of other civilizations. In his work on the Arabic geographies of the great period, André Miquel has shown that, if their history is distorted into only two periods, pre- and post-Prophet, their geography is also perceived such that the Islamic countries 'are the navel or the centre of the world'. The same was also true of China, with the notion of the Middle Empire; nevertheless, the Moslems gave this idea a more explicit formulation, and, seen from their point of view, it is in a sense justified.

As André Miquel shows, the arrangement of climatic regions by Arabic geographers is such that the fourth climate, Iraq's, is found in the centre, for three regions are further to the north and three south. The Arabic-Iraq unit – 'navel of the world' – consti-tutes the first of the world kingdoms; the four others are China, Turkey, India and Byzantium. Moreover, it is in Iraq that the sun shines at its best and purest. It is better supplied than any other state. The emperor of China, the best-obeyed, is a king of men; the Turk is a king of ferocious beasts – a reference to men as well as animals; the king of India is a master of elephants and wis-dom; the king of Byzantium rules over handsome men and alchemy. But the king of the Arabs is the best provided of all. Defining peoples negatively, the geographer Ibn El Farih denies to the Turks loyalty, to the Byzantines generosity, to the Khazars modesty, to the blacks seriousness, to the Slavs courage and to the Indians chastity.

The geographical tradition is closely linked to historical memory and shows the vision of others which the Arabs formerly had. André Miquel writes:

> Gahiz, followed by Ibn El Farih and Mas'udi set the tone in describing particular characteristics. The Chinese are a people of technology and artisanry; the Indians of theoretical science, mathematics and its derivatives, astronomy and music; for the Byzantines, again, astronomy is a characteristic but this time with medicine, philosophy and alchemy, for they are the heirs of the Greeks who were themselves technicians; Iran's inheritance is that of ethics and politics; and finally war belongs to the Turks. In the Arab case, they themselves recognize – without objection – the true gift of poetry, foreshadowed by Sem (Chaldea), which inherited the gift of prophecy and true religion. This is the vital difference between themselves and the rest of the world, one which gives them consciousness of superiority.

As Arab geographers describe and analyse the treasures of India and China, their attitudes are confirmed. All these foreign countries may be civilized, but they do not understand the essence of life, that is the harmony between the will of God and that of the believer.

> If their social structures are praiseworthy, it is only by accident. Without a real reason for existing, these worlds are not worthy of comparison with Islam. And if, indeed, there are different *degrees* of human behaviour, there are no degrees in faith, – one is either Moslem or not, and that is the only true distinction.

THE LESSON OF ISLAM

In Islamic countries, the first kind of instruction is Islamic. Later on, this can still take up to as much as a third of the teaching time (in Saudi Arabia for instance); on average it takes up about a tenth, though sometimes less, as in Tunisia. The basis of this teaching is the Koran. Children learn a simplified version of it by memory from the age of twelve or thirteen years.

In fact the nature of the teaching of the Koran varies considerably from country to country and varies even more in relation to history. History can be dissociated from the Koran, at least in one method, for it takes the form of stories about the origin of the tribe, which looks back to a period not so much historical as mythical (for example in Morocco, Tunisia and certain countries of Black Africa).

As regards the teaching of the Koran itself, in Sudan or Nigeria, the text of the Koran only constitutes one possible approach. Its exegesis, the *Tafsir* comes first – it takes together some scattered elements, such as the history of Yusef (Joseph), the ascension of Mahomet through the seven heavens towards the throne of God, the *Isra*, or descent through the seven hells, in which Mahomet resists temptation and rises towards God, accompanied by Gabriel. The *Tafsir* also describes the epic of Alexander (Iskander), the possessor of two horns, who seeks the wells of life in the company of Khidr, or Khadir, who was Sage of Islam. These tales form the substance of the written or oral record taught to the children of Islam from the Bashkirs to the Hausa of Nigeria. Knowledge of the sources of law, the *Hadith*, is also a basis of learning. From the very earliest ages children thus learn everything to do with marriage, divorce, inheritance and all the most important aspects of life.

'Why did Allah, in his wisdom, allow Moslems alone the right to have several wives?' asks the teacher.

'Because then the Moslems would have many children and so would be more numerous than the Christians. . . .'
'Not bad, not bad . . . And you, Ahmed, what do you think?'
'Because there are more women than men.'
'Yes, but what else? What do you think, Anwar?'
'Because Allah, in his great wisdom, saw that the Moslems truly loved women, so that a single one would not satisfy them.'
(Witnessed by Bernard Williams)

Through this educational procedure, the Moslems' social and cultural behaviour is inextricably linked with religious conviction (a characteristic also found in Japan). They are also taught the *Ficq*, the law of the Koran, and so understand its practice, unlike the case of the westerner, who is law-less, and for whom law – though he is expected to know it – in practice is dissociated from simple knowledge and is left to specialists. Such specialists – the *ulemas* – do exist in Islamic countries, but they do not have the monopoly of the law, but are simple technicians.

To this knowledge is added a more literary learning, such as the *Mahdi*, or the panegyrics, which every Islamic culture creates of its own accord; or biography, which plays a vital role wherever Islam and Abraham mix; or the *Wa'azu*, homilies and warnings as to the meaning of life and death, the emptiness and futility of the world, the inevitability of death, and the necessity of repentance.

In Nigeria, other factors round off this first stage of teaching, which is given sometimes in the *makarantum ilmi* (which differ from the Koran schools), and sometimes simply by teachers who, in Black Africa for instance, have obtained the *ijaza*, that is a licence which qualifies and permits them to teach the above subjects, and several others, such as geography, the *Prolegomena* of Ibn Khaldun, astrology, etc. In Kano, the course of Islamic studies at the university groups these subjects together and adds to them the history of Islamization, theology, the history of religious orders, particularly of the Sufi, and the history of present-day political movements in the Islamic countries.

If we compare an Iraqi and an Egyptian textbook, the chapter on the Arabs before Islam, it is clear that, from the very start, there are big discrepancies. On the purely Arab soil of Baghdad, pre-Islamic history is speedily covered, even though Iraq is the old Chaldea and Mesopotamia. Only the regime of Saddam Hussein, which regarded itself as lay, restored the ancestral lands and Nebuchadnezzar to honour. The identification with the Arabs is nevertheless clear. In Egypt, the textbook on the same period is unmistakably condescending towards the primitive Arabians.

TWO VISIONS OF THE ARABS
IRAQ

The Arab world is one of the oldest places on earth, a place where the very first peoples created civilizations, towns and states: it is the cradle of history.

Its inhabitants have always been Arabs; and in the Arab world, waves of emigration populated the empty spaces; they were the originators of Arabia.

There have been many foreign invaders of the Arab world: in 1539 BC the Achaemenids conquered Babel and spread across the whole Arab world. Later on, the Persians conquered Iraq; and the Romans took Egypt, Syria and North Africa.

Only Arabia has always remained independent, together with the Yemen.

The people of the Yemen organized irrigation and established commercial links with Africa and Asia. The Arabians emigrated northwards and westwards; the queen of Sheba and her subjects left the Yemen after the collapse of the Marib dam, and it was at that time that the Kinda tribes created an emirate in the north of the country and so managed to repel invaders. But this state soon fell under the domination of the Ethiopians and the Persians. After that, there no longer existed a centralized nation but a number of Arab communities and principalities with trading stations along the commercial routes.

THE EGYPTIAN VERSION

Arabia is the country from which the Prophet departed, and the chief original area of the Arabs. Before the arrival of the Prophet, they led a simple tribal existence. They lived in tents, continually wandering with camels in search of water. The Khoraish were one of the largest tribes of the north; some of these tribes traded from the Yemen to Syria via Yasreb (Medina) and Makkah.

At that time there was no single God: Arabs worshipped the moon and the trees and others worshipped the sun or statues. The tribes went off on pilgrimage to Makkah, around which there were many statues.

Some Arabs were Jews and Christians. There was not a single state or government, but each tribe had its chief. Wars were frequent between the chiefs and there were also a number of vendettas.

There were a number of worthy traditions amongst them, such as hospitality, fidelity, protection of one's neighbour and respect for elders; but there were also bad habits, such as a spirit of vendetta, a tendency to drink and gamble, and the burying alive of girls.

Because of these things, God sent them the Prophet.

THE AUTHORIZED VERSION OF THE ARAB 'CONQUEST': A LIBERATION

Under the first four caliphs, Arab lands were freed from Roman imperialism. The Arabs recovered the Fertile Crescent.

In Iraq, Ibn Harissa had defended the country against the

Persians; in Syria, there had been several uprisings against the Byzantine Emperor and when the Arab Islamic nation appeared the Prophet was able to unify the whole Arab people, which aroused such enthusiasm that it was then quite easy to liberate all brothers still under foreign domination.

Abu Bakr had sent El Nuaddin into Iraq. The Romans matched the Arab forces and brought up some of their best troops. Nevertheless, Khalid's army defeated them at the battle of Yarmuk, and so freed the country up to the Jordan. On Abu Bakr's death, Palestine was liberated. Omar, his successor, then went to Jerusalem. Some Christians asked him to come and pray in their church. But he refused at first, for he did not want them to believe he would change their churches into mosques. He preferred to go and pray at another spot. This did not fail to increase the admiration of Jerusalem's people. The Moslems then built a mosque next to the church.

In the west, Moawiya carried on a war of liberation and reached Barka in Libya. The liberation of Tunisia was accompanied by the foundation of Kairouan by Obka ben Whafi, as a point from which the Arabs could reach the Atlantic further west.

Moawiya built a great navy to combat Byzantium and attacked the Mediterranean islands so as to cut the imperial route to Egypt. With 700 ships he attacked Cyprus and Rhodes and threatened Constantinople.

Arabization continued with the caliph Abd El Malik el Marwan, who established the Arab language as the official language of the Islamic Arab State at the expense of Greek in Syria, Coptic in Egypt and Persian in Iraq. To establish a bureaucracy, he called in young Arab intellectuals. Foreigners realized the danger of the situation and wanted to stop the process of Arabization; but they were unable to do so. The Arab language thus became the language of the state, society, culture and science.

THE ARABS IN ASIA

Eastern conquests were also pursued. Abd El Marwan had given this task to Kotayeba who reached Bukhara and Samarkand and even reached the Chinese border. Further south, another army reached India, where many mosques were built and part of the population was converted to Islam.

Meanwhile, the Buyids, who had attacked the Abbasid state in Iran, established a state which soon stretched as far as Baghdad (conquered in 956 – the year of the Hegira – in the reign of Caliph Mustapha).

Iraq remained under their rule and the people became divided, for state power encouraged sects to develop. These princes rewrote and distorted the history of the Arabs; but discontent and anarchy increased, the decline of the state was accelerated and the Seljuk Turks conquered it in 447 (1069). The state fell to pieces, and the Crusaders profited from this to conquer Syria and threaten Egypt. The Abbasid caliph continued to fight them but in 528 (1150) he was killed.

The Arab conquests, only the first years of which are described, are here presented essentially as 'liberation'. It is true that, just before the Arabs' arrival, Byzantine oppression was barely endured by the people of Syria, Egypt and even Ifriqiya. The reasons were both financial and religious. Financially these provinces had been squeezed dry by Constantinople, for the Byzantine state needed money to pay for mercenaries, who pushed back the barbarians to the north and the Sassanid empire in the east, for the Persians had resumed conquest early in the seventh century and had threatened Alexandria and even Constantinople in 622. In Syria and Egypt alike, peoples who had been only superficially Hellenized and still more superficially Romanized were greatly aggravated, especially when, at the Council of Chalcedon and the Ecthesis of 638, Emperor

Heraclius instituted monotheism as a state doctrine and banned any debate as to the plurality of powers and wills.

In Egypt and Africa (present-day Tunisia), the endemic religious schism was prelude to political schism and the Arabs were warmly welcomed as liberators, for they left people free to choose their faith. In Egypt, the Arabs ensured Coptic loyalties and even presented the Copts with orthodox churches. In Syria, the Arabs were warmly welcomed. Only the barbarians resisted their conquest, much as they had constantly opposed the Roman and Byzantine occupation.

Iran was exhausted after the long wars with Byzantium, and the Sassanids, divided amongst themselves, were defeated: the King of Kings fell back after a series of battles, towards the easternmost borders of his empire, where he was assassinated.

The Iranian resistance was only displayed later – in fact, throughout the Omayyad empire, defeated nationalities resumed their fight from the ninth and tenth centuries, often in the guise of Islamic sectarianism. The Buyid dynasty, for example, was a semi-Iranian dynasty which became Shiite.

Whereas Islamization met enthusiasm rather than resistance, the process of Arabization was a completely different story: in a way, the Abbasid triumph expressed a transition from an Arab empire to an empire that was Moslem but not necessarily Arab. As to the origin of the Abbasids, or the massacre of the Omayyads, the books written for the young Arabs of Iraq are silent.

The differences between Iraq and Egypt for this period of study are minimal, and amount only to a vaguely anti-Arab gloss on the Egyptian side. Thus, 'Abu Bakr reorganized the state, for, after the death of Mahomet, the Arabs had returned to worshipping the idols and the country was threatened with a step backwards.'

The compilation of the Koran, which the historians credit to Othman, is associated with earlier reigns: 'The Koran was learnt by heart, but this tradition began to disappear in the continuing wars and conquests. The Koran was written down on palm leaves, animal bones and camel-skins; so that these should not be lost, they were then gathered together in a single book.' Othman is also credited with the organization of the State, the lightening of taxes and the freedom of worship 'in return for payment of a tax'. He was 'harsh towards members of great families who grew rich at the expense of the poor; in the evenings he disguised himself so as to see for himself what was going on, without being recognized.'

> With the reign of Othman things began to change. He was too good-natured and negligent; he unfairly favoured his own family. There were revolts, for example, by the governor of Kufa. The rebels demanded his abdication: a delegation came and he was assassinated in the course of the disputes. From then on there was growing division amongst the Moslems, which led to war among them.

The fourth caliph, Ali, had not taken part in the plot against Othman, but did not condemn the murder. The notables of Makkah rebelled, led by Ayesha, the Prophet's widow, who hated Ali; the would-be avengers of the caliph were ranged behind Moawiya, the governor of Syria. The first revolt was put down after the 'Battle of the Camel', so called because the most energetic fighting took place around Ayesha's own camel. Ali was forced, none the less, to collect his supporters around Kufa, in lower Iraq, and so to abandon Arabia. The outcome of the second, and greater, revolt was decided at the Battle of Siffin (657) when Moawiya's supporters hoisted the pages of the Koran on their lances; the supporters of Ali interpreted this gesture as an appeal to the judgement of God, as an arbiter. But if that was Ali's view, some of his supporters also disagreed, for they would not allow mere mortals to anticipate a judgement of God and they refused the proffered arbitration. Such were the 'secessionists', or 'Kharijites'. The Adroh arbitration acquitted Othman, and so condemned Ali's acceptance of the caliphate. Before fighting Moawiya, Ali had first meant to cut the Kharijites down to size, and it was this which led to his murder.

The Omayyad dynasty began with the proclamation of Moawiya as caliph in 660, while the supporters of Ali and his family, the Shiites, seceded. But Ali's eldest son, Hassan, rallied to Moawiya, and there was almost no trouble so long as he lived and Moawiya himself reigned. But everything changed on Moawiya's death. His son, Yazid, succeeded, but, on Hassan's death, his younger brother, Hussein, second son of Fatima, took up the challenge and war began again. In fact, even before the fighting started, and without Yazid's involvement, Hussein was killed in an ambush at Kerbela. Yazid was widely blamed as 'usurper' and murderer of the Prophet's grandson; the Shiites then had the sanctity of suffering – martyrdom.

Not much of this figures in the textbooks for young Arabs in Iraq, though it is officially Sunni and recognizes Omayyad legitimacy. By contrast, in Iran, as will be shown, a special place is given to the murder and martyrdom of Hussein, whose story also crossed the mountain barriers of the Caucasus and of the Hindu Kush. Even now, in the Moslem republics of Soviet Asia, Shiite children have games in which they act out Hussein, to the great indignation of their Soviet masters, rather than the great deeds of Alexander Nevski.

THE ARABIZATION OF ISLAMIC HISTORY

The last chapter of the history textbook for the youngest Iraqi children deals with the 'Abbasid Renaissance' during the reign of Al-Nasir Ledin Allah. The period of the Seljuk Turks who replaced the Persian Buyids takes only a few lines, although it lasted two-and-a-half centuries, from 945 to 1180. The identification of Islam with the Arabs is confirmed by the choice of title:

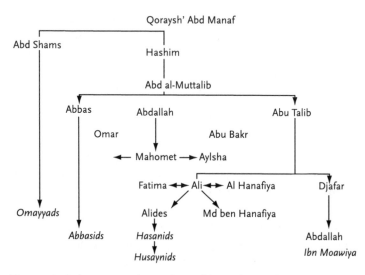

Figure 1 Arab dynasties and genealogy of the Mahomet family

a more glorious past is given to Al-Nasir Ledin Allah, an Arab, than to the great Abbasid caliphs from the seventh to the ninth centuries; El Mansour, Harun al-Rashid, etc., i.e. the period of true Abbasid grandeur, although these caliphs were Persian.

> Several caliphs succeeded each other and gave strength and greatness to the Abbasids, particularly Al-Nasir Ledin Allah, caliph in 1180. He reorganized the army and the administration and helped Saladin to fight against the Crusaders. He succeeded in reuniting the Islamic world after the disunity of the Buyid period.

Here is the first allusion to the schisms within Islam:

> He made no distinction between the different sects, created a popular militia (we shall come back to these points), encouraged physical education and sport and was interested in the youth. He revived the spirit of the Moslem world.

His Arab policy: One day, he was seen in the cemeteries of
Baghdad, visiting the ruins of the city. He ordered that anything
foreign [that is, not Arabic, but Turkish] should be removed. All
the Islamic princes agreed with him on this. One of his sons,
after his death, built El Mustanzir, the first university in the
world.

During his reign, the Mongols of Hulagu occupied Baghdad
in 1258.

With the fall of Baghdad the Arab state disappeared under
the weight of imperialist domination which lasted until 14 July
1958. [A sentence which ends the book.]

Here is a complete Arabization of history, for if the Mongols
were invaders and infidels, the Turks, who came to the rescue,
were Moslems who had already held the caliphate. It is also
worth noting that this history does not give Egypt its due; for,
if in 1258 the Arab world was almost entirely occupied, Egypt
remained untouched as the refuge and hope of Islam. Moreover, it was Egypt's army which defeated the Mongols in 1260
and chased them out of the Arab world. This was a victory
which saved Islam and yet the children of Iraq are not told
of it.

Following on from this, the sixth-form textbook begins with
an introduction on Abdu Abdallah Tarif Idrissi, the Arab geographer born in Ceuta in 1099: 'He grew up in Cordoba and
visited North Africa and Central Asia. Roger II, King of Sicily,
heard of him and invited him to reside with him in Palermo,
where he ended his life.' There he drew a map of the world and
wrote the Delight of one who wishes to visit all the regions of the world
(Nuzgat el-mushtaq fikhtiraq el-afaq).

Thus the Arabs were able to show the entire world what their
researches had achieved.

Cyprus and Andalucia were the places from which Arab

culture was radiated to Europe, which learnt a great deal about other peoples.

The Europeans did not know the routes towards these peoples and had to use the Arab routes. During the fifteenth century they looked for others: this is the period of the great discoveries.

When the Arabs left Andalucia, their culture remained so that the Spanish and Portuguese were able to use the work of Arab geographers and Arab naval skills. By the fifteenth century sailors thus discovered the north-west coast of Africa. They reached the Cape of Good Hope and went on to India.

To safeguard their trade with eastern India, the Portuguese needed to defeat the Arabs who dominated the routes to the Orient.

With this war between Arabs and Portuguese, it may be said that the period of imperialism had started, from which the Arab people has suffered until today.

At the beginning of this work, as at the end of the earlier one, the relationship of past to present is a constant concern of history and its teaching. The repeated allusions to Andalucian Spain, like the reference to the geographer Abdu Abdallah Tarif Idrissi, and the absence, in contrast, of any mention whatsoever of the great historian Ibn Khaldun, are tied up with the other objective, the glorification of the Arab nation.

In contemporaries' eyes, Andalucia was not thought especially remarkable in the Islamic world. Its grandeur was altogether a 'myth' which only appeared much later in the nineteenth century. Bernard Lewis has clearly shown this in his *History Remembered, Recovered, Invented*. From the beginning of the seventeenth century, after Al Maggari had praised Andalucia for the final time, it was not mentioned in traditional Moslem literature. The discovery of its 'greatness' took place between 1840 and 1886, and was the work of the English, who reprinted the works of Al Maggari. Quite soon, Abdul Hamid II, sultan of Turkey, sent messengers to Spain to recover Arab manuscripts of the Omayyad period. 'Discovering the greatness of Moslem Spain through European historians was, for the Arabs, a difficult pill to swallow.' They swallowed it – the more so as the knowledge of forgotten Andalucia came with flattering commentaries as to Arabs' tolerance, a judgement probably exaggerated, but one which has done well. Besides, since it came from Jews, it had a practical function, not least as a measure of the Christian persecutors' cruelty.

MOSLEMS AND JEWS

That Moslem anti-semitism was less than Christian anti-semitism has plenty of evidence; for instance, in the work of the historian Ibn Khaldun. True, from early childhood the young Moslem recites the fourth Sura, where there is anathema on the Jews. 'They broke their promises and denied the power of the Lord. They killed the Prophets and said that, in our hearts, we are uncircumcised. The Lord branded their forehead with the seal of ignominy.' And in the fifth Sura we find Mahomet saying: 'Know that the most ardent enemies of True Belief are the Jews and polytheists. You know that Christians are just, charitable and capable of love, like the True Believers.'

However, Ibn Khaldun amends the Prophet's announcements. He considers the Jews as belonging 'to the great families of this earth, counting all the prophets from Abraham to Moses among its ancestors', they were exiled from their home and experienced servitude for centuries. And yet they never ceased to be fully conscious of their own nobility, even when they lost their *Asabiya*, i.e. the communal spirit, which, according to Ibn Khaldun, was the most powerful force of all, accounting for societies' birth and permanence. 'The roguery and harshness of today's

Jews', writes Ibn Khaldun in the fourteenth century, 'are the result of exile, dependence and their way of life.'

He notes that the Jews have once before been regenerated, which defines his view of history and gives a prognostication for the future. According to him, history is a cycle, in which nations' creation, survival, influence on others, decadence and decline all follow in succession: a conception of history which comes from the Bible, though without prejudice to the Jews' future. This idea is stressed by the *Prolegomena* (*Muquadimma*), and also applies to other peoples, which makes the Arabs much like anyone else.

That a North African historian said in the fourteenth century that the Arabs were entering upon a period of decadence, and that their revival by the Turks, also Moslems, was a gift from God, was clearly not designed to please the Arabs either of his day or of ours.

In the history textbooks written for Iraqi children, it is not Ibn Khaldun, the greatest of all 'Arab' historians who is at the centre, but rather Abdu Abdallah Tarif Idrissi, the famous geographer.

THE CAUSE OF THE ARABS' MISFORTUNES: IMPERIALISM

What is imperialism? asks the Iraqi book:

> History gives evidence of the domination of certain countries over other lands and peoples to their own advantage and without considering the interests of the conquered or dominated people. We call this imperialism. The imperialists are like leeches which suck your blood.
>
> Our own Arab world has been subjected to this imperialist wave, which takes many forms, both direct, since the Portuguese conquests, and indirect, since the sending of missionaries into Syria, which gave the French a foothold there.

The Portuguese were first to penetrate the Arab world. . . .

Then there were the Ottomans. The Arabs were busy defending themselves against European imperialism when the Ottomans invaded, in 1516. They conquered Syria and Egypt, then Arabia and the Yemen, and, in 1534, Iraq.

Their power stretched to the Maghreb because the bey of Algeria collaborated with them and so became head of the Ottoman fleet.

By the end of the sixteenth century, the domination of the Ottomans over the Maghreb was total.

Then came the Dutch. . . .

Then the English. . . .

Finally the French came, and landed in Egypt in Bonaparte's time.

In Iraq, as in Egypt and throughout the Islamic world, imperialism holds prime place in the collective consciousness, and particularly the memory of the wars against the conquerors. In Iraq, the period of Turkish occupation has been more or less exorcized, but not in Egypt. There, early in the nineteenth century, Mehmet Ali gained independence from the sultan and constructed an empire out of lands belonging to his nominal suzerain, Mahmoud II; his son, Ibrahim, extended it to Libya and Tunisia.

EGYPT: THE VANGUARD OF ANTI-IMPERIALIST STRUGGLE FROM MEHMET ALI TO NASSER

'From his simple *vilayet* (province) in the Ottoman empire of 1805, i.e. from a place even lower in the hierarchy than the odjaks, Mehmet Ali built an empire.' But it was his son, Ibrahim, who spoke the same language as Mahomet and identified the empire with the Arab renaissance. A coalition of European powers led by the British put an end to his plan to reunite the

Arab world (1833). Nevertheless, father and son had transformed Egypt into a modern country, both industrially and militarily; it was as advanced, in the first half of the nineteenth century, as the chief European states themselves. In spite of the sudden check to Egypt's industrial and military development, 'the push towards an independent national state had been made; it affected spirit and institutions alike.' (Abd-El-Malek)

From then on, the history of Egypt developed under the shadow of colonialism and imperialism; but the impetus gained during the first third of the nineteenth century was to make it once again the engine of the Arab-Islamic regeneration after the Turkish empire's final defeat in 1918. Political independence was regained in 1936, but Egypt could not again take the lead in the Arab world until it had destroyed the symbol of imperial economic expropriation in the Arab world, the Suez Canal. Even then, in Iraqi or Syrian eyes, Egypt was not truly Arab – as to Moslems it is not a truly Islamic country.

In the Egyptian's view, the country was already an Islamic leader with the great victory of 1260 – a turning-point in world history – and through the glories of the Nile valley, especially Cairo University, the very centre of Islam.

Egypt was Islamic again during Mehmet Ali's time and, later, with Ibrahim and then Nasser.

NASSER, A CARTOON-STRIP HERO

Not surprisingly, Nasser himself even became the hero of a strip cartoon. We see the birth of a boy named Nasser in a lower-class quarter of Alexandria. His family had come from Asyut. He studies hard at school, passes his examinations in 1936, but is unable to enter military school because of his ideas and because he is the son of an ordinary family. So he studies law instead; however, thanks to the reforms of Nachas Pacha, he is finally able to enter the army.

The textbook version:

> He was transferred to Upper Egypt and made two good friends there – Zakharia Moheddin and Anwar El Sadat. Once the war was over, our three musketeers formed 'The Movement of Free Officers'. When in 1948 Britain withdrew from Palestine, they realized that the moment had come to defend the rights of the Arabs. On 15 May 1948, the Arab armies entered Palestine to liberate it, in spite of the few arms at their disposal and their lack of organization. During the war, Nasser, a young officer, met the grand Mufti of Jerusalem: 'I put my unit at the service of Palestine to fight for its liberation.' 'We were fighting in Palestine', Nasser recalls, 'but our dreams were in Egypt; our shots were directed against the enemy, but our souls were in Egypt. For we then discovered the truth; we had no munitions left. . . . An order had been given to advance on Harak Duiden which the Israelis were attacking, but before we could even start the attack, the Cairo newspapers announced it to the world and Felluga was surrounded. . . . I thought of Egypt and its problems. Our country was another surrounded Felluga. The upshot of it all was the occupation of Arab lands and thousands of Palestinian refugees'. . . . Within the army, the free officers therefore set up a programme for the revolution: (1) to fight imperialism and its accomplices, (2) to fight the feudalists, (3) to fight the domination of capital, (4) to create a powerful national army, (5) to establish social justice, (6) to set up political democracy.

Once the war was over, the free officers continued their activities, whereas the politicians went on with their in-fighting. After the WAFD had won the elections of 1950, the British were asked to evacuate the Suez Canal. Behind the scenes, Fuad, the minister of the interior, was encouraging demonstrations by the people, and subsequently by the Fedahin. 'I knew then that to hold the movement back was impossible: events were unfolding at great speed and the climate was favourable to revolution.' On the canal, the Fedahin stepped up their activity and, on 15 January 1952, they blew up a munitions depot at Tel El Kebir. On 25 January, British tanks encircled the barracks and fifty soldiers were killed. At the time of the Cairo fire, the authorities did nothing; 'accordingly, on 2 July at 23.00 hours, while King Faruk and his ministers were in Alexandria, troops following our plans moved in on the strategic points and the radio-station and arrested the ministers, so that within less than two hours Cairo was in the hands of the Free Officers.'

'The plan has worked' – Neguib was named commander-in-chief and Sadat declared on behalf of the group: 'Today Egypt has at last emerged from a dark period of its history.'

> The Free Officers wanted to punish Faruk.
>
> 'I don't want any bloodshed, let him go', Nasser ordered.
>
> 'Our problem, first of all, is how to resolve our relations with the British.'
>
> 'The evacuation of your troops is the only basis for good relations between our two countries', said Neguib.
>
> Churchill then interrupted the negotiations:
>
> 'Great Britain will not abandon its interests in the Orient', he said.
>
> 'Independence is not negotiable', replied Neguib.
>
> An officer then said to Nasser:
>
> 'It is time to return to the barracks.'

While the Moslem Brotherhood opposed the revolution, and even fomented a plot against Nasser, on 18 February 1955 Israel attacked Gaza. Nasser then met Tito and, with him, laid the basis for a policy of non-alignment, which was soon to be widely adopted by the Third World at the Bandung Conference.

'Communism is indeed a threat to our country, but imperialism was even more dangerous.'

To arm, and to build the dam of the Upper Nile, Egypt had asked for help from Europe and the USA.

Reading the paper in the morning, Nasser learned that, without warning, Pineau and Foster Dulles had decided not to lend their help. At the Revolutionary Council Nasser proposed three solutions: nationalize the canal, nationalize half the canal, threaten to nationalize the canal. 'Then I looked at Mr Black and imagined that he was Ferdinand de Lesseps'; while the Council was in discussion, our soldier comrades were on their way to the canal to take it. Nasser made a great speech: 'We are going to recover our rights over the dam and we are not going to give them up.' And he burst into laughter, a mocking sarcastic laughter, which avenged Egypt and the Arab world for the humiliations they had undergone.

'Eden and the British wanted revenge, as did Guy Mollet, for Nasser was helping the Algerian patriots.' Nasser hoped that the Americans would stop them and that, without America, they would not dare act. 'It was then that Israel attacked Egypt again, but the eighteen countries that used the canal condemned the action; Shepilov threatened the British and French who had to evacuate the canal with their tails between their legs.' 'The whole world had risen against the British and French, including even the Moslems of Russia (sic).'

Nasser, the victorious hero, was a strategist and a diplomat. After the 'union' with Syria, formed to 'forestall communism', he feared an attack from Turkey, 'but we will defend ourselves'. 'Dulles acts without thinking', Krushchev told him, 'but neither of us wants a war, so be careful.' When in 1961 Syria was separated from Egypt, Nasser decided against military intervention.

He intended to remain a peaceful hero. After the six-day war he resigned, but the people called him back and, once more, he won peace and assured the Palestinians of his aid.

This account is of course written in strip-cartoon style. But there are also several omissions. For example, the state of Israel is not even mentioned, nor is its recognition by the UN in 1948, when the peoples' democracies and the USSR participated in the vote. It was precisely to stop Israel from coming into existence that, on 15 May 1948, troops from Egypt, Iraq, Syria, Lebanon and Transjordan invaded the country, and not just the forces of King Abdullah, the only ones actually mentioned. The troops were pushed back and the UN ordered a ceasefire which was rejected by the Arabs. Then again, the plans for the partition of Palestine were rejected by both sides in turn. A further omission is the failure of Nasser's economic policy in the United Arab Republic, and of his social reforms in Egypt; there is, again, silence as to the dissolution of the Moslem Brotherhood – which happened before the attempt on Nasser's life, which they plotted; silence, too, on the imprisonment of Egyptian communist leaders, and the total ban on their party, whereas a principle of the Free Officers had been the installation of true political democracy within the country. This was not effectively instituted until 1976, by Sadat, and then only partially, since only two political parties are legalized in Egypt ('that is enough') and since the communist party is still forbidden there.

Just what Nasser represented outside Egypt, for the Arab world at large, can be seen in the magnificent films of Muhammed Chukri Jamil. In *The Walls*, the small shopkeepers of Baghdad are entirely transformed by the cataclysmic enthusiasm which culminated in the nationalization of Suez. Beginning with the school and some workshops, the movement won over the young and penetrated the political world right into the seraglio. The police of Nuri es Said, the 'Englishman', used informers and 'thugs' to terrorize the patriots; whereas the big merchant exported rice that the poor needed to eat and, to gain the contract, offered a big bribe to the negotiator. It becomes clear that imperialism and tyranny help the profiteers; and the only 'healthy' elements are those which rise against the oppressors.

Just after Suez, there was a revolt in Baghdad. It was bloodily put down. In *The Walls*, scenes alternate in a powerfully-orchestrated way, and a musical accompaniment of great resonance marks the marriage of the master, the mounting of the insurrection, and the funerals of the victims of the repression. *The Walls* shows admirably how an area of Baghdad had become conscious of the great days of the Arab world. The Baghdad Pact is constantly attacked, and so is Nuri es Said. Imperialism remains anonymous, neither England nor America being cited. Everything happens as though the Arab nation had really existed in 1918, and had been destroyed by imperialism and Zionism. Everything happens, that is, as though, before imperialism, the Arabs had never been subjected to the Turk, and, before that, to the Mongols.

FROM THE CRUSADES TO ISRAEL

In these books and films, 'imperialism' appears with the arrival of Portuguese voyagers and merchants in the Arab-Islamic world. The European perspective, however, is rather to differentiate between the preindustrial European expansion overseas, in the sixteenth, seventeenth and eighteenth centuries, which did not reach the Islamic-Arab world, and imperialism proper, which enveloped the whole world, bit into the fringes of the Turkish empire and was closely linked with industrialization. By taking imperialism back to the fifteenth century, and in failing to make any distinction between non-territorial expansion (say the Portuguese in the Indian Ocean) and territorial expansion, Arab-Islamic historians can thus explain the economic 'backwardness' of the East in comparison to the West and attribute it to the Great Discoveries. Is such an explanation legitimate? Whether it is or not, it certainly obscures the effects of the Ottoman conquest which are skipped over, even though the empire lasted several centuries and though the Arab renaissance, in the nineteenth century, had been essentially anti-Turkish and even involved Moslems and Christians (in the Lebanon).

Another tradition takes 'imperialism' back even further, to the Crusades. This tradition is relatively recent for, during that long period which stretches from the twelfth to the nineteenth century, Islam was ignorant of the very concept of a crusade. In comparison with the other wars which the Arabs fought in all far-flung corners of their empire, these Christian wars were nothing special. The idea and the concept of the crusade, Gabrieli has shown, are notions which the Moslems incorporated only later on into their history, and saw it as a sort of revenge by the Christians for the Arab conquests. In Iraq, this entire era, the military epic and victory over the Crusaders is seen as a feat of the Arab nation as a whole, and part of the *Jihad* or holy war of 'Arabdom', '*uruba*.

Obviously the difficulty, as it happens, is that the 'liberators' of the Arab lands from the Crusaders were not Arabs at all, but their conquerors, the Turkish house of the Zengids and the Kurdish house of the Ayubites. History books for Arabs also omit the Kurdish origins of Saladin: they make him out to have been an Arab – after all, his generosity, his nobility and his cavalier spirit are supposed to be the outstanding features of the Arab people. These historical works concede that the Arab emirs, such as Usama Munqidh, collaborated with the Franks and did not fight them: in this way the books stress the role of the masses, the 'peoples' militias', and their rage at the treaty of 1229, when the emir handed Jerusalem to the emperor Frederick II.

In Egypt, stress is also laid on the Crusades – particularly St Louis's – which threatened the country. The Crusade appears as the starting-point of the Egyptian renaissance; it led to an era when Egypt became leader of the Arab world. Thus the Egyptians saved Islam by defeating the Mongols in 1260, and again by defeating the Franks at El Mansoura. The truth of the matter is that in both cases it was not Egyptians who decided these battles, but Mamelukes, i.e. Cherkess and Turkish slaves who became the soldiers and then masters of Egypt. Though ruled by the Turks, Egypt was, as we have seen, none the less the first 'Arab' state to free itself in the time of Mehmet Ali. It then won the leading position in the Arab world, a position it has never since lost, as was to be shown in the prominence of Nasser and the first United Arab Republic.

In any case, the eastern historians say, the harm done to the Arab world, first by the Crusades and then imperialism, is immeasurable. They make a pun and assert that whereas the West took from them any advantages (ghunm), and learnt Moslem culture, science and fortress-architecture, the East had from this only harm (ghurm); the West sowed ruins. While they had brought Europe from infancy to maturity (Hitti), the Crusades only led Asia to ruin.

The Arab historians say that the same humiliation will be the fate of any imitator of the Franks attacking Islam and the Arabs. Even in 1911, Al-Himara of Beirut had a cartoon showing Saladin defending the Arabs in the Gezreel valley against Joshua Hankin's Zionists. Soon enough, the rantings of a General Gouraud or a General Allenby, of a Louis Madelin or of a Kipling, with their 'Rule Britannia' or 'French presence', had to give place to two independent states, Syria and Iraq.

The lesson is obvious. Just as the Arabs won in the past by exhausting and destroying the Crusaders and regaining their territory, so the Arabs will win today, will absorb the imperialist's positions and swallow up Israel.

What is there left of the Latin states in Syria, and what remains of the French in Algeria?

DID THE FRENCH EVER COLONIZE ALGERIA?

The women can, here, have the first lines, collected by Assia Djebar, in her *Nouba des femmes du Mont Chenoua*. They do not write history. They do not even talk it aloud, but rather whisper it; it is their wombs which for centuries past have produced the men and women of the Djurjura.

Assia Djebar shows them grouped round the huge tent, telling stories to their children, about ancestors, the tribe, and resistance to the Christian (never French) who disturbed the rhythm and the unchanging patterns of life on the Chenoua mountain.

Stealthily, Assia Djebar's camera takes us into the heart of an unknown world, to the group of women whose tragic and war-like infants have been their only contribution to history – during the anti-French rising of 1860 and that of a century later, when the French were expelled once for all. The wounds are still there, and the first only just healed.

These women have not really changed since Delacroix's painting *Femmes d'Alger*. The seraglio has been reconstituted, together with the rule of invisibility and silence. Cloistered in this way, they must neither talk nor know; otherwise they would be like serpents to which poison has been given.

Assia Djebar's photography is the revolt of a Mudjadin against her own ignorance of history and cruel blindfolding. It also shows, as she meant it to, that one hundred years of French presence have had no more effect on this Arab village of tents than a tick on the tail of a camel.

INVERTED HISTORY

History taught to Algerians is for obvious reasons quite different from the North African history that is taught in France. The French version takes much from the Roman tradition, of which the French were consciously the heirs; and this is the only point of agreement, for the Algerian often describes the French as Roumi. Otherwise, generally speaking, *Je connais l'Algérie* presents children with a view of the past which not only differs from European historiography, but is its exact opposite, a counterpoint.

From the start, stress is placed upon the antiquity of three African states. Before the coming of Rome, there were Phoenicians who 'landed' in North Africa and founded 'factories'. At that time, and during the wars between Rome and Carthage, the rest of North Africa was divided into three kingdoms: a Moorish kingdom to the west of Moulouya; a Masaesilian kingdom centred on Tafna; and a Massilian kingdom to the east, which ruled over Numidia with Cirta as its capital. King Massinissa ruled from 248 to 203 BC. He resumed the Carthaginian conquests with the slogan 'Africa for the Africans'; he 'transformed the country while encouraging agriculture and the development of towns'.

> After the death of Massinissa, Rome, which annexed Carthage, undertook to dominate the kingdoms of the Maghreb. Jugurtha eliminated his cousins who were 'too subservient to Rome', and 'seized the throne of Numidia'. He refused to bend towards the wishes of the Romans and waged war for seven years while pursuing a tactic of ambushes and harassment. . . . The treacherous king of the Moors, Bocchus (*sciliet* the king of Morocco), delivered him to the Romans who took him prisoner in 105. . . . The Roman legions were constantly exposed to resistance from the hostile populace and, after the second century, uprising followed uprising until in 428 the invading Vandals came to sweep away 'the remains of the decadent Roman empire'. The Vandal period was one of tyrannical occupation 'but its reputation for atrocities was probably exaggerated, since it was made up by enemies'. It was ended by the Reconquest (*Reconquista*) ordered from Byzantium by the

emperor Justinian and realized in 553 by his general Belisarius. The Byzantine period of rule was marked by a very harsh exploitation of the country, by revolts and by the disorders provoked by oppression. It was a period of decline.

'THE ARAB MIDDLE AGES WERE A PERIOD OF PROSPERITY'

Such is the title of the chapter which opens with the Arab 'conquest' (not the 'liberation', as in the Iraqi or Egyptian works) under the aegis of Uqba Ben Nafi, and the foundation of Kairouan in 670.

The Kahina, queen of the Aurès in Numidia, raised troops and led the resistance to the Arab armies. She was at first victorious and beat them to the edge of the Meskiana and back into Tripolitania. Then, under repeated attack, 'she finally died in 702 on the field of battle with the caliph's powerful army. On the eve of the last battle she had *ordered* her son to join the ranks of the victor.'

After that comes 'a fast-moving and sometimes confusing period of history where kingdoms and dynasties rise up and disappear, some of them weak and some powerful'. It was also a period of great economic and cultural development, in which arts and sciences flourished.

In 776, the Persian Abderraman Ibn Rostem founded a Kharijite kingdom at Tahert. It was at odds with the dominant current of Islam, but prospered until its successors, defeated in 909 by the Fatimids of Egypt, were forced to flee to the south, where they founded the towns of the M'zab.

The Zirids and Hammadits created two dynasties which then fought over the land, whether in alliance with Cairo or Baghdad. They managed to maintain local power and to beat off the invasions of Beni Hillal in the eleventh century.

Then came the 'conquest of North Africa right up to Algeria by the Almoravids from the Mauritanian desert; they ruled over Moslem Spain which they defended against the Christian Kings.'

In the twelfth century the Almohad movement dominated Spain and North Africa for a hundred years.

In 1235 the Abdelwadites of Tlemcen created both a new dynasty and an independent kingdom which in spite of attacks from the Merinid sultans of Fez . . . lasted for nearly three centuries, until 1554.

Tlemcen, capital of this kingdom, was a prosperous city and the most important economic centre of the Maghreb. It lay at the crossroads of an international, well-organized trading network between Europe and the Sudan, whence came ivory, spices, slaves and, above all, gold. It is presumably from there that the Tlemcenian custom comes of weighing young brides against piles of gold ornaments.

This analysis is radically different from the traditional western vision, which comes from Sallust or Livy. To read them, with their exclusive interest in the history of Rome in Africa, and not in Arab North Africa, you might suppose that Africa was divided between the Carthaginian and Roman causes. In the book for young Algerians, the Berbers at least have their own historical development; they are not just 'indirectly present' (P. Nora). The Berbers, who feared the Phoenicians and Romans, represent 'Africa for the Africans'. Through these works, they can be seen in revolt against Carthaginians, Romans, Byzantines and then Arabs, and finally the French. Their identity is shown in the foundation of these three kingdoms, whose existence predates the arrival of the Romans; it was again demonstrated after the Arab conquests by the renaissance of these kingdoms and empires which 'lasted for several centuries' despite dangers and invasions. In the intervals the population was forced to retire into the interior, leaving the coast and the plains to the invaders; in the case of a lengthier occupation, the desert became the last refuge, until the Reconquest. If a new invader appeared, the Maghrebians would be there to help him chase out the former oppressor. When Rome arrived, they chased out Carthage; when the Vandals came, they chased out the Romans; and with the Arabs, the Byzantines were expelled. Religion to some extent enabled the Maghreb to bear the strain of foreign occupation – first under Rome, then with Aryanism in the Vandals' time, and then with Kharijism in the Islamic period.

The Kharijites, chased out by the Fatimids of Egypt, took refuge in the oasis towns of the south, the M'zab. At that time, *nomadism was certainly not associated with the desert and with pillage, as in the French tradition, but with urban commerce and liberty.*

In the same way, local power, the preserve of the tribes, or the village, by no means represented a primitive level of political organization which 'the Berber never overcame', as is affirmed or maintained by colonial history, but, rather, represented an advanced level of organization such as is necessitated by foreign occupation. Here, then, are two characteristics which have been admirably delineated by the Maghrebian historian Abdallah Laroui.

Such history is quite the reverse of that presented in Europe, where the period in which the Islamic Maghreb enjoyed its greatness is called the 'dark ages', and where the eras of foreign domination are considered as 'times of peace and progress'. Its organization into states appears natural, destroyed only by invaders, and was refounded after the expulsion *manu militari* of these invaders. Here then is a vision of history which destroys the comfortable images of the West, which are associated with the 'backwardness' of the Maghreb, its 'incapacity' to organize itself into states and the 'curse' which struck it with the triple invasion of the Vandals, the Arabs and the Hilali, as contrasted with the better era that came with the Foreign Legion and the *Pieds-Noirs*.

'ALGÉRIE FRANÇAISE'

The 'French' period takes up two chapters, one for the conquest and one for the 'revolution of November 1954', as if between these two dates there were nothing but a void, neither French, nor Algerian, with no colonists and no progress.

> French colonization began in 1830 and was only imposed after hard fighting. The French fleet landed at Sidi Ferruch, Abd el Kader resisted, the Sheikh el Mokhrani rose in resistance: such are the episodes of this section of history. Sheikh el Mokhrani died on the field of battle on 5 May 1871; but the fighting continued for nearly a year, led by Si Aziz and Bou Mezrag, the former caliph of Abd el Kader . . . it ended in bloody suppression: summary executions, villages burnt, settlements pillaged, cattle expropriated. The occupation of land spread rapidly. . . . Deprived of their goods, the Algerians were pushed back to the mountains and the dry areas. From 1920 onwards, the Algerian movement took on a new vigour. The North African Star, founded in 1926 and banned in 1937, developed into the Party of the Algerian People (PPA) and made nationalist claims. The *Ulema* movement, founded in 1931, fought a vigorous campaign, under the leadership of Sheikh Ben Badis, for a national culture and character. The UDMA and MTLD fought with weapons of propaganda and electioneering. But the thwarting of their efforts forced the MTLD to create the Secret Organization (OS) in readiness for armed struggle.

Thus there is no transition between the conquest and the war of liberation. 'The Algerians have no nation: let France give them one, and they will not look for another', said Ferhat Abbas. As to this 'non-nation' there is nothing said – in fact there is nothing on Ferhat Abbas or Messali Hadj, the founders of the UDMA, or the North African Star, nor on the Algerian trade unions, nor on the Algerian Communist Party, nor Nasser nor Islam, and there is not even a mention for Ben Bella, Khider, Boudiaf or Ait Ahmed. The only people cited are the dead, those killed during the 'revolution'. French people are simply not mentioned.

Except, that is, to mention that in 1830, an agreement had been signed guaranteeing the liberty and the possessions of the Algerians. 'It was not respected.' There is of course mention of the French troops in 1830, the resistance to French soldiers, and the struggle against the French military; the million and a half deaths, the hundreds of thousands of refugees, the border areas made uninhabitable, the countryside ravaged by destruction are all mentioned – 'a heavy price paid by the Algerian people for the conquest of liberty and independence'.

On the 'French achievement' there is, of course, hardly a word. 'What does it matter that there is electricity in my house, if my house is not mine,' said Ferhat Abbas.

Nothing figures of the presence of Frenchmen – not a word to make the reader think that a million Frenchmen lived for nearly a century in this country, that they procreated, worked, prospered, 'despite Arab rights and honour', and who, having mocked and humiliated the Arabs, were expelled in the outcome of a long and harsh war. Now, children must be preserved from knowledge of the punishment and the rape.

6

THE PERSIAN AND TURKISH VARIANTS

THE ARABIC-MUSLIM WORLD AND IRAN

A brief chronology, 550 BC–AD 1936

550	Cyrus King of the Persians.
521	Darius I extends the Achaemenid empire to the Indus.
490–480	Persian Wars.
334	Alexander the Great occupies the Persian empire.
250	Revolt of the Arsacid Parthians against the Seleucid heirs of Alexander.
2nd C.	Dynasty of the Ptolemies in Egypt.
1st C. BC	Conquest of the East by Rome.
53 BC	Crassus defeated by the Parthians at Carrhae.
1st C. AD	Evangelization of the East.
AD 224	Ardeshir founds the Sassanid dynasty.
3rd–6th C.	Late Roman empire. Extension of Sassanid empire to Yemen.

451	Invasion of the Huns.
610	Chosroes II occupies Jerusalem, Egypt, Armenia. Zenith of the Sassanid Empire.
628	Byzantine reconquest under Heraclius.
632	Mahomet.
633	Beginning of Arab conquests.
651	End of Sassanids.
680	Arab dynasty of the Omayyads. Massacre at Kerbela. Birth of Shiism.
751	Zenith and end of Arab conquests: battles of Poitiers (Gaul) and Talas (China).
Second half of 8th C.	Reign of Abbasids: Harun al-Rashid.
9th C.	Saffarids and Samanids of Iran. Breakup of the 'Arab' empire.
945	Dynasty of the Buyids.
969	Fatimids of Egypt.
End of 9th C.	Conversion of Turks to Islam.
1055	Entry of Seljuk Turks into Baghdad.
1071	Victory of Turks over Byzantium at Manzikert.
1180–1204	Saladin, 3rd and 4th Crusades.
1221	Genghis Khan at Bukhara.
1258	Fall of Baghdad.
1260	The Mamelukes of Egypt repulse the Mongols.
Beginning of 15th C.	Egypt becomes the cultural centre of the Moslem world.
1453	Death of Timur.
1453	Fall of Constantinople. Triumph of Turkish empire.
1501	Renaissance of Persia: Ismail Shah Safenid blocks the expansion of the Turkish empire.

1512	Zenith of the three Moslem empires: Turkish, Persian, Mongol.
1569	Battle of Lepanto.
1580–1620	Shah Abbas of Ispahan retakes Baghdad. Foundation of Ispahan.
1683	The Turks threaten Vienna.
1722	Invasion of the Afghans.
1736	Nadir Shah of Persia occupies Delhi.
1800	Bonaparte in Egypt.
1813–28	Russo-Persian Wars: Treaty of Turkmenistan.
1830	The French in Algeria.
1833	Autonomy of Egypt under Mehmet Ali and Ibrahim. Treaty of Unkiar Skellesi: the Turkish empire becomes the 'sick man of Europe'.
Mid-19th C.	Renaissance of Arab National Movement.
1881–1904	Conquest of Tunisia and Morocco by France.
1883–1914	Seizure of Egypt by the British.
1906	Movement of Young Turks.
1907	Iran divided into zones of influence between Russia and England.
1915	Sykes-Picot agreements on the partition of the Turkish empire.
1916	Hussein proclaimed king of the Arabs.
1917	Balfour Declaration on a Jewish homeland in Palestine.
1918	Franco-British protectorates throughout the Arab world: Syria, Iraq, Lebanon. Breakup of Ottoman empire.
1918–23	Renaissance of Pan-Turkish movement.
1936	Egypt becomes independent.

Of all the Islamic countries, it was certainly Iran that stood at the greatest distance from the Arabs. Whereas in Egypt, or even in the Maghreb, national identities are sometimes dissolved into a larger cultural identity, where Egypt could happily play the role of leader of the Arab world, in Iran, dissociation from the Arabs is a vital part of the mentality and of perceived history, even though the first historians wrote in Arabic, and though, before the Arabs, there were no Iranian historians.

As in Algeria since Islamization, the national character was distinguished by a schism, though clearly hostility towards the Arabs and then the Turks has been much stronger than dislike of the Sunni Moslems. This fact is evident in the school textbooks. In Iran, the great epoch against which the country measures itself is not the Islamic era, but rather the Sassanid period, which the Arabs brought to an end. The European historical viewpoint is that the Achaemenid era was the greatest in Persian history, though only in so far as its inheritance was taken over and reproduced by Greece, Rome and the Renaissance. Seen in different eyes, the Iranians' own choice can be justified, however, for the Sassanid epoch was the only time when Persia shone with an unrivalled brilliance, since the Roman empire, in its decline, was falling victim to the barbarian invasions. However, within a century, Sassanid Persia collapsed against the Arabs. Just as is the case in Egypt, pre-Islamic history takes a large place in the books. From the outset it is precisely and categorically asserted that the Iranians are of Aryan race.

THE PERSIANS AS ARYANS AND FOUNDERS OF THE FIRST GREAT RELIGION

'The Aryans, at the dawn of history' is the title of the first chapter of a historical work in use at Pahlavi university.

> four thousand years ago, several tribes arrived from the plains and mountains of the North. These tribes were Aryan, and were the ancestors of today's Iranians. . . . Recent archaeological

work has shown that the Persians of that day had a brilliant civilization, distinguished by its architecture.

The greatness of Iran predates that of Islam; the Persians were not always Moslem.

The Persians, like all ancient peoples, worshipped several gods, but Zoroaster gave the Iranian nation a new vision. Ahura Mazda was the great God, and his commandments were written down in a Holy Book called *Avesta*, which taught three fundamental principles: the good word, the good deed, and precise thinking.

Thus Iran is presented as founder of the first great religion, and is therefore also defined as the first of the great empires. Earlier on 'the brave Medes had expelled the Assyrians [for which we are no doubt meant to read 'Iraqis'] and so became independent again'. The Iranian past is put at some distance from the Semites, and comes correspondingly nearer to the West. This is shown in the history of the Achaemenid empire, which is taken from Greek and Roman sources. Myths and legends associated with the birth of Rome recur here. Thus, with the birth of Cyrus:

King Astyaj had a daughter named Mandan. One evening he dreamed that in her womb she bore a tree that could cover the whole of Asia (in Herodotus, we read that 'from his daughter came a torrent that flooded the whole of Asia'); in a second dream, it was a vine that grew out of his daughter's body. He called one of his magi and asked, 'What is the meaning of this dream?' The magus replied, 'Mandan will bear a son who will be the greatest of all kings; he will take your own lands, and with them, the whole world.' Magus was afraid, sent his daughter off to the west, and married her to Cambyses; when she conceived a child, the cruel grandfather ordered her to abandon the child in a forest, to be devoured by wild beasts. But the servant who had been given this task secretly gave the infant to a forester, whose own new-born child had just died, and who now adopted the baby. Cyrus's destiny was secured: he grew up big and strong, and soon attacked Astyaj on account of his excessive taxation. Cyrus won, and organized one of the most up-to-date armies of his day, for he even had huge chariots, drawn by sixteen bulls. The kings of Babylon, Lydia and Egypt allied against him but he beat them all and conquered Babylon. Sixty years ago an edict of Cyrus's was rediscovered, in which he proclaimed the liberty of nations. In this way, the Jews regained their freedom after seventy years' oppression at the hands of the Assyrians.

For a western reader, the account of Darius and his successors has a surprise in store, since it refers to his greatness, sense of justice, the Babylonian revolt, and the growth of his empire. 'He left for Europe where, several times, he led his army into battle, occupying Macedonia and part of what is today Romania.' There is no mention of Hellas, Xerxes, the conflict with the Greeks, or the battles of Marathon and Salamis. The whole conflict of 'Greeks' and 'Barbarians' is left out, together with any reference to the political and cultural rivalry of these other Aryans who founded western civilization. None the less, the book dwells at length on the resistance to Roman invasion: it is held up as a model of courage and glory. After the Seleucids and the Arsacids, there were more and more wars with Rome. 'The Roman army, though it conquered Europe and Africa, never managed, even under Antoninus, to take the slightest fringe of Iranian territory.'

Persia's greatness inspired the Ardeshir family. It dreamt of restoring the Achaemenid empire, and of recreating Iran's religious identity through the revival of Mazdaism. 'Ardeshir defeated the Romans several times and occupied Armenia. His successor, Sapor, captured the emperor Valerian, who, in a fresco, is depicted kneeling before Sapor's horse.' In the reign of Sapor II, 'the Great', the Persian empire triumphed over two enemies at once:

> the Arabs from the south who were broken several times in the field, and the Byzantine empire, which, secretly, he had seen for himself: one day, Sapor II disguised himself and went to Constantinople. He was identified, and thrown into prison, but managed to escape. He came with an army to the capital's outskirts; the emperor Julian attacked him again and again, and was slain. Sapor II reigned for seventy years, during which there were ten Roman emperors.

STRENGTH AND TOLERANCE: THE VIRTUES OF THE SASSANID EMPIRE

> So that his son should not be brought up in enervating luxury, Yasdegard handed his education to an Arab emir, the governor of one of the empire's provinces. This made the boy a true horseman and hunter. He and his brother fought over the crown, and a decision was made that the crown should go to whichever of the two managed to retrieve it from a den of lions. Behram won . . . he fought off the Yellow-skins (Huns), reached the Indian frontier, granted liberty to all Christian peoples who wished to keep their faith, and made universal peace.

This care to highlight the tolerance of the King of Kings is constantly displayed, whereas in reality the enforcement of Mazdaism was never stronger than in the sixth century, especially in Christian Armenia. The 'Pact of Peace' drawn up between Heraclius and Chosroes was in fact only a partition of Armenia between Byzantium and Ctesiphon. 'The Holy Cross was returned to the Romans, and Heraclius himself took it back to Jerusalem.'

THE ARAB CONQUEST

Of the Arab conquest and the fall of the Sassanids, as with any great disaster, there were premonitions.

> In the time of Piruz, the empire suffered a great drought; to fight famine, the King of Kings bought food abroad, and forced the rich to share their supplies, instituting a ceremony, *Abrezagan*, to commemorate the return of the rains. But he committed a very ugly crime in killing his brother and other Sassanid princes so that there should be no claimants for the throne other than his own children. In fact, he had already killed his elder brother, Ormazd III, and had called in the Turks to help him to capture the throne. He was punished for this, for he died of the plague. . . . Several years later, the Sassanid empire fell into hopeless chaos – twelve monarchs came swiftly, one after the other, and two of them were women.

In 632, Yasdegard III came to the throne, as last of the Sassanids. In the twelfth year of the Hegira, the Moslems started to attack, and they defeated the governors, who were quarrelling among themselves. Yasdegard was forced to flee to the eastern provinces; the Arabs seized his capital, and the King of Kings found refuge far away, near Merv. 'There he sought asylum from a miller who did let him stay, but, on seeing his jewels and clothing, killed and robbed him during the night.' So ended the last great Sassanid kingdom. The Zoroastrian religion was cut back and 'in Iran a new era blossomed'. Mahyar Djavoherian well remembers how, at school, he was taught Islam and the story of the Arab conquest.

> Our first image of the Arabs was one of peasant ruffians – disorderly and unorganized, living from pillage in the desert; they were savages who wandered around on camels whereas

the great Persian army had powerful cavalry. The Iranians' defeat was not the fault of their king, but happened because their many wars had weakened them ... the Arabs simply exploited the situation ... and then again they were inspired by faith, a fanaticism that could lead them to the ends of the earth.

THE IMAM ALI, A TRUE IRANIAN PEASANT

The history of Mahomet is a kind of Vulgate. In Shiite Iran, however, the caliphs Abu Bakr, Omar and Othman were succeeded by Ali, who took the title of imam – 'the first Shiite imam'; and, as Mahyar says, 'the school picture of Ali is exactly like an Iranian peasant'. Everything is shown as if Mahomet did not have any proper successors before Ali; the schoolteacher explained to Mahyar that the Arabs disliked Ali because he was associated with the Prophet through his wife, Fatima, daughter of Mahomet, whereas the Arabs despised girls, and often buried them at birth. Mahomet was the first Arab to respect girls, and he gave his own daughter to Ali. Ali was taught the art of government, and the 'words of Ali', or Nahjol-Balagi, were models for governors, just as Mahomet's 'words' had been before.

'Ali, thus glorified, sought to safeguard Islam; he always fought renegades, and was killed by one of his enemies.' The essential episode is this:

On the death of Moawiya, the imam Hussein, son of Ali, declared a *jihad*. He went to Kufa to collect an army, but the town's inhabitants would not keep their promise, and abandoned the Prophet's grandson, who stood alone, with seventy-two relatives. He died valiantly with them in a battle that has no counterpart in history: he had been cruelly betrayed.

From that time onwards, Islam was divided, between the Shiites who were faithful to Ali and had twelve subsequent imams, and the Sunni, who claim that there were four caliphs after Mahomet. It is common for Shiites to hold up the last two caliphs for ridicule and blasphemy. During Ashwa, at Mesched, the Shiite sanctuary, Omar is made to look absurd, dressed in red, and showered with insults in Persian. To say that someone is 'an Omar' or 'looks like Omar' is a great insult. The Sunni way of prayer is also ridiculed: they pray with their arms folded, whereas the Shiites pray with them down.

This is an anti-Arab tradition. Among the evil were the 'renegades' whom Ali fought (i.e. the Syrian Arab, Moawiya); and their contempt for women is also seen as a negative quality. Finally, the town of Kufa is in Mesopotamia, i.e. Arab Iraq. Here we see the root of an antagonism that splits Iran from the rest of the Moslem world, especially Iraq, where the Sunni predominate. What is perturbing is that Iran did not really become Shiite for good until eight centuries later, when the main enemy was no longer the Arab but the Turk, who had taken over the Sunni mantle. History, as this shows, brings the past to life for present-day purposes. In the textbook published by Pahlavi university, there is utter silence as to the fact that, after the Kerbela massacre, Moslem Persia as a whole, for several centuries to come, adhered to the Sunni cause.

THE GLORY OF MOSLEM PERSIA

For the whole period up to the Mongol invasions in the thirteenth century, history, as taught to children, is marked by hostility towards the Arab conqueror.

> The caliphs gradually lost their power. The Abbasids, who descended from the Prophet's uncle, were greatly loved, and the Iranians were even more opposed to the Omayyads than the other Moslems. . . . Abdu Muslem Chorasan and his brave soldiers fought the Omayyads; the whole of Iran, up to

> Mesopotamia, rose in revolt. In 750, the Omayyad caliphs were killed ... five centuries of Abbasid rule began ... Caliph Mansur ordered Chosroes's palace to be razed to the ground, and a magnificent palace of brick was built at Baghdad. It was so well-constructed that even the Arabs could not demolish it.

The book goes directly from the massacre at Kerbela to the accession of Abdu Muslem Chorassan, and telescopes the entire Omayyad era, just as it does with Iranian dependence on the Arab masters of Damascus. Under the Abbasids, as we have seen, the empire gradually changed from an Arab to a Moslem state, in which the non-Arab peoples were freed. The agent of this 'revolution' was in fact a Persian, of the Chorassan family. The Abbasid period therefore receives full treatment, whereas in the Baghdad textbooks, the exact opposite is true, for the period is skipped over. 'Iran had accepted Islam, but not the local commanders', i.e. the Arabs; and after the conquest 'the Iranians constantly strove for independence. Some princes did obey Baghdad, but only in appearance, so that Iran could win back her freedom.'

'Four great dynasties assisted the recovery of independence: the Taherids after 208 (830), the Saffarids and Samanids after 259 (881) and the Buyids from 322 to 447 (963–1069).' Harun al-Rashid was famous for the *Thousand and One Nights* but he also revived Persian court life of the Sassanid period, and so coloured the whole Moslem world with the refinements of Persian civilization, though it had disintegrated. He was succeeded by Mamun (191–211, i.e. 813–33). 'The son of Harun al-Rashid was Persian on his mother's side. He became caliph and killed Amin at Baghdad.' In fact, Amin was the half-brother of Mamun, and his mother was an Arab, whereas Mamun was the son of Harun al-Rashid's second wife, a Persian slave. Harun al-Rashid had foreseen a conflict and the formation of two quarrelling clans, and so divided his inheritance into two parts, the greater of which was given to the elder son, Amin, who meant to keep his brother, who was living in Meshed, under close control. Soon, it came to war between the half-brothers, and Mamun won, though only after overcoming fierce resistance by Arab Baghdad; he tried to institute, officially, the *mutazil* doctrine to reconcile Shiites and Sunni, but failed in this.

> The Iranians loved Ali's descendants, and Mamun declared as his successor the eighth imam of the Shiites, Al-Rida (a descendant of Hussein). The imam Al-Rida was, however, murdered in a little village by poisoned grapes. Since his death, Shiites have made the pilgrimage to Meshed, where his tomb is. . . .
>
> With cunning and hypocrisy, the Baghdad caliphs tried to divide the Iranians, and fomented conflict between the Saffarids and the Samanids, dynasties who ruled, respectively, the centre and north-east. Once, one of the Saffarids, Amir Munis, was captured by the Samanids. In his prison, a warder prepared his meal; but a dog, attracted by the smell, stuck his muzzle into the saucepan, was burnt, and ran off with his muzzle still stuck in the pot. 'The world has turned upside down, you see', said Amir Muhis to the warder, 'Yesterday, the greatest cooks came one by one to serve me their very best dishes, and now a dog runs off with my bowl.'

THE RESTORATION OF ANCIENT (PRE-ARAB) PERSIAN GLORY

'The Samanid state, centred on Bokhara, had an extraordinarily brilliant period in the tenth century.' Like the Saffarids, the Samanids construed a Sassanid provenance for themselves after they had taken up the succession of the Tahirids. At the Samanid court, there grew up a neo-Persian literature, of which the

Shahnama of Ferdusi and the musical poetry of Rudaki were famous instances.

> It is said that when Mahmud established the Ghaznavid dynasty (which replaced the Samanids) and had to remunerate Ferdusi, he offered the same number of coins as his predecessor had given Ferdusi, but in silver, not, as had been the case, gold. Ferdusi saw this as a bad omen, and fled. The prince felt repentant, but when his messengers finally caught up with Ferdusi to pay him the difference, the poet was already dead. . . . In the Elburz, in the west of the country, there lived the Mazandaran heroes, brave horsemen who, from their mountainous heights, looked down over the Arabs, who did not dare challenge them. The Persians' greatest desire was to regain the greatness they had enjoyed before the Arabs, and to chase out the Abbasids, with their wickedness and cruelty. The Mazandaran kings, such as Maziar, had tried to achieve this, but in vain, but in 334 (945) an army led by Ahmad did enter Baghdad. The caliph was overthrown, and for a hundred years the caliphate of Baghdad was in the hands of Buyid generals, who came originally from Gilan, on the Caspian. . . . It was at this time that Avicenna lived. He was the great Persian physician, and lived firstly at the royal court, then at Bokhara in the Samanid state, and finally at Isfahan. His books, such as *Ar-shifa* ('Healing') were an important scientific source in the Europe of that time.

The Ghaznavids were kings who had 'strength and courage'; they conquered the Chorassan, the Sistan, and western India. Masud, a Moslem and Muhajid, went several times into India, where they destroyed statues and idols, but they protected artists and scholars, among them the great astronomer Biruni, who wrote a book on the culture, religion and manners of the Indians (*Fa'rihk-el-Hind*). The Ghaznavids were finally overthrown by the great Turek-Bey, hero of the Seljuks, who, by 1055, governed a state that stretched from Turkestan to the Mediterranean. He was of Turkish race, though Iranianized, and he became the first sultan. His successor, Alp Arslan, attacked the Byzantine army in 1071 and crushed it (at Manzikert), and the Persian troops captured its commander, the emperor Romanus Diogenes. The sultan nevertheless freed him. In this era lived the great poet Omar Khayyam, who was also an astronomer and mathematician. He wrote a universal calendar, and his literary epic, the *Rubaiyat*, was translated by Edward Fitzgerald in 1859.

THE ASSASSINS (OR HASHISH-SMOKERS)

In this period, the Ismaili sect established a secret organization, the Assassins which, under the leadership of Hassan Ibn el-Sabbah, conspired to attack the government.

> The organization was highly centralized, and its combatants, the *feddayin*, murdered a great number of highly-placed people, including kings. They lived in an inaccessible and impregnable keep, and were all disciples of Hassan Ibn el-Sabbah, who sent them out to kill his enemies. The name 'Assassin' comes from the Arab word *hashashun*, or 'smoker of hashish', a drug that the sect's members used to anticipate in spirit the joys of Paradise, and to intoxicate themselves before committing their wild deeds. They struck terror for more than a century, although, on the Mongol invasions, their reign came to an end, and their lair was destroyed.

THE SAFFAVID RESTORATION (1501)

Iran did not officially become Shiite until the succession of the Saffavid dynasty in 1501. There had been more or less constant sympathy for the descendants of Ali even if, in the books written for schools, you do not find systematic hostility towards the Sunni rulers who, after all, in the Samanid case, guaranteed the survival and spread of Persian culture, Shu'ubiya.

National feeling is thus stronger than the attachment to Shia Islam. This is all the more apparent, given that, although the Arabs and the Mongol invaders are condemned – 'they destroyed everything' – the Turks are spared such hostility. Contrary to what a reader might conclude from earlier textbooks, it was not the Iranian-Afghan Ghaznavids, but rather the Seljuk Turks who, having defeated the Ghaznavids at Dandanqan (1040), expelled the Buyids from Baghdad and so took the succession of authentically Iranian monarchs. In fact the fall of the Buyids put an end to the Iranian interlude in the caliphate. However, the Turks, unlike the Arabs, adopted and spread Persian culture. 'They gave it a supra-national prestige', says B. Spuler, and identified themselves with the Persian empire, whose greatness they intended to restore. The Turks even gave their sovereign the title 'sultan and Padishah', to distinguish him from the caliphs, from whom legitimacy stemmed, and it was in Persia that the first sultan ruled.

The Mongol interlude in Iran lasted for more than a century and a half. For the Islamic countries as a whole, it finally ruined the leadership of Baghdad, and gave Egypt its first era of preeminence; Iran, though ruined by the Mongols, succeeded, as Greece had done before, in taming its ferocious conqueror and thus preserving its culture, though equally it lost its status as a great nation. Once again, liberation came from the northern provinces, indeed from a Kurdish family that spoke Azeri and 'were called Sayyids, or descendants of the Prophet through the seventh imam. With the help of the Qizilbachs (who wore red turbans in twelve folds) they gradually extended their power over Iran and founded the Saffavid dynasty, who were loyal Shiites.' These Saffavids were in fact chiefs of a religious order, the Tariqa, who were Sufi in inspiration. They fought in the struggle of the Turkmen 'White Sheep' and 'Black Sheep', and then made war on the Mongols, entered Tabriz and declared Azerbaijan Shiite. From Azerbaijan, the Saffavid state extended across Persia, and in 1501 Ismail was proclaimed shah of Iran.

'In the war against the Sunni Ottomans, he fought so bravely at the battle of Khaldiran that, with only his sword, he split one of the enemy cannon.' In reality, he had indeed regarded artillery as unchivalrous, openly charged the enemy weapons, and was defeated; but the glorious defeat made his reputation. The nation's greatness was preserved throughout the long reign of Tah Masp, which unfortunately consisted of endless wars that impoverished the country, for the shah used 'scorched-earth' tactics to fend off both the Ottomans in the west and the Uzbeks in the east; power lay in the hands of the Qizilbach faction, Turkmen soldiers who violently disliked the Persians. Ismail tried to put a stop to this by replacing the Qizilbachs with a body of Ghulam, or Georgians captured during the successful campaigns for Tiflis, and then converted to Islam. The Georgian female captives formed the new harem; the children of the Georgian women fought for power with the children of the Turkmen ones. But supplanting the Qizilbachs was not easy: '"You cannot build a tent for the Shah out of old skins", said Ismail; but he died, poisoned.'

GREATNESS AND DECLINE

In the reign of Abbas, called 'the Great', the Persian state rediscovered its vigour and glory.

He was a knight, a famous monarch, and a lover of the arts; he made Iran a great state, and Isfahan became one of the great artistic capitals of the world. He build hundreds of miles of roads, bridges and caravanserais; in Isfahan alone there were 162 mosques, 48 schools, 1,802 caravanserais and 273 public baths. He called in foreign experts and employed them to construct a powerful army. In 1031 (1653), with English help, he took Ormuzd, which had fallen to the Portuguese, and he also expelled the Russians from the Mazenderan. However his successor, Hussein, was weak and effeminate; he did harm to the country, for he allowed his army to be destroyed by the Afghans. Hussein offered them Isfahan and with his own hands put the royal crown on the head of his conqueror, Mahmud.

This passage only presents the respectable side of the story's essentials; for children could hardly be told that, by the time of Ismail II, rivalries of the harem reflected conflicts of power between Qizilbachs, Persians and Georgians, who were now masters of the state. In this feverish climate, Hussein's own sister slipped poison into the hashish and Indian hemp of her brother; Abbas had had his father and two brothers blinded; and yet this degeneracy gave birth to a literature and a form of erotic art to which the Persian miniatures of the Bizhad school are an immortal testimony.

The dynasty ended its reign in an apocalypse: at the siege of Isfahan, 8,000 people died of hunger or disease, four times as many people as died in the battle itself. Mahmud had a further 3,000 Qizilbachs executed, and then ordered the massacre of the entire Saffavid family, bar three – in all, seventeen people. Then he himself went mad and was overthrown by a cousin, Ashrad, who made peace with the Ottomans and ceded some imperial provinces to them.

Several years later, this Afghan interlude came to an end when a chief of the Qajar tribe raised the Saffavid flag and, having defeated the usurper, Ashrad, took the Saffavid throne and was proclaimed Nadir Shah in 1736. He cleared Iran of both the Russians, who had settled on the Caspian coast, and the Ottomans, who were still poised to invade and who had made common cause with the Afghans, Sunni like themselves. In particular, Nadir Shah undertook an expedition to India, and occupied Delhi, which he looted of its fabulous treasures, as trophies. It was the greatest pillaging in history.

Such marks of decadence come thick and fast. The court's sumptuary expenses, and the need for soldiers to fight the Qizil-bachs, led to changes that favoured crown lands at the expense of the state's domains, and taxation fell increasingly heavily on the people, though it profited the wazirs or the shah rather than the state. The Qajar dynasty attempted to bring some order into the country's administration, and to advance centralization in the western monarchies' manner, but that produced only more resistance from the large tribes. The wealth brought by 'the Persian route' was in any case destroyed in the crisis of the eighteenth century, for the Afghan episode terminated large-scale trade.

THE ARRIVAL OF RUSSIANS AND BRITISH

This weakening of the nation opened it up to new invaders, the British and Russians, who had different motives for intervention, but whose intervention had much the same effect. Persia, faced with this double threat, could not call on the Turks for help, since they were Sunni, nor on the Afghans, whom it hoped to reconquer. Almost as a forewarning of what was to come, Peter the Great and the Ottomans concluded a treaty to partition Persia, in 1724. It presaged the treaty of 1907 when the British took over from the Ottomans.

Until the early nineteenth century, Persia had not had to fear the Russians. As late as 1795, when Heraclius of Georgia asked for Russian protection against Persia, Aga Muhammed Khan, the first Qajar, at once put Tiflis to the sack as a reprisal. The shah was beaten in the great war of 1813, in which he lost Derbent and Baku, and was forbidden to keep a naval force in the Caspian.

He tried for revenge in 1826, but was once again defeated, and the Persians were forced to cede Erivan and to sign the treaty of Turcomanchai in 1828. The balance of power, now, had changed.

Russia intervened increasingly in the internal affairs of Persia. It worked for the secession of still-Iranian Azerbaijan (around Tabriz) and stepped into the problem of Persian succession by adopting Abbas Mirza's cause, at the time of the Gulistan treaty in 1813. Turks and Persians failed to unite against the common enemy, for the Ottomans were Sunni and the Qajars, Shiite. The 'Shadow of God on earth' (the official title of the shah who now, unlike the Saffavids, was no longer a descendant of Ali) appealed to the British, whose interest was to defend Persia against Russian penetration towards the southern coast or the route to India. However, British designs on Afghanistan 'for the protection of India' against Russian intrigues ran directly counter to the Persian aim, and it even came to war when Nazir Al-din marched on Herat in 1856.

Whereas the British 'ally' turned into a new rival, Russian penetration of Central Asia threatened the very existence of Persia. The Russians also contested British economic penetration of the area. Combined with these two dangers was the shah's own inability to deal with the crisis, for this caused Persians to question the nature of their regime, and to demand reform. In the towns, there emerged a public opinion greatly resentful of the humiliation caused by foreign encroachments. The explosion happened in 1890, when the shah granted a tobacco monopoly to a British company. Foreign corruption and penetration prompted an alliance between shopkeepers, who saw their livelihoods threatened, and the Shiite clergy, who detested the subversion of Islamic identity which had occurred through the country's modernization. It was an alliance closely similar to that of ninety years later, when the Pahlavi dynasty fell.

POETRY: THE PILLAR OF PATRIOTIC HISTORY

In Iran, the defence of Persian, as the national language, was always one of the principles at stake in the confrontation with the Arabs, ever since the nationalist-religious *Shu'ubiya* movement. In the ninth century, the Samanids, who came from a family of Zoroastrian priests, encouraged a cultural renaissance of the Persian language, as shown in the works of Rudaki and Daqiqi, which were written in Arabic characters, to keep an inter-Islamic link, but were in the Persian language. In the tenth century, the *Shahnama* epic of Ferdusi acted as a catalyst, for it gave Persian its classical form and made an epic of the eternal combat between Iran and the Turanian world, which was the myth of the pre-Islamic kings. In Ferdusi's day, Persia was a sizeable country, and Mahmud's greatness was associated with the Persian renaissance. But, soon, there came another invasion, this time by the Turks, to whom Amir Mu'izzi addressed pathetic appeals; before the ruins of Ctesiphon, Khaqai spoke of the lost grandeur of the Sassanids and the stolen glory of Iran.

From then on, lost glory was a dominant theme, and patriotic poetry was auxiliary to history, which it kept in the forefront of memories. For many years, it is true, this patriotism amounted only to love-poetry in Persian, such as that written by a Saadi or a Hafez. But poetry served the cause of militant patriotism, as in the case of Fath 'Ali's minister, who was executed by the third Qajar shah. He had sung of 'this country's fatal destiny, which at one time sends a brave army to Tiflis, and at another allows Russian hordes to conquer Tabriz'; or, again, 'our soldiers look healthy and ruddy-faced, but towards the Russians these mincing weaklings show only their backsides.' It was the humiliation inflicted by the Russians after the 'ignominious treaties' of Gulistan in 1813 and Turcomanchai in 1828 that caused this revival of patriotic poetry. Hatred of the Russians and the British supplanted the ill-feeling against the Arabs. This literature was born with the French Revolution and was linked with the liberal movement; it was one of the fermenting agents of patriotism, the other being the teaching of the Shiite clergy. In Adib-e-Pishawari's case the two agents met, and such poetry clearly forged the revolutionary temper of 1905 and 1920.

'I have a fond memory', wrote S. R. Shafat in 1952, 'how, as school-boys, we used to hear the verses of Adib-al-Mamalek, who then wrote under the pseudonym "Amiri". His powerful poems sang of the old glory of Iran, and lamented her present decline; revolutionary orators also cited these verses, which had a strong response from the masses.' This also was true of the poems of Mirza Agha Khan: 'Is not our country upside-down, and has it not become a haunt of demons? Have not tyranny and lawlessness increased, to leave the people in misery? Has the king not become a beggar, his country a desert and his people a desperate mass?'

These poems' chief themes can be found together in a very popular operetta of the 1920s, *Resurrection*. Here, ancient traditions and Zoroastrianism were portrayed as the very essence of the Iranian nation. The King of Kings and Zoroaster, returning to earth, are appalled to see how the country they founded has degenerated, and the piece ends with a long monologue by Zoroaster, in which he prays for the country's regeneration. History, given the lack of historical literature, has been a matter for poetry in Iran for many years.

The Persians' resentment towards their own government has been all the more keenly felt, in the last two centuries, as in many other fields their culture, which formerly had swept all before it, had continually fallen back and given place to other cultures, even the Turks'. In Turkestan, only the Tadjiks, since Islamization, continued to speak a language close to Persian, but elsewhere Turkish gained ground, even in Persian territory: as W. Barthold has noted, 'If, for instance, Turkish and Persian were spoken in the same village, Turkish gradually became the common language.' Persian survived only in one bastion: it was the language of culture and of bureaucracy.

TURKEY: GLORIFICATION OF THE HUNS AND OF THE NOMADIC CIVILIZATIONS

The pride of the Turks is immeasurable; they ruled the Arabs, threatened the very existence of Christendom, and for five centuries formed the greatest of empires. The Ottoman collapse in 1918 has not lessened that pride very much, and the history taught to Turkish children shows this.

Atatürk's secularization, and the contempt shown towards the Arabs – who failed to win their freedom save through foreign intervention – sets off the model of Turkish history, still more than the Iranian model, from the version supplied to other Islamic peoples, even though for many people the secularization is only superficial, and though the 'Turkification' of Ottoman history is a recent phenomenon, dating only from the later nineteenth century, for until then the empire had incarnated the eternity of Islam.

Since Atatürk, the origins of the nation have been associated, not with Islam, but rather with two different sources. There is, first of all, Anatolia, with a rediscovery of the civilizations that preceded the Turks there, including the most ancient of them, the Hittites; next, there is Central Asia: Turkish school-history glorifies the nomadic civilizations which broke upon the West, especially the Huns. This is a complete reversal of the traditional view held by the West, Persia and China, of the Huns, the first Turkic people.

As a matter of fact, apart from such information as we can glean from Orkhon's tomb-inscription of the eighth century, nothing is known of the Huns which does not come from peoples whom they had subjected. The primary sources are entirely Chinese, Armenian, Byzantine or Arab. How would we react to a history of France derived entirely from enemy sources?

History as taught in Turkish schools is the only one which rates the Huns highly and speaks warmly of the nomadic empires, from Attila to Tamerlane. 'The memory of Attila remains that of an extremely well-meaning and inspired king: a great man, a dominator of history.' In the fifth century the empire of the Huns, 'which in turn subjected both Byzantium and the Roman empire of the West', is presented as a territorial state with a double frontier – one contiguous with the empire, and the other touching the tributary nations. The terms of the treaty with Byzantium in 434 are supposed to show the two states as equal, both of them highly-organized and with a similar status. The Huns' incursions are presented, not as a devastating tornado, but as a fundamental fact of Euro-Asiatic society. Thus for instance the Huns laid the basis of chivalry (*vide* the *Nibelungen*) and many habits and structures of organization which, after the collapse of the empire, gave rise to states which have existed ever since, such as the Magyars and the Georgians.

This vision of the past will, it is supposed, illumine the future of the Turkic peoples even after the other end of this history has been described – the collapse of the Ottoman empire, the greatest, and no doubt the most tolerant, of multi-national states ever known. True, Pan-Turanianism did fail, after Enver Pasha's vain effort to restore the unity of the Turkish world from Anatolia to Kazan.

Still, even in the textbook of 1976 published at Istanbul, the survival of the myth is clear. There is, reproduced, a map of the Turkish population in 1963, where each point represents 100,000 Turks and in which a continuous dotted line shows the borders of an imaginary state in which Turks might constitute 'a majority of the population'. It stretches from Anatolia to (Soviet) Central Asia and Sinkiang. In its midst is a tiny white spot: today's Armenia.

7

FROM CHRIST THE KING TO THE NATION-STATE: HISTORY IN EUROPEAN EYES

We have already encountered the European historical perspective several times, and shall encounter it several times again, but only in respect of its relationship to the rest of the world. Other aspects of this history, its content and function can, in the context of the space available to me, only be scrutinized in a limited way.

We have first of all to look at its focus, if only to show that the history of historians is not the only history. Bernard Guénée, in his *Histoire et culture historique dans l'occident médiéval* (History and Historical Culture in the Medieval West) notes that, together with a common foundation, started by Cassiodorus, but distinguishing the historical culture of the West for the next thousand years (it includes Flavius Josephus and Eusebius) there is a kind of sub-history as well. It is written, not in Latin, but in the vernacular, in prose or verse – for instance, the history of

England since Brutus, written by Robert Manning in English verse in 1338, 'not for scholars, but for ordinary people'.

The connection with Rome lasted until the fifteenth century at least; until then, in effect, historical works were concerned with the Ancient World, or the history of the church, i.e. sanctified history; even the royal civil servants did not have other works of history than these, particularly in France. It was only in the fifteenth century 'that the history of their country became a general passion among all educated Frenchmen', so that it took on, as elsewhere, the functions which it still has today: glorification of the nation and legitimation of the state. However, written documents are not the only focus of modern historical consciousness. In Spain, for instance, festivals have an important role in the popular memory, and the same is true of England, with the theatre – Shakespeare above all. Painting and film now feature in this process, and in Nazi Germany they had an important part in shaping the popular consciousness of history, or rather the history that governments tried to inculcate into children. In France, there is a multiple focus, but the problem does not consist solely of that complication: it is whether attraction towards history, or fear of it, will gain the upper hand.

SPAIN: THE FESTIVAL OF HISTORICAL WITNESS

Leaving Islam, but remaining for a time in Spain, we encounter a culture impregnated with Moorish or Moslem civilization. In Molvizar, above Motril, there were watchmen who, for centuries, surveyed any possible arrival of the Moorish fleet. Here is a characteristic scene:

Sentry	Halt. Who goes there?
Moorish Ambassador	A Moor who wants, at once – for he has had to wait – to announce his embassy to your lord, if he has not already fled his castle.

Christian King	Let him come at once, to the first step. There he can tell us the business of his embassy.
Moorish Ambassador	May Allah protect you, valiant king of Molvizar, Castile and Aragon, defender of Jesus and his Laws. . . . Tell me who protects this castle which has provoked our rage. If he will not die, he would do better to run; if he will not, then I have to tell you that you will all be struck by terror. I swear by Allah that even the cinders of the sea will tremble, for I shall punish the outrages that have been inflicted on Great Turkey by Isabella and Ferdinand in expelling my family from their own land. My king shall come and conquer Spain, and shall show the Christian that he will face harsh punishment for his arrogance.

Spanish children can hear this rant every year, not at school, but in the very *plaza* of their own town. In Molvizar, near Motril, defenders of the Christian faith have repeated such speeches and actions from the past since time immemorial. The performance is not the kind of commemoration which the French would understand, with troops marching past a ramrod-stiff president of the Republic or sub-prefect on 14 July. In Molvizar the citizens of the place, helmeted, and covered in ancient capes, re-enact what their ancestors did and said, and they thus recall the Moorish challenge, their own defeat, their revenge and the final victory. Every city reenacts the vital moments of *Moros y Cristianos*, adding variations to suit the locality. The play is enacted in the long summer days when, from the heights of the Andalucian *cordilleras*, watchmen announced the arrival of the Turkish or Moorish armadas, and now, from Castilla to Jaca, from Bocairente to Cóceras, nearly fifty cities still enact *Moros y Cristianos*, several centuries after the event.

History here, more than elsewhere, is an integral part of the life of a Spanish town. It forms the basis of a whole festival. Of the 2,500 to 3,000 festivals which fill the Spanish calendar, religion easily accounts for the majority, and popular festivals come a close second to historical pageants. *Moros y Cristianos* marked the national past, and so comes first, though other great moments of Spanish history are also recorded even if the passage of time has to some degree distorted their images – whether in the Iberian-Celtic festival of San Pedro Maurique or the ceremony that marks the ending of the tribute paid by Galicia to Castile in 1852. There are other festivals in between, commemorating, for instance, the Roman feat of arms at Cogollas Vega, in the battle of Clavijo, the victory of El Cid, the coronation of the Catholic Kings, the discovery of America, the victory of Lepanto, or the war of independence that defeated Napoleon, and so forth.

Such history is not a scholarly or controlled representation of past events; it is quite simply a popular memory, for it is relatively spontaneous, and is not a reconstruction such as school-books might supply.

There is, however, a clear link between the content of these festivals and the subjects taught at primary school. In Antonio Álvarez Perez's *Enciclopedía primer grado* (168th edition, 1965) religion plays as important a role as history; it accounts for the first forty-four pages of text, whereas the whole history of Spain has thirty-seven. Within the space allotted to the history, it is the triumph of Christ the King that takes up the finest pages, and includes both Arab invasion and Reconquest. Anything concerning the church's mission of conversion equally gains the priority, whether with Santiago de Compostella, Teresa of Avila or the mission to the Americas: 'After the conquests of Cortez and Pizarro, they achieved something no less great, for, with a patience and a self-sacrificing spirit unique in history, our brothers taught the Indians to read, write and pray.'

In this work, which was designed for children aged between

seven and eight, the whole of Spanish history is seen as one long struggle for liberation. To Spain's enemies, though they were frequently victorious, she 'taught the meaning of heroism . . . even as early as the siege of Saguntum by Hannibal, when all died rather than surrender. . . . for the first time Spain, through the voices of Saguntum's people, taught the world that a people capable of dying could never be slaves.' In Numantia, Spain once more succumbed to the Romans and 'Viriatus chose to die rather than surrender.' The tale is repeated several times throughout history, up to the heroism of the defenders of Saragosa, who resisted Napoleon.

The history of Spain ends in another *guerra de liberación* – 'begun by Franco on 18 July 1936 to free Spain from its enemies and make it One, Great and Free'. In Spanish history, in this school-version, the Caudillo is alone 'unrivalled': he 'put an end to the attacks on the church, to the murders and daily strikes that threatened to turn the country over to the communists'.

This summary of the text is not even a caricature, and its coarseness is not simply a reflection of the way in which history is taught under dictatorships. Democracies, too, make an effort to jettison the embarrassing parts of their own pasts, and the same is true, as we shall see, of socialist regimes. There is a set of subjects that must not be raised, and even young children gain experience of this. Much is made of the conquest of Mexico and Peru, but where is it ever said that they were subsequently lost? Why is nothing further said of the Spanish empire? Are we to suppose that it never existed at all, from Cuba to Manila and Guinea? There is no mention of the extermination of the Indians or of their slavery; and this affects even Spain, for Spanish children are left in the dark as to the fate of the Jews and Moriscos, whether expelled or forcibly converted to Christianity. Children would not even learn, at least not from school-history, that Spain, by the will of the people in 1931, became a republic. True, since Spanish history is identified with that of Castile, it may be that many pupils would not consider such history to be their own, if they come from Catalonia, the Basque country, or Galicia.

NAZI CINEMA

The role played in Spain by festivals or in Great Britain by the theatre or novels was filled in Germany by opera and cinema. For German children, consciousness of the past owed much, for the Thirty Years' War, to Schiller, and, for the notion that the German people was somehow ethnically predestined, as *Urvolk*, to greatness, to Fichte, its initiator. However, the diffusion of a panoramic vision of the Middle Ages and the origins of the Germanic people was really Wagner's work: his music-drama gave roots to the myth of the Rhine in German consciousness, and led the Germans into communion with this myth. In the Hitler period, this Wagnerian spectacle was modernized as *Triumph of the Will* and *The Olympics* (*Olympia*) and it perpetuated a craving for community which the traditionally disunited Germans had always wished to experience, though this time they experienced it in the services of a Leader sent by Providence.

More generally, the Nazi regime clearly gave weight to theatre and film, especially as a way of educating youth. After April 1934 the Hitler Youth of Cologne favoured the use of film in education (*Jugend-filmstunde*), a programme that soon became established in all branches of the Hitler Youth movement. Dr Rust, the minister of education, soon organized the showing of carefully-selected films in German schools, and by 1936 70,000 schools were making use of 16 mm projectors, with over 500 different films, of which 227 were for schools, and 330 for universities; 10,000 copies were made of these films. The extent of this effort can easily be seen in the fact that, in today's 'audio-visual age', in France, films such as *Mourir à Madrid* (F. Rossif) or *1936: le grand tournament* (H. de Turenne) are allowed only in a handful of copies for educational purposes, and there certainly are not 70,000 16mm projectors available to primary or secondary schools – it would amount to 800 per *département*.

> Nothing betters film in penetrating our schools with our ideas (said Rust). . . . Film must introduce them to the problems of our age, and give them a knowledge of Germany's past greatness and an understanding of the necessity of the Third Reich. The National-Socialist state has deliberately and definitively chosen to make films the main instrument for transmission of its ideology.

This being so, it would be difficult to argue that the National-Socialist vision of history did not really penetrate education, although this has been seriously suggested: after all, the first textbooks inspired by Nazism appeared only in 1937, and the series was not finished until 1941, such that, in consequence, no young Germans could allegedly be conscious of the basic conception in these works. But historical knowledge is not passed on solely by school-books, nor are political attitudes and actions wholly dependent on book-learning. The negative test can also be applied. After Nazism's overthrow, the Germans could hardly mourn the adored *Führer*, but they did completely telescope the teaching of modern history; it was altogether ruled out of the curriculum, and the taboo was total. One inquiry showed that, for the very young, the name 'Hitler' received the response 'Never heard of him.' The interdict can be seen still further back in the past, and includes study of the origins of the First World War. There was an explosion of rage when Fritz Fischer published a work showing with incontrovertible documentary evidence that in 1914 Germany had had extraordinary expansionist aims, the implication being that Hitler's conquests had not been a mere 'accident of history' or the work of a megalomaniac, but the realization of an idea shared by a large part of German society. This raised the overall problem of German responsibility, which the general silence on the subject of Hitler had been designed to avoid. Later on, in the 1960s, one of the mainsprings of revolt of young people against their elders in Germany was the questioning of the elders as to what they had done in the war, for the young wished to know how they could reject responsibility for the extermination of the Jews. E. Leiser's film, *Mein Kampf*, acted as a subversive agent within families, for it revealed to young Germans, whose emancipation was beginning in these dark cinema-halls, what horrors had been committed by the Gestapo and even by the army in the Warsaw ghetto and the concentration camps. Thereafter, many other films were used to explain the phenomenon of general adhesion to Nazism – Peter Fleischmann's *Bavarian Hunting Scene* and V. Brandler's *I Love You and Kill You* being only two examples. A decade further on, *Holocaust* showed German society, as a whole, how it should openly approach the problems of the Nazi era.

But the schools themselves had no, or almost no, part in this. It is therefore important to look at the textbooks of the Nazi era, and juxtapose them with the books of preceding and succeeding eras, for it is true that the Nazis were trained in Weimar's schools, while today's German leaders were educated in Nazi schools, and there can hardly be a very great discontinuity between the textbook contents of before, during and after Hitler – or rather, not as great as might be supposed. Quite simply, between 1933 and 1945, certain exaggerations were taken to the point of caricature and some specific lies were assumed, with greater or lesser cynicism or good faith than at other times or in different regimes.

Rainer Riemenschneider has shown that the school-books of Hitler's time were directly inspired by *Mein Kampf*, and that was also true of the historical films put out in this period. Dietrich Klagges, author of these books, even stated that *Mein Kampf* was worthy of comparison with Copernicus, 'because it offers the key to a clear and obvious interpretation of history'. According to Hitler, 'the basis of our historical vision must be made clear, whereas in the present educational system, which in 99 per cent of cases is appalling, all that you remember amounts to a few facts, dates and names . . . the essentials are not taught at all. . . . But it is vital to outline the main paths of historical evolution', and universal history 'must revolve around the notion of race; Greek and Roman history should be taught, but only in the context of racial development of Aryan peoples; their history is a continual struggle to maintain race-purity which is constantly exposed to the evil conspiracy of inferior races trying to infiltrate the body of a healthy people.'

Above all, says *Mein Kampf*,

> Our system of education has not been adapted to make our people's historical development revolve around a few great names . . . it must be reshaped, so that attention can be concentrated on great heroes, and go beyond 'objective presentation', towards the more urgent goal of inspiring national pride. . . . An inventor ought not to be praised merely for being an inventor, but for his contribution to the national community, as *Volksgenosse*. . . . We should select the greatest of our heroes and present them to youth in such a striking way that they are seen as pillars of a resolute nationalism. . . . The German, on leaving school, should not be a weakling, a pacifist, a democrat, or anything of that kind, but a German, through and through. . . . There is no doubt that the world is heading for a cataclysm: will this conflict benefit the Aryan, or the Eternal Jew? History should not be learned as a list; it should inspire.

One educational innovation, for the youngest children, was to present history as a process going back through time: Adolf Hitler became the first true hero, and it is in him that history culminates. Next comes Leo Schlageter, a 'resister' against the

French occupation of the Ruhr, who was shot by the French in 1923 and became a national hero and 'victim of the Diktat of Versailles'. Then comes Bismarck 'who, at his death, hoped that one day his work would be completed', and so it goes on, back through Frederick the Great, Luther, Charlemagne, etc., to Arminius, who was the exact equivalent of Vercingetorix in Gaul or Viriates in Spain, and 'who, in the depths of the Germanic forests, fought a strong Roman army. Arminius hoped that all Germans would be united, but they remained divided, and this cost them dear. They dreamed of re-union, and . . . finally, one day, it came.' Such glorification of the race, the German people, amounts to a distinct subversion of the earlier-accepted historical 'Vulgate' in at least three ways.

One of these is the problem of religion and the role of Luther. The Reformation was considered not as a properly religious problem but as 'the first German Revolution, directed against foreign oppression by Rome . . . an essentially national and polit-ical rising, in which the renewal of faith was a means towards creation of a new man, the German citizen.' Luther wished to preside over the birth of a new church, a German national one (much as Hitler would have liked to institute) but that was impossible until Germany had been freed from the pope. Moreover at this time, the Reich's image had been constantly tarnished and debased since the end of the Hohenstauffan; it was a despised and divided country, an easy prey to foreigners; the pope played on such divisions, and Luther – like Hitler, a ple-beian – became the mouthpiece of the first German Revolution.

Secondly, the French Revolution is virtually expunged from history. In fact, the few paragraphs on it make it out to have been dependent on the American Revolution, for the stress is upon 'the powerful effect that it had on France', and the events of 1789 are reduced to a list of upheavals and agitations, culminat-ing in 'the recognition of popular right as the foundation of the constitution'. The universal aspect of the principles of 1789 and the echo they received elsewhere (e.g. beyond the Rhine) are firmly ignored because, as we have seen, the German Revolution originated with Luther, and is therefore much older. In no sense is the French Revolution to be taken as an example; it is different to the American Revolution, which liberated the people from foreign oppression. The young German, since he is kept in ignorance as to the kind of theoretical debates thrown up by the French Revolution, 'is in no danger of becoming a democrat, or anything of that sort'.

Finally, *Einkreisungspolitik*, or 'encirclement', to which Germany was victim throughout the length of her existence, formed the third aspect of teaching given to young Germans. Of course, belief in such a threat predated Nazism, which, on this point, had only to bring an existing rage to boiling point. Long before 1914 German children were being taught that their national land was a graveyard of Slavs, and that since time immemorial the German people had been haunted by a fear of the Slavs' resurrection. Conquering and colonizing in the past, the German nation now saw itself as a bulwark of civilization against the eastern masses. It stood by and anxiously watched the western Slavs wax and multiply, and wiped out all trace of their existence in the territories which had so recently belonged to the Slavs, such as Pomerania or Lusatia. Like the French, Germans believed at first that the real danger was in the East and the idea of a *Drang nach Osten* was promoted to guarantee the eternity of a German presence throughout Central Europe. But now, German children had to learn of a second enemy, this time in the West. Goethe wrote in his memoirs that during his childhood the greatest catastrophe had been the French occupation of Koblenz. 'Today', said a book published around 1910, 'English mercantilism and French hatred are joined with Russian ambition against the poor German empire.' 'The Fatherland is encircled . . . but God has always struck down Germany's enemies, as with Napoleon at Leipzig', the centenary of which was celebrated with pomp just before the Great War. 'That is why we Germans have nothing to fear except God. Healthy and strong, the Germans have nothing to fear from their western neighbours.' Yearly, from 1872 to 1914, they celebrated 'Sedan Day', which recalled their victory over France, whose importance thereafter declined, and which could be written off as frivolous. The war, 'though predictable, was not willed by Germany, the Kaiser did everything to avoid it'. It was Edward VII who organized the strangling of Germany, for he was jealous of her irresistible prosperity and expansion: Ernst Lissauer's *Hassgesang* ('Song of Hatred') showed the grudge borne by so many Germans against an England which refused to share its world domination.

In the aftermath of the First World War, after the Versailles *Diktat*, anger and frustration mounted: essays, school textbooks, and films untiringly branded the permanent enemies of the German people, to whom were now added, in Nazi works, the communists, Freemasons and Jews. Until the war, only domestic enemies were attacked – as for instance in the series *Gestern und Heute*, where subversion of the state and of morality during the Weimar period was analysed systematically, according to the 'grand and healthy' achievements of the Third Reich. To tighten up the resolution of Youth, and to prepare young men for the new battle, pacifist films such as *All Quiet on the Western Front* were forbidden, while, to counteract the effect of Pabst's *Westfront*, UFA produced *Stosstrupp 1917* and *Ein Mann will nach Deutschland*, to glorify German heroism in the years 1914–18, and to condemn the selfishness of home-front 'shirkers'. Anti-Soviet films, such as *Frühling* (1934) and *KGB* were few, and production of them was interrupted by the Pact; but after 1939 a huge wave of antisemitic and anti-British films broke on the screen. These films were for young soldiers, or for their families if they had gone to the front.

These films were perhaps the purest expression of the Nazi ideology and vision of history. Goebbels himself supervised their production; the most 'magnificent' means were allotted to the production, so that these 'super-productions' outstripped all that Hollywood or the Soviet Union had managed to do until then, in order to keep 'the masses' enthusiasm' at boiling-point. For *Kolberg* – which tells the story of a town's heroic resistance to Napoleon – Veit Harlan deployed 6,000 horses and 187,000 soldiers.

IMPOSTURE TRIUMPHANT

Subversion of historical truth appears in many of its traditional forms, whether in distortion by omission (for instance, in *Kolberg* nothing is said of British help to the besieged garrison) or by simple invention (the introduction of an urban tax (Excise), which was so hated, is presented in *Jud Süss* as 'an idea that could only have come from Jews' although that tax existed in several European countries in the eighteenth century). Some forms of historical lie were, however, peculiar to the Nazi style: forms of subversion that cannot be equated with other forms of propaganda. This is all the more remarkable, given that the historical films were always prefaced by a 'notice' to the effect that they were 'based on historical fact', and that one of the historical advisers, Wolfgang Liebeneiner, even gained the title 'Professor'.

FALSIFICATION BY INVERSION OF REALITY

In *Jud Süss*, Süss, having grown in power, and become minister of the duke, rapes Dorothea, the daughter of Councillor Sturm, and then she commits suicide. In fact it was Süss's own daughter who killed herself, having been raped by the duke. In the same film, the press-gang sets to work to recruit mercenaries, but this occurred not at Süss's suggestion, but at the initiative of the duke who, in the film, ascribes the whole affair to the Jews' machinations.

INCULPATION OF OTHERS

The obverse of all this was the criminality of the regime, the concentration camps and 'total war'. In *Ueber Alles in der Welt*, we see life in Paris on the day war is declared, on 3 September 1939: Germans are hunted down by the police, and locked in the Colombes stadium, together with Jews who have been similarly rounded up. In *Ohm Krüger*, the plebeian ways of the Boers make them equivalent to the Nazis, while the lasciviousness and luxury of the British makes them 'the Jews of the Aryan world'. Lord Kitchener is credited with inventing 'total war' (just then, the Germans had destroyed Coventry) and the British are also accused of 'inventing' concentration camps.

In this final example, the allegation runs counter to both truth and legend. The British did indeed create the first concentration camps during their Boer wars; but at that time they had neither the same function nor the same organization as the Nazi camps. Civilians were indeed locked up in appalling circumstances, and typhus and typhoid fever raged. In contrast to the Nazi camps, however, there was no 'final solution' worked out for the captives, who were to be liberated in the normal way once the war had been ended; and this was in fact done. An invented counterpart makes its appearance in *Ohm Krüger*, where there is a suggestion that, in the camps, mothers were separated from their children. But the Nazis, rather than the British, did this.

FRANCE: THE TEMPTATION OR THE FEAR OF HISTORY?

Messenger	My honourable lords, health to you all!
	Sad tidings bring I to you out of France,
	Of loss, of slaughter, and discomfiture;
Bedford	Me they concern; Regent I am of France.
	Give me my steeled coat: I'll fight for France.

> Away with these disgraceful wailing robes!
> Wounds will I lend the French instead of eyes,
> To weep their intermissive miseries.

This extract from *Henry VI* has its equivalents in several other parts of Shakespeare. There is every reason for history in England to be Francophobe, since, for several centuries, Shakespeare was the greatest English classic, a modern Homer, whose word, for all Englishmen, counted as the outstanding national treasure. France has no Shakespeare; nevertheless, her classical theatre also shows both a fear of, and an attraction towards, history. Of course, it ostensibly dealt with Rome or Spain, but behind the action of the play everyone could detect contemporary problems. This is not done directly, as in Shakespeare, which means that it loses some of the function of a *Henry V* or a *Henry VI* (and not, say, *Julius Caesar*), i.e. to frighten us. Through the plays of Shakespeare, and also through Sir Walter Scott, a retrospective vision of the British past is embedded in the popular memory.

The French, though they lacked a Shakespeare (or a Wagner, as in Germany), still had their Latin inheritance. Their Walter Scott is Alexandre Dumas, who had obvious counterparts, from Victor Hugo to the popular historical novelists of today. When French colonial expansion occurred, the picture was rounded off by more exotic heroes, as in Jules Verne or Paul d'Ivoi; and another vehicle was the strip-cartoon which, for many years, has taken history more as a framework than as a theme. It may slip into an earlier age (*La famille Fenouillard*, *Tintin* and, now, *Astérix* which today is the best-selling French publication, with over 30,000,000 sales to its credit). Even though Astérix takes in post-Gallic periods from time to time, he remains the hero of a period of which the history is not a matter of contention. Still, the fear of the past in France is still clear, in whatever form it is written.

Evidence for this is manifest whenever a powerful work emerges: there is always something of a storm, whether in Abel

Gance's *Bonaparte* or *Le Chagrin et le pitié*, for civil war was somehow ever-present. It is easy to see why television prefers adaptations of historical novels: 'We cannot allow such passions to recur', said the censoring ministry with regard to a showing of *Madame Jeanne*. Television does of course put on documentaries and *La Caméra explore le temps*, but only a few of its doings are likely to cause 'commotion'. It must also be said that the cinema, which is supposed to be more independent (though from whom?), is not more daring. Jean-Pierre Jeancolas has studied the films made in France since television has had a national role, i.e. since about 1958, and he remarks that the cinema 'has been feeble in response to history'. True, there were *Lacombe Lucien* and *Staviski*; there was *Allio* and *Tavernier*, but who saw those? History-as-problem has a smaller audience in France than history-as-story or history-as-dream.

How, then, are we to account for the present-day success of history, a success which can be seen in the astonishing popularity of reviews, magazines and cartoons? Conversely, why are people so afraid of analytical or critical history? In *The Great War*, in 1969, I wrote that

> The French genius, a historian might morosely conclude, is not so much for war as for civil war. Except in 1914, France had never known a long and truly patriotic war. She of all nations might most glorify arms, but history, both recent and distant, shows that she fought no war that was not sooner or later cross-bred into civil war. The Second World War is an obvious case in point. So were the Revolution and the Empire, Joan of Arc and Burgundians, Henri IV, the League and the epoch of Richelieu. Even in 1870 there was a group that, openly or secretly, wanted the government to be defeated. This was not true in 1914–18; then, there was no 'foreigners' party'.

If that was true of the history of France, it also applies to history in France. History is one of the main areas of civil war, the origins of which can be explained at various levels. The example of Joan of Arc shows this. At one level, though even then with fissures, there is the century of Joan of Arc herself, when she was known simply as Jeanne Darc. Her adventure called into existence three quarrelling groups, the king, the rationalists and the faithful. The quarrel was born at that time, but it continued in various ways thereafter.

An American historian, George Huppert, has shown that, as regards Joan of Arc, historians of the fifteenth and sixteenth centuries in France failed to use readily-available documents, especially of her trial. Official historians even, in practice, ignored the Maid. In Gilles's *Annales* (1553) Joan played a very minor part in a drama, the major protagonist of which was the king himself. Gilles does not mention the trial for heresy and witchcraft, and there is no talk of miracles: the king's triumph could not possibly be explicable in terms of witchcraft or miracle. Monarch, lawyers and historians had all to find a national, not a clerical basis for the king's legitimacy. Gaguin, somewhat later, talked of English cruelty and of Joan's virtue: otherwise Charles might have been supposed to owe his throne to the forces of evil. He allows Joan to help him in the struggle; but royal service required that the heroine should be laicized, and made less important.

The difficulty is clearly that of comprehending how a simple farm-girl could have managed several armies. De Haillan provided the first rational explanation for this, and said that the miracle of Joan was 'assumed' or 'staged and manufactured by clever military men . . . such is the force of religion and superstition.' They saw, in other words, how the king might profit from Joan's arrival, and turned her into a 'miracle' which, for a time, worked. According to Huppert, the 'pious' version of this came into being somewhat later, with Belleforest's *Annales*. Here, Joan becomes a complete innocent, a poor little shepherdess chosen by God as the instrument of His will for, as was later testified by the historian Mezerey, who had His ear, God wished to save the Dauphin. Joan, as agent of Providence, thus went from miracle to miracle; if she was finally taken, it was because her mission had been completed, for she ought to have 'gone back where she belonged' since she had done what she had been meant to do once the king was crowned. 'She was, however, stubborn; and God, who insists on utter obedience, had no reason to go on performing miracles for her.'

Some centuries later, after the fall of the monarchy, Joan ceased to be a matter of embarrassment for the Republic. Thus, two alternative versions survived together, a religious one, and a secular one. The Catholics were indeed embarrassed by Rouen, the trial, and Joan's condemnation by Bishop Cauchon, her executioner. Several Catholics smuggled this archbishop out of the picture, as Amalvi demonstrates, or else they stressed that the church itself expelled him from its body. The really guilty men were thus seen to be the English, the eternal enemy of France, and besides, in the outcome, Protestant.

What embarrassed the secular side was the 'voice' of Domrémy. In the lay picture, Saint Michael, or Saint Catherine, is eliminated: the claim is that these were internal voices, which the most advanced laymen described as 'hallucinations'.

The stern republican Ernest Lavisse, who was the apostle of Revenge against Germany, who wished to unite all, including Catholic, opinion tried to find an agreed version: 'Joan heard *someone* telling her to be good and wise. . . . She *thought* she heard voices from heaven, and they spoke to her of France's misfortunes.' The trial was the work 'of the wicked Bishop Cauchon'. (The edition of 1904 was contemporaneous with the beginnings of the Entente cordiale, and the English had to be humoured.) As she was going to the stake, 'Joan told the wicked bishop of *Beauvais*: "Bishop, I am dying for your sake".' But the Catholics' honour was saved, for Lavisse had a monk come upon the scene. Just as Joan stepped onto a pile of timber, a monk came up to her: 'Let me see him as I die', said Joan; and, with her last breath, she called, 'Jesus'. Ernest Lavisse was well-informed in the same way as Mezerey, because no eye-witness account has survived of the death of Joan. She did die at the stake, but the rest was made up.

It was precisely at this time that the Thalamas affair raged, showing how strongly people reacted to any questioning of the pious Vulgate. Thalamas, an *agrégé* in history, had set his class Joan of Arc as essay-subject. One pupil wrote, 'She is one of religion's glories, not some pagan goddess of patriotism. . . . She saw in the king only Christ's lieutenant, and she came to lead France back to Christ.' Thalamas would not allow this interpretation, and what he admitted saying was: 'Miracles should not be introduced into history. As historian, I am not required to believe in God, who is not a historical personality. Joan did not come to conquer France for Christ, she was a very natural character, a decent peasant-girl. She thought she heard voices that she declared were of heavenly origin.' Since the pupil had ignored the trial, Thalamas filled the gap by adding that 'today such a trial would seem iniquitous.'

> At the Lycée Condorcet, where Thalamas teaches, [wrote the *Revue de l'enseignement primaire*] there are undoubtedly families that are reactionary, clerical, of advanced fanaticism, and prejudiced against the master. Pupil No. 8, the chief witness for the indictment, stated that his teacher had said, 'I do not believe in your God, and still less in his vicars.' Still, that same pupil had said a few days before that 'the teacher said he did not require, as historian, to believe in God.'

M. Chaumie, the headmaster, made Thalamas look foolish: 'He has been wanting in tact and sense of proportion.' Teachers, both secondary and primary, were troubled by this. At the municipal council of Paris, Chassaigne-Goyon intervened to say that

> The demonstration of the teachers in Thalamas's favour is in reality directed against Joan of Arc, because she is the embodiment of patriotism. . . . It is time to act energetically, and tell these people, who have perverted their proper work as state servants, what is what, for tomorrow they'll be saying that the very flag is just an old bit of cloth, that the army is a rubbish-heap and patriotism a nonsense.

A socialist and anti-clerical, M. Faillet, also condemned Thalamas for

> He has done damage to the glory of France, which is criminal. There is nothing to be said for pedants who mock the divine mission of a sublime, patriotic visionary. But you, gentlemen on the Right, remember that Joan of Arc is not your property. Do not forget that it was through your bishops that the Church captured her, condemned her, and committed her to the stake. You lay claim to Joan; but for five centuries you had forgotten her, and you commit sacrilege. She belongs to the French fatherland, whereas for you the fatherland is Rome, the Church and the Vatican.

Once Thalamas had been reprimanded, 'no teacher from that time on could feel safe. We could all be denounced by any malignant schoolboy, or any informer, whether clever or dim.' The Thalamas affair could equally well have arisen over any one of the historical figures disputed between believers and sceptics – Clovis, Blandine, Fénelon (educator or revolutionary?). The dispute arose over Christian heroes written off by the anti-clericals, and, similarly, over lay heroes unrecognized by Christians; it also arose over other matters – Protestants and Catholics, modernists and traditionalists, revolutionaries and reactionaries, militarists and pacifists, socialists and republicans, or, in this century, fascists and communists, the Vichy and Resistance quarrels provoked by 'collaboration', or the Algerian war.

In the case of Joan of Arc there is almost a contemporary problem, in that, during the 1930s, through the Leagues, Joan sowed discord among Frenchmen; under Vichy, she was adopted both by Pétain and the Resistance. If this was the case with Joan, how much more so with greater and more recent issues – the Reformation, for instance, and the various conflicts, ably described by Philippe Joutard's team, to which it gave rise; or the French Revolution, the various myths and interpretations of which have recently been skilfully catalogued by Alice Gérard; not to mention the debate on French imperialism, or on Vichy.

But even the distant past can create violent dissension. The very origins of the French are a case in point: 'Where the eighteenth century saw noble Franks as the incarnation of the liberties of the German forests against despotic Christian monarchy, the nineteenth century perceived the Gauls as champions of democratic freedom'; nowadays there is a new 'front'. Centralization has been pushed too far for more than a century. Some areas have been systematically promoted, to the detriment of others that were sacrificed to crudely 'growth-oriented' ideology; there has accordingly been a reaction in favour of provincial identities, and the establishment of an alternative history. Its basis is to challenge the Jacobin equation of history-as-progress with the growth of the centralizing state. Robert Lafont, the pioneer in this field, C. Gendre and F. Javelier have shown how systematically such allegedly objective history simply omitted inconvenient facts: for instance, that the 'Breton marriage' was part of a power-game, that, though Corsica was 'bought', it then had to be tamed, or that the County of Toulouse was attached to the royal domain in such a way as to confine free Catalonia, in 1793, to its trans-Pyrenean part. 'Jacobin' practices of this kind recurred, in an ostensibly socialist cause, 150 years later as regards the Soviet border peoples (see below, on Armenia).

Gradually, several versions of history, varying by degrees from the Vulgate, emerged, and they display the varieties of historical memory among Frenchmen united (or divided) around the scholarly Pantheon so brilliantly described by Amalvi. This was not merely chaotic. A multiplicity of opinions is simply the expression of democratic life, but it seemed on the one hand to deny, by definition, the very nature of knowledge and any scientific basis, while on the other hand it appeared to challenge the state, which objected. Like so many Bayards, history teachers fought right and left to create a kind of 'historical truth' at least conforming to 'the facts'. But choosing facts was itself an ideological act. We can easily see why it was in France that the '*Annales* school' first triumphed, since it aimed at a clinical analysis of the past.

Traditional history in Lavisse's manner laid itself open. To Africans, it produced the dictum 'Our ancestors, the Gauls', and to young French people in 1958, as Pierre Nora has shown, it 'omitted' to mention collaboration, Vichy or Pétain in discussion of the Second World War. The state, it is said in France, dislikes history and its debates, and on the Right they do not care for philosophy either. On the assumption that 'the human sciences' had progressed, a new form of history, that of 'civilization', has been added to the curriculum. What, for historians, was a step forward as against mere chronology or repetition of truisms, soon became, in bureaucratic hands, an instrument for destroying the whole structure. The claim was made that history hitherto had stuffed brains, not refined them, and themes, rather than periods, became the new object of study.

Here again, allusion to the 'progress of the human sciences' was a pretext for 'de-ideologizing' history and turning it into 'a science'; but this apparent advance occurred once more at the expense of the established corpus of knowledge, i.e. the nation's own memory and consciousness. This consciousness is itself an object of history, even if it rests on contested or questionable facts, as we have seen in the case of Joan of Arc. Such matters were now ruled out: the curriculum was said to be 'overloaded'. Just as the bureaucrats unhesitatingly sacrifice the Midi or secondary railway-lines, so also, in the primary schools, history was eliminated, and 'awareness studies' were substituted, history becoming optional.

History-teaching had a similar challenge from the media. Interest on the part of television was directed, with a few outstanding exceptions, towards sterilized, unproblematical history. Such history, far from discussing the origins of our own times and (at least in France) its problems, was simply presented as a dream, a sort of exotic escape that served for evening relaxation of the tired citizenry. This began to have some influence as a parallel form of historical knowledge, because it could use methods to capture audiences which 'the talking head' of a teacher could not compete with. Faced with the challenge from this parallel school, the teaching profession at first did not bother, and adopted a haughty, condescending attitude towards television, much as its predecessors had done towards the cinema. Nevertheless, teachers, despite themselves, changed from makers of rules into mere mediators.

Publishers complemented the blows struck by the media; perceiving the crisis in education displayed in May 1968, they took to launching a new sort of book, where documents and statistics, as well as study by themes, came to take the place of narrative history which was now supposed to be outdated, discredited and on the way to anaemia. In particular, instead of complementing the performances of the media, publishers tried to compete with television (much as railways tried to compete with aircraft) and filled their books with pictures, large efforts in colour, so that school-books became a sort of 'spectacular' or 'pageset'. Just as a television programme has to fill up exactly fifty-two minutes, or thirteen, or twenty-six, so each chapter now had to have the same number of pages, and each page the same number of insets and photographs. From history in indigestible bulk, we have moved to prepackaged history, its portions as minuscule as those of *nouvelle cuisine* – tricky little confections, with their own incomprehensibly pretentious presentation. Lay-out mattered more than text, and the book became an object, like history itself.

Given books like this, the rivalry of television, and the growing supervision of guide-lines, inspectors, bureaucrats and various societies, history was pretty well killed off. The system created chaos: children 'know no history'. In compensation came a swarm of magazines, part-works and strip-cartoons dealing with 'the old days' according to contemporary prejudice.

But a powerful rebellion occurred, well-led by the Association of History Teachers. It spoke for the use of film in teaching, for up-valuing contemporary studies, for making history compulsory once more and for sensible division of the curriculum; in so doing, it won over all sorts of historians and gained some victories. In the meantime, of course, history had acquired some new weaponry. It had learnt a great deal from the balance-sheet and the experience of the previous twenty years had not necessarily been wholly negative – that it could hardly have been. Reflection on history and its methods, above all on its function and functioning, had been more profound, whether through Foucault or the *Annales* school or Paul Veyne or the defence and attack of the so-called Marxist approach. The storm that passed over history did not leave only ruins.

To find out for myself what 'awareness studies' amounted to, I attended a history class at a primary school in my own suburban district, Saint-Germain-en-Laye. It was an agreeable surprise. Ampère is a school just like any other. It was not specially selected or recommended, but was simply the nearest one – my daughter, Isabelle, had attended it. I turned up unexpectedly, had a warm welcome from the headmaster and staff, and sat in on several lessons the next day.

In the second-year general course for nine- to ten-year-olds under Aline Josse, the class had to reconstitute the history of France, through that of Saint-Germain itself. Every stone, every doorway and town prospect acquired meaning, and the changes that had taken place in the town were all located in space and time, and placed in an overall perspective. In one of Marguerite Trublin's classes, on the Middle Ages, I arrived just when tournaments were being discussed. Using a scene from Enguerrand de Marigny in 1310 the children reconstituted other aspects of life of the nobility: study of a miniature on tournaments caused an exercise worthy of Roland Barthes, which revolved around the word 'tournament' and different styles of history, and put the question, what can be learned from a juxtaposition of the commentary, the story and the picture?

The work of Nicole Darman, who taught the first year, of eight- and nine-year-olds, was breath-taking. As before, the lesson was not delivered ex cathedra; instead, 'awareness' was sought. These thirty small boys and girls, in two hours, and with only a dozen pictures from the Renaissance to refer to, did extraordinarily well, so well that it is worth recording what, in their own collective words, they achieved. How it would have pleased Pierre Francastel to see this! I was present when they drew up this essay, and I have transcribed it as it was, omitting only spelling errors:

> Question: Why are the fifteenth and sixteenth centuries called 'The Renaissance'? By looking at our documents, we noted that if, in the Middle Ages, man was essentially concerned for his salvation (Héloïse) from the early fourteenth century he became more interested in the world around him (Jean-Marc) and in himself (Cécile). From Fra Angelico and his *Deposition* (1435) to Titian's *Madonna with Rabbit* (1530) the landscape

became increasingly important (Pascal). The painters wanted to represent space (Stéphanie) as, for instance, by the presence of a mirror in Van Eyck's *Arnolfini* (Amélie) or through perspective (*Chancellor Rolin*). The abundance of portraits is also notable (Valérie) – of bourgeois and peasants in Breughel (Nicolas) but especially of noblemen and princesses, as with Raphael and Piero della Francesca. Artists also liked to show themselves in a flattering light (Emmanuel) as in Dürer's self-portrait. Sometimes a religious scene simply became an excuse for this, Veronese's *Wedding at Cana*. The sculptors, as in antiquity (Olivier) were interested in showing the human body (Sophie). In architecture we see the castles appearing as places of pleasure (Anne-France), e.g. Chambord or Chenonceaux. The old functions of the fortress are there only for decorative purposes. During the Renaissance, the scientific spirit developed (Marina) with Leonardo da Vinci's machines. Galileo announced, contrary to Church doctrines, that the earth moved round the sun.

I was quite amazed. Does all this – Saint-Germain, tournaments, Renaissance, palaces – represent fear of or attraction to history? This kind of method could hardly be applied to teach the Revolution or fascism, or the Commune, or collaboration. Nevertheless, I have high hopes that it will be applied, so that people, as adults, will gain an understanding of the world through their own efforts – an awareness that is worth more than all forms of imposed knowledge, whether in the form of a book, a lesson or a film.

Note In England, history is less anti-French than it is anti-British in France. Pierre Daninos in his *History Lesson* noted that the British celebrated Joan of Arc as 'the most courageous woman of all time . . . a heroine of history, a saint. . . . Piers Plowman, a breviary of English schoolchildren, remarked that the English could, here, only remember their ancestors with shame.' The only point on which the English version insists, and which the French one ignores, is the humiliation which Joan encountered in May 1428: haunted by her 'voices' she went to see a nobleman of the region (perhaps the Lord of Vaucouleurs) who asked the people who had brought her to give her a beating and send her back to her father. Daninos's remarks are confirmed by other books, such as the English History written by Rudyard Kipling and C. R. L. Fletcher, which describe Joan as 'a daughter of God' who 'led a pure life and was able to communicate her sense of mission to others' while 'the English burnt her as a witch, but in all good French (and English) hearts she lives on.' Passages on the French Revolution show the severity of English feeling towards France – it is the old story of France trying to dominate the world, from the very outset. Grievances against the king were of course quite right, and the Ancien Régime did collapse all at once. In the name of natural law, or imaginary rights, a new gospel was preached; all government was tyrannical, religion a mere sham; down with 'them' and up with 'us', the 'us' being the blood-thirsty masses from Paris and elsewhere. The image of Napoleon, in contrast, is more understanding. Suzanne Baudemont has systematically studied British works of the Victorian period and writes that 'Indulgence for a romantic destiny, admiration for military genius, gratitude for the restoration of order and religion – all of it a far cry (except in the pacifist, Pollard) from "the Corsican ogre" whom we might have expected to encounter more often.' In France, Anglophobia starts from earliest childhood, from the story of endless conflict with a neighbour whom no one has ever finally defeated. The British even defeated the heroes of our own national Pantheon – Joan of Arc, Napoleon, Colonel Marchand, etc. and 'expelled the French from India, Canada, etc.' so that they appear throughout history as 'winners', which is not equally true of France! British arms were always one ahead: archers triumphed over cavalry at

Crécy, the navy over the French army in the eighteenth century, and money over the armed forces in the eighteenth and nineteenth centuries, for the British had a decisive advantage during this period in their industrialization and technology. Jules Verne well expressed the admiring envy for the English that Frenchmen experienced at the turn of this century, even though today there is much surreptitious mockery in France at the 'decline' of their rivals.

8

ASPECTS AND VARIATIONS
OF SOVIET HISTORY

'Historians are dangerous, and capable of turning everything topsyturvy. They have to be watched': thus Khrushchev in 1956, at the time of de-Stalinization. The remark admirably sums up the place of history in the USSR. At the best of times, it is under supervision. The difference with other authoritarian regimes is not just that the Party, rather than the state, is the supervising agent; there is also the fact that the regime claims to incarnate the very movement of history, and to be history's own interpreter. The leadership could never allow historians to produce versions different from its own: if they even try, the Party hurls anathema.

All this is a long way from Karl Marx. He wished to turn history into a science: in Engel's words, 'Just as Darwin discovered the laws of evolution in nature, Marx discovered those of evolution in society.' Indeed, the concept of class-struggle was borrowed from that of natural selection.

The Marxian analysis led towards an identification and

recognition of the means of production as chief determinants of the historical process. The means of production created social classes, and their struggle was the 'motor' of history and the transformation of means and forms of production: 'Relations between men owe nothing to their individual wills, for . . . relations of production correspond to a distinct stage of the productive forces . . . and it is the means of material production that determine the social, political and intellectual process. Consciousness does not determine social existence; rather, social existence determines consciousness.'

With such premises, the great periods of history can be defined: slavery, feudalism, capitalism, and, from capitalism's inevitable fall, socialism. Each and every society can therefore be subjected to a periodization in terms of means and forms of production. This implicitly challenges the role of individuals in history: Marx himself never dealt directly with this question, but he did derive a conception of history in which individuals, who were moved by necessary laws, hardly had any place. 'Men make their own history, but do not make it as they want.' However, unlike natural history, human history is moved by objectives and by passions. Nevertheless, thought Marx and Engels, 'these affect only particular events at certain eras; and this does not alter the fact that history is governed by general laws.' G. V. Plekhanov in turn approached this problem, and took the Marxist matrix, to change its shape somewhat, for he insisted that leaders' personal qualities could give specific features to historical events, which gave some support to future practicians of the 'cult of personality'.

None of this has any obvious connection with the need to put history under surveillance. The creation of revolutionary institutions – the International, socialist parties, etc. – showed the revolutionaries' need to organize the movement of history and 'help' it towards its inevitable transformation. Thereafter, these bodies' tactics were linked to their judgement of the historical situation, and their success was linked with the quality of their judgement. Before 1914, the teaching of Marx, Engels and Kautsky inspired the Germans, and Franz Mehring, in his *History of Germany since the Middle Ages*, was the first Marxist historian, or historian-politician, to show what the new history could achieve. His work was translated into several languages, particularly Russian, and was unquestionably influential.

The Russian Marxists, who were first to carry out a revolution, did more than write history: they made it, and so gained a prestige that made them the leading interpreters of historical development. They held sole power after October 1917, and so counted as true prophets who had been right all along. Other socialist bodies objected to this view, and they could easily show that Russia had not passed through the stage of capitalism and so was not ripe for socialism. Thereafter, the political debate became a historical one, and the Bolsheviks did not mean to let historians' history invalidate the leaders' own judgements as to the history that was about to happen. The Party, as incarnation of the working class and the historical process, had taken power only because its analysis had been right: its power was knowledge; it could only be infallible; and reality was to conform to this diagnosis. Any non-conforming history had to be changed, for any questioning, based on history, would render illegitimate both the Party's policy and 'line', and hence also the Party's right to govern at all. It therefore mattered to keep an eye on what historians were doing, especially in questions of the Party's own history, for the Party was both the incarnation and the source of history.

VARIATIONS ON PARTY HISTORY

There were already, before 1917, various histories of the Party or of Russian social democracy, particularly Lyadov's. The situation changed when a single faction, the Bolsheviks, took power and in that sense it was Zinoviev who wrote the first history (it stopped in October 1917, and was written in 1922–3). At that time, the notion of an 'official' history defined as the only 'scientific' one, had not yet emerged, and Zinoviev's book dealt with problems in a way that, subsequently, is suggestive, for his vision of Party history was that of a very close companion of Lenin's (Zinoviev was sarcastically known as 'His Master's Voice'). Zinoviev wondered what was, and what should be, the basis of a political party: for him, it was not a voluntary association of people with similar views, or of 'adherents of a common programme', for these would mean only subjective bodies with no historical foundation, but rather 'the fighting organization of a social class'; so many classes, so many parties. The corollary was of course to wonder why there were so many workers' parties: how was this possible? Was it because there were conflicts of interest within the workers' ranks? A further problem involved the Socialist-Revolutionary Party. That it called itself a workers' party, then a peasants' party, and finally the party of the working intelligentsia seemed to be the height of absurdity. But it was an absurdity soon, under Stalin, to be adopted by the Communist (Bolshevik) Party itself, in which it was to be copied by other communist parties that adopted that kind of identity. Incidentally, Zinoviev's account even acknowledged the Bund, or Jewish Socialist Workers' Party 'which at the darkest hour of the Tsarist reaction was the first to rise and give battle'. He also saluted Plekhanov, and, despite his 'errors', Martov.

Such questioning and such respects have never figured in the history taught to Soviet children, who grow up in ignorance of them. Both leaders and people have been educated with a history drawn up much later, the Short History which was written with Stalin's own assistance in the 1930s, and was endlessly reprinted as a whole or in extracts. The Soviet Union of today has inherited the book, though both Khrushchev, in 1959, and latterly Brezhnev altered it in ways needed to legitimize their policies.

For the historian of the Communist Party has, in the USSR, much the same function as a theologian in an Islamic or Christian country: the object of his teaching is to reinforce and add stature to the existing institutions. This function is not formally required by the Soviet system, but its leaders, Stalin in particular, insisted upon it in an extreme degree, so that the past was transformed and distorted according to the twists and turns of the political 'line', which had always to be explained by the necessities of history-in-the-making.

The effects of such variations – which are sometimes tantamount to lies – can be seen in the book's treatment of the Bolsheviks' enemies, Mensheviks, anarchists, socialist-revolutionaries, etc. and, in still more distorted caricature, its treatment of Trotsky. Trotsky is simply avoided, almost expelled from history, whenever he agrees with the Party, or strengthens it, or agrees with Lenin. Thus, in the *Short History* Trotsky's election as president of the Soviet in September 1917 disappears; so does the famous document in which Lenin praised Trotsky in October 1917; for greater safety, any trace of this document is eliminated, and taken out of public libraries, together with the record of the Sixth Congress at which Trotsky figured; and his role as commander of the Red Army similarly vanishes, together with the victory of Kazan ('The Red Valmy') in the Civil War, etc.

Conversely, his part is deliberately increased each time he comes into conflict with Lenin, even if their disagreement was trivial and momentary: Trotsky has to bear the burden of anything that might tarnish the image of the Soviet Republic. In the period of the Revolution and the Civil War, for instance, 'he wished to shoot many communists (in 1919) who were involved in military matters and did not have the good fortune to please him; thus he played the enemy's game.' In itself, the fact is authentic, but his role as commander of the Red Army was not confined to this.

In the school-book for class nine (which is equivalent to our highest form) Trotsky's name comes up three times in the 160 pages covering the period from 1917 to 1932. Before October 1917, there is an observation that Trotsky 'proposed not acting before the meeting of the Second Congress of Soviets, until that Congress had had a chance to decide as to power-taking: it was not due to meet until 25 October. Trotsky's proposal therefore put the Revolution's success at some risk.' Again, over the negotiations at Brest-Litovsk, 'Lenin disagreed with Trotsky's and Bukharin's ideas' . . . 'The country being in great danger, Trotsky declared (to the Germans) that the Soviet Republic would not sign peace and submit to the Germans' demands, which was treacherous, for he knew that the Soviet leaders had decided to conclude peace after all.' In the textbook, there is not a word as to Trotsky's role as founder and organizer of the Red Army, although some of its commanders are cited by name – on the eastern front, Kuibyshev and Gusev, on other fronts Voroshilov and Stalin. The third occasion for mention of Trotsky is an attack on him for wishing to militarize the trade unions.

As might be imagined, Trotsky is not the only victim of 'variation' of the historical record. Others among Lenin's companions, murdered during the Moscow show-trials, are also made to disappear, except for fleeting references to any disagreement with Lenin: thus Kamenev is 'against the October rising' although he was elected by the Bolsheviks, including Lenin, as president of the Second Congress of Soviets, i.e. the personification of the Bolsheviks' seizure of power. The same is true of Zinoviev, Rykov and several more. On the other hand, some Bolsheviks who died before Lenin – Sverdlov, Volodarsky, etc. – are quoted more often than they merit.

As regards other revolutionary bodies – the SRs, Mensheviks, anarchists and the like – they figure only to commit deeds that harm the Revolution. But the truly striking feature is the almost total disappearance of Stalin. Whereas in the Short History of 1938–59, he was always at Lenin's side ('Lenin and Stalin' even, in a way, replacing 'Lenin and Trotsky'), since Khrushchev and de-Stalinization his name has disappeared from school-books, even more completely than Trotsky's, which at least comes up whenever there is some deed to be judged negatively.

In the fourth-class textbook of 1956 (destined for thirteen- or fourteen-year-olds) Stalin appears only twice in all between 1917 and 1953. He figures among the five, including Lenin, who organized the October rising: the others were Sverdlov, Dzierżyński and Bubnov. He also appears as one of the five who organized defence against the whites' 'the Fatherland in danger', the others being Lenin, Voroshilov, Frunze and Kors. His name is not mentioned in the context of collectivization, the Five Year Plans, or even the Second World War, except in the battle of Stalingrad. In the ninth-class book (which stops in 1938) we find the same names even more advancedly absent – if the expression fits – in the same context. This is tantamount almost to a supplementary Leninization of history. As regards 1917, mention is made of names like Yemelyanov, who hid Lenin, or even the Andreyev who remembers that at the Second Congress, in October 1917, Lenin was cheered. But the big names do not appear.

In such history, individuals come and go at the whim of those who succeed them. This is of course not just characteristic of Soviet–Marxist types of history. The 'whites' history has done the same, and even highly liberal governments also: in France, for instance, Georges Bidault simply disappeared from the Gaullist memory some time ago, for just after the generals' coup in Algeria his picture was blurred out in a documentary to commemorate the Liberation, when, at de Gaulle's side, he walked down the Champs Elysées. The difference between such aberrations and the history taught in the USSR is that outside the

USSR, several versions of the truth co-exist: this is not the case in the USSR where only a single version is tolerated. In particular, the whole set of institutions for studying history in the USSR is designed to carry out these changes to make them appear correct, and to adjust the past to the needs of the present.

Throwing out Trotsky and then Stalin 'onto the rubbish heap of history' replacing them by the omnipresent and anonymous Party, and quoting Lenin as gospel is only the visible aspect of this phenomenon. But what of the phenomena and events that are completely manipulated out of sight? What of the Kronstadt rising when the Soviet and the inhabitants of the great revolutionary town rose against the Bolshevik autocracy? Or the Comintern, presided over from the start by Zinoviev, the very existence of which makes incredible the Soviet will towards peaceful co-existence? Practically none of these things is mentioned in the *Short History* of 1938 and no mention at all is made of them in the later works designed as school textbooks. Of course, despite Khrushchev, the horrors of enforced collectivization, the wholesale deportations or massacre of several small nationalities of the Caucasus, and the disappearance of the Crimean Tatars are not recognized as facts worthy of recall.

RETROSPECTIVE CHANGE

It is also important that such obvious and legible manipulation requires constitutional change in the vision of the pre-1917 period. This is a much more subtle and demanding matter, which is more difficult to effect.

Western historiography also makes use of gradations in hindsight. It has been said, of the change in the character of the First World War, that 'the fighting of 1914 echoed that of 1870; in 1918 it looked forward to 1940'. A comparative study of the fighting in 1914 and 1918 if written in 1970 would not analyse it in the same terms as a study written in 1919. Inevitably, there are selections of detail, omissions, additions and new interpretations. But these omissions and additions have nothing in common with Soviet practices, in which the factor that counts, and reshapes interpretation of the past is not just hindsight, which affects the Soviet historians, as it does all professionals, but also a need to adjust to the determinist dogmas concerning phases of history. Before 1925 this meant organizing the facts so that a coherent analogy could be drawn between the Russian and French Revolutions; in particular, historical matter has to be shaped according to the demands and requirements of power-politics.

Georges Enteen and T. Kondratieva have shown these mechanisms at work, and analysed the various interpretations of particular problems in Russian history, according to Soviet political development. The example chosen is that of Russian imperialism before 1914.

In origin, the debate was purely academic, and the question was to what extent Russian imperialism before 1914 was itself dependent on western capital. Some historians played down the role of western capital, but others regarded it as vital and decisive. Vanag constructed a theory of Russia's subordinate status, while Goldman saw Russian imperialism as a branch of western imperialism and Lenin, when he referred to it in 1914, even gave it inverted commas to show that it existed, but was military and feudal, functioning quite differently from the British or German models. Sidorov, on the other hand, regarded Russia in 1914 as autonomous; the war made her more imperialistic, but also more dependent, so that the October Revolution saved Russia from absorption by the West.

The first turning-point: 1927

The defeat of the Chinese communists, after that of other communists in Europe, ruled out a socialist revolution in the near future. According to Stalin, China was at the stage of a democratic bourgeois revolution, and consequently might liquidate feudalism and expel foreigners, but was not ready for the socialist stage. Since, now, the Soviet Union itself was attempting socialism, its stage of development could hardly be equated with that of semi-colonial nations; and to say that, before 1914, Russia's was a 'dependent imperialism' could only mean that she was too backward to establish a form of socialism on her own, for that simply gave arguments to the Trotskyites. Thus Sidorov's theory was seen as right, and those of Vanag and Pokrovsky wrong. They turned into 'bourgeois falsifiers' and both died, it seems, in the camps, whereas Sidorov joined the Academy of Sciences.

The second turning-point: 1933–6

Stalin suddenly abandoned Sidorov's theories and adopted the semi-colonial line. Why? At the Sixth Conference of Comintern in 1927, it had been argued that the colonial and semi-colonial countries lacked the bases for socialism. Such arguments gave a certain credibility, in Central Europe and elsewhere, to the legitimation of Fascism, which was then triumphant and appeared as a regeneration force. But once Hitler turned out to be the chief threat to the USSR, the Soviet Union sought to show that its interests were similar to those of other countries threatened by the Nazis, and played the role of protector of small peoples. The semi-colonial theory, which showed Russia liberating herself from foreign capital, once more became a convenient way of demonstrating that the Soviet Union was by nature an ally of nations threatened by German super-imperialism. It was now good form to insist on the background character of the Russian nation in 1914, as Lyashchenko did, and to show that there were other ways towards regeneration than Fascism. Vanag and Pokrovsky were rehabilitated.

1956: A new turning-point

After Stalin's death, historians expected liberalization of the regime, and supposed that the positive elements of their research might allow a proper assessment of the question, and perhaps some model-building. Gefter and P. V. Volobuev provided an increasing amount of detail, showing the importance of the great monopolies in Russia before 1917. But was this not to suggest that, after all, progress under socialism had not been as remarkable as the government claimed? These historians were soon removed from their posts.

The study of Russian imperialism in 1914 is just one example of the kind of fluctuation that history undergoes, and the same exercise might just as well be applied to other problems in Russian history – the reforms of Peter the Great, the emergence of the Oprichnina (was it 'bureaucracy'?) and much else. Peter the Great, for instance, was seen in a very critical light by Karamzin, for having weakened Russia's identity; and then again by Pokrovsky, for having launched Russian expansionism. Next, Lyashchenko rehabilitated Peter in the era of the Great Patriotic War as the inheritor of Alexander Nevsky and precursor of Stalin. Another instance is the campaign of Napoleon in 1812. It was traditionally shown as a victory for Russian patriotism. However, Soviet historiography from Pokrovsky to Tarle and Pionkovsky reinterpreted it as a series of blunders, dressed up as inspired tactics and having nothing to do with national spirit: 'There was no real popular participation in the fighting. The peasants only took up arms when they found their geese and chickens being taken without payment.' The war had been willed by the commercial Russian nobility in order to establish a British type of capitalism on Russian soil, whereas Napoleon brought liberty to the Russian peasantry along with the enlightenment and progress that had been won through the French Revolution.

There was a sudden change in 1936 when it came to mobilizing Soviet patriotism: without explaining why or how, Tarle abruptly refuted his own ideas, and glorified the Russian heroism and genius of Kutuzov, because Napoleon's attack on Russia 'was the most imperialist of all the campaigns aiming, as it did, to make a vassal Poland and Lithuania serve as spring-boards for the interests of the upper bourgeoisie in France'.

In the school-books for the eighth class (1977 edition) the patriotic version of the 1936 type is dominant, and is decked out with tales of peasant bravery in the 'partisan' movement. All history is thus made to yield to the patterns and requirements of politics. It is easy enough to see why the regime mistrusts even historians who publish only documents, for that in itself can be demonstrative, and question the legitimacy of the regime. Such people are 'dangerous' and have to be made harmless. Because Soviet historians have had to learn how to protect themselves, they have acquired professional skills and enviable abilities, for they must manage an art of double-writing, such that their work can be taken in both one sense and, if need be, its opposite. Like politicians, they are true professionals.

MARXIST HISTORY AND EDUCATIONAL NECESSITY

Marxist history in the USSR was limited for some years to Party history. It had, however, to extend its horizons and examine the more remote past, and to confront a different history which had no immediate relevance to the problems of Soviet politics. Indeed, Lenin's own works were a characteristic example of the constant grafting of Party history and Russian history which was properly a matter for professionals. Control over such history developed only slowly and uncomfortably, because there was always a difficulty: the non-Marxist historians were professionals, a Tarle or a Platonov being better-equipped than Marxist historians to analyse an event such as the Berezina or the Time of

Troubles, whereas in the first twenty years of the Soviet regime the Marxists who wrote history, such as Pokrovsky, inevitably worked towards abstractions and the establishment of sociological models defining feudalism, capitalism, imperialism, etc.

To make the masses identify with the regime and let Stalin appear as true heir of the defenders of the Fatherland, a different kind of history was needed, more inspiring and consonant with the popular memory. Already in 1934 the Communist Party attacked the Marxist historians for their dry-as-dust dogmatic approach.

> Historical lessons have not been made enjoyable or lively. No effort has been made to describe the chief facts and events in their chronological order, interspersed with tales of outstanding personalities. Instead, children have been burdened with abstract definitions of economic and social development and sociological patterns have taken the place of patriotic history. . . . History should inspire children and give them a lively image of the events that led towards the Marxist vision of history. There is no other way.

A further instruction announces that

> A good historical education should convince people that capitalism must go bankrupt . . . and that everywhere, in science, agriculture, industry, peace and war the Soviet people leads all others, its achievements being unequalled in history. . . . War and military matters should be stressed so as to maintain Soviet patriotism.

This explains why school textbooks have two aspects. The history of the Party and the building of socialism is in constant flux, and is, as it were, on a short circuit, the terms of which alter the closer it approaches the present day. The other history, planted onto this, is also subject to change as the present captures it, but the cycle of change is slower. Not only are narrative and anecdote not abandoned, they are set up as examples for children. At the crossroads of these two types of history stands Lenin. On the one side, his theoretical writings are quoted and analysed; anecdote has only a limited role; and the nearest it comes to any sort of life is the story of one Andreyev, who remembers that when Lenin appeared at the Second Congress, delegates stood up and cheered. On the other hand, to inspire children, there is an endless amount of story-telling: *Lenin and Geese, Lenin and Children, Lenin and Cats*, etc.

> 'Do you have a cat?' Vladimir Ilich asked my daughter, Lelia, while they were strolling in the garden of our *dacha* where we had asked him to stay. 'Yes, Viaska. We call him Vassili Ivanovich; there he is', replied Lelia, pointing to a large black cat, which was proceeding from the kitchen in a dignified manner. He was nearly all black, with a white patch under the chin; his paws were white, like little mantles, and so was the furry tip of his tail. 'What a big beast,' exclaimed Vladimir Ilich, 'What a beautiful animal. Great lazy creature!' 'What do you mean, Vladimir Ilich', Lelia broke in, 'He catches mice very well'. 'And so he should', said Vladimir Ilich, 'Let's see what tricks he can do'. And Vladimir Ilich took hold of the cat, tickled it under the cheek, scratched it behind the ears and stroked it. Viaska agreed to all this quite amicably; he began gently to nibble one of Vladimir Ilich's fingers while, rolling onto his back, he tried to push with his back paws.

Such literature dates from the early 1920s; a reading-book for young peasant children, *Novy Put*, tells stories about Lenin. In January, there is a passage on Lenin's death; in April, on his return to Russia; in October, on the Petrograd rising. Edifying homilies as to the need for work in the communes, the struggle against alcoholism, etc. constitute children's first experience of historical teaching.

WORLD HISTORY AND SOVIET HISTORY

Later on at school, world history and Soviet history are taught in alternation. This combination produces a complete vision of countries' past which is the most systematic in the world. The Soviet textbooks are vaguely reminiscent of French works of the Malet-Isaac or Halphen-Segnac type. They are classical, even though they are designed to a Marxist pattern. The general historical works assign a relatively sizeable part to extra-European cultures (see in the appendix to this chapter the table of contents from a work on the period 1640–1870) and give a better balance between the histories of different societies, Africa, India, Asia, Europe, than do other such works. This is of course an effort to see such societies' development within the framework of a large-scale Marxist periodization, and is not meant as a challenge. For the Russian textbooks on the USSR are themselves Russian, indeed very Russian, in inspiration even if Soviet patriotism increasingly takes over from Great-Russian nationalism.

It is helped by the fundamental principle of history in Marxist countries, the theory of the lesser evil (*Naimensheye zlo*) which can be used to justify Old Russia's successive expansion – what, without this, would have happened to Armenians or Georgians? Would they not simply have fallen victim to the Turks or Turkmenies? That theory is still alive, for in 1980 it was used to justify intervention in Afghanistan, to save the Afghans from feudalism and the 'Pakistani menace'.

These themes can be seen in the fourth-year textbook version of the origins of Russia and of her union with the Ukraine; later on, they can be seen again in the university textbooks' presentation of the Second World War.

THE FOURTH-CLASS BOOK: INTRODUCTION TO SOVIET HISTORY

The country in which we are born and in which we live is called the Union of Soviet Socialist Republics. It is our Fatherland. Our fathers and forefathers have lived and worked here from time immemorial. Their labouring built our towns and our countryside, our villages, our factories, our *kolkhozy*, our schools, our theatres and our sports-stadiums – everything that we use in life. The people of the Soviet Union are the owners of their country, for everything belongs to the people – the land, the forests, the seas, the rivers, the factories and businesses. In the factories, machines are made. They are our factories and our machines. The combine harvesters you see are our own combine harvesters, and they reap our harvest in the fields.

It was not always like this. The working people have not always been masters of their country. People have not always lived as we live today. What can we learn from historians about the life of people in past ages?

The mystery of the red hill

In the Caucasus, near the town of Erivan, the capital of Soviet Armenia, there is a large red hill. The inhabitants of the surrounding country looked for precious stones on it. Often, they came across skulls or old bits of pottery or arrow-tips of bronze or gold. How did all this happen? Experts came and found iron swords and head-bands made of bearskin; one expert found an inscription from the old fortress of the town of Teshebaini and pots in which grain had been stored. The people who lived there had settled over 3,000 years ago: that was the red hill's secret.

In the desert of Central Asia

In Central Asia there is little water. Everything depends on water. Where it exists, there are rivers, flowers and cotton; where it has gone, all life perishes with it and vast, arid regions grow up. However, Soviet explorers, venturing into inaccessible country, discovered now-buried ancient towns, villages and water-systems. Historians have been able to reconstitute three Central Asian states which disappeared over 2,000 years ago.

The culture of the birch-tree

The Old Russian town of Novgorod is more than 1,000 years old. Soviet scientists excavated there, and, in the marshland, found remains of very old houses. They also found some writing carved on wood, real letters, written six to eight centuries ago. Many very interesting things can be learnt about this civilization of the birch-tree.

The frontiers of history

It is not just excavation that lets us see how people lived in the old days. Here is a newspaper, a century old. In it, we can find the following notice: 'For sale: a peasant aged twenty-five, his wife and three children', or 'For sale: two coachmen, three horses and a pack of hunting-dogs'. At this time, peasants belonged to their owners and worked for them. The owners bought and sold them as a labour-force. Here is a pamphlet, an appeal to the workers. It was printed fifty years ago, in secret. At this time, the workers and peasants of our country lived under the tyranny of the Tsar and other oppressors. 'Down with the Tsar, liberty for the people', say these pamphlets. It was the Bolshevik Party that encouraged workers to attack their oppressors.

> Here again is a proclamation. It is written in tiny letters. It was written by Vladimir Ilich Lenin on 26 October 1917. On that day, the workers, led by the Communist Party, threw off their yoke. In this proclamation you find recorded a decision of the victorious people 'To form a government of workers and peasants to lead the country'. In this history book we shall learn about the past life of the people of our country, their work, their struggle against enemies, their fight for a free and happy life, and their battles for the future.

From the very start, then, the regime awards itself high merit: communal ownership of the means of production, transformation of life since the October Revolution, role of the Bolshevik Party and of Lenin all receiving emphasis. Above all, the principle is laid down of identifying government, for the purposes of legitimation, with workers and peasants.

OLD RUSSIA

'If a Russian, a Ukrainian and a Byelorussian meet and talk, each in their own language, they can understand each other for they come from the same racial family. They are Slavs, peoples who lived between the Black Sea and the Baltic.' A framework is thus laid down, such that the Baltic falls within the eastern-Slav purlieu. The book goes on to explain that 'from the start, the land belonged to everybody; but gradually some people obtained more of it than others. These were the boyars.' From the first pages, then, the boyars appear as land-grabbers. The princes had still more land, and so the peasantry had to pay heavy tribute:

> One day Prince Igor imposed a heavy tax on his people and returned to his capital, Kiev. On the way back, he reckoned that the tax should have been higher, and he turned about. When the peasants heard that the prince was coming back for a

further tax, they said, 'When the wolf has tasted one ewe he will eat the whole flock. If we do not kill the prince he will suck us dry.' The people rose in revolt, and the prince was killed. But there were always other princes, and other boyars. Igor's widow raised another *druzhina* and the rebels were cruelly punished. In this era, the country suffered the attacks of nomads, Khazars and Pechenegs, who wrecked and burned everything. Igor's son, Svyatoslav, spent his life in fending them off. He knew no fear, underwent everything and slept on the ground, his saddle by his side. The warriors loved this brave prince, and he managed to push back the nomads to the country's borders. . . . In old Kiev, the capital, which was one of the largest cities of its day, and a major centre of trade, the church played a great part. Not for nothing did the princes show such consideration for the church. Its servants helped the princes and boyars keep the people down. They said that, in the sky, there was a God who would punish all those who did not obey the princes and boyars. The people believed them and their stories, for they feared the church's threats. In these centuries, the Russian state grew, and cities also increased, both in number – Novgorod, Ryazan, Vladimir – and in size, like Kiev. The peasants worked and the boyars and princes grew richer. With the aid of their *druzhiny* the princes guaranteed government and justice, and they controlled the police. But soon, other princes grew more powerful, and the cities ceased to obey the prince of Kiev. Early in the thirteenth century, these little states fought each other and their wars devastated the country. The state was large, but not solid.

MARXISM VERSUS MARX

Thus, nothing is said as to the Varangians who, according to tradition, founded the Russian state. The idea that these invaders

– at that, from Germany and Scandinavia – could have been founders of the first Russian state is hardly acceptable to patriotic feeling, whether Russian or Soviet. For many years, Russian historians condemned this 'Norman' view of things, and it is altogether concealed from children, even for purposes of refutation. The Varangians are certainly mentioned to older pupils, but only once the Russian state has been established: 'These invaders looted several European countries and penetrated Russian soil, ruining it, and forcing open a passage from the Baltic to the Black Sea. They occupied Novgorod and other cities; some of them went back home, but the rest mingled with the Russians and adopted the Slav language and customs.' Finally, for adults, the denial of any Varangian political role as absurd proceeds from Marxist first principles.

> In one legend, Slav tribes invited Rurik, Sineus and Truvor to govern them. This myth was used by some historians of German origin, working in Russia during the eighteenth century, to show contempt for everything Russian and to demonstrate that the Russians were unable to set up their own state. They claimed that the Normans – Scandinavian groups who took to maritime piracy in the ninth century – were the true founders of the Russian state, and that before their arrival the Slavs had been savages. . . . *But this could not have been the origin of the Russian state since the state is always the outcome of internal developments inside a society, and cannot be imported from without.* The Varangian troops of the old Russian princes had little influence on the social composition and civilization of the country, for they were few in number and came from a lower level of social and economic development. Besides, the Varangians assimilated quickly with the Russians.

This passage is all the odder for its complete inversion of the relationship between Varangians and Russians. The problem of the origins of the Russian state is in fact still an open question. What is certain, at least, is that if the existence of Rurik has never been proven, his successors, the princes of Kiev, certainly existed, and were Varangians. The curious point in this matter, fought over between Normans and anti-Normans with mountains of scholarly ammunition for over a century, is that Marx, when writing before these disputes, took for granted the idea that the Russian state had Varangian origins, and that the Normans had been civilizers: that, even though 'the state is always the outcome of internal developments inside societies and cannot be imported from without'. It is an unpublished instance of Marx contradicting himself.

THE LEADERSHIP OF MOSCOW

In this book, the boyars come under constant fire: they are always involved with whatever misfortune is being inflicted on Old Russia. In this, the Marxist conception of history and national *amour-propre* coincide, since the institution of boyars came directly from the Varangian *druzhiny*.

The church is clearly stated to have been 'associated with the mighty', although there is no reminder that it was also bound up with Byzantium, which converted Russia to Orthodoxy and gave her a collective identity, partly based on religion. The Russians maintained their religion whatever territory they inhabited, whether around Kiev or around Moscow, or still further west. In fact the unification and centralization of Russia was originally the work of the church, said Klyuchevsky. This attachment to Byzantium later strengthened both Moscow and the princes who accepted its rule.

As far as the unification of the Russian lands by Moscow is concerned, Soviet children know only one single fact, the geographical situation. It is not even stated that the prince of Moscow, before rebelling under Ivan III, sought and won the Tatars' favour in acquiring the privilege of levying tribute, with all of the advantages it implied (Ivan I was known as 'money-bags'). For older children, the amount of factual information is greater and the presentation is more analytical, following Marxist precepts: everything starts with 'feudalism' and then explains it; its birth, development, consolidation and achievements offer a universal explanation of all the situations presented. Thereafter, the framework is extended, and patriotism is no longer a Russian monopoly, for it occurs in the Caucasus and in Central Asia, where the same three factors are brought into operation: feudalism, peasant risings, foreign invasions. Only, for older children, a fourth factor is added: religion.

It first comes up in the section on the early Russians when, finally, the question of Byzantium can no longer be avoided: 'One of Prince Oleg's horse-raids reached the great city. . . . The power of the Russian forces terrified its inhabitants . . . they asked for terms.' There was intermarriage and trade.

> At this time, Russia was still pagan, but this religion was of no service to the princes' power; it was different from Christianity which argued the Divine Right of Kings. Vladimir, son of Svyatoslav, became Christian and made Christianity the state religion in 988. The people opposed the new faith . . . but Christianity was imposed by force. . . . In Novgorod the church had half the city burned down and for many years it was said that Putyata baptized by the sword, and Dobryna by fire.

> The clergy was learned. . . . The country's culture developed more quickly than under paganism. But

> '*Christianity upheld feudal power over the peasantry and strengthened the power of the princes*'.

THE CAUCASUS: THE ARAB THREAT

'The peoples of Transcaucasia, which was threatened by the Arabs, were subjected to feudalism and never managed to combine to defend their independence. Azerbaijan, Armenia and Georgia were all conquered.' As in Russia later on, the peasants of Azerbaijan revolted against their feudal oppressors. They were led by the intrepid Babek, who beat the caliph's armies, 'which the feudalists, being allies of the foreigner, had supported'. The general uprising soon affected Armenia and Georgia. The Arabs captured Babek's son and summoned Babek to surrender, but his proud reply was: 'Better one more day of liberty than forty years of slavery.' This peasant war lasted for over twenty years.

> When, finally, he was beaten and captured, the conquerors cut off his right arm with an axe. With his left hand he painted his face with his own blood and said, 'When a man dies, he becomes pale. I will not have enemies see me go pale.'
>
> In Central Asia, the Arabs also appeared as conquerors, pillaging and destroying whole towns and villages. Thousands of people were killed or were taken away as slaves. According to one witness of the times, a single conqueror deprived the country of more than 100,000 people who were carried off to slavery. The local feudal lords were now serving the conquerors, and from now on the peasants had not only one oppressor but two: their feudal lords and the Arabs. Each used the Islamic religion as an agent of oppression.

THE TATARS

Apart from Kiev there were other states, in the Caucasus and in Central Asia. They, first, had to face the 'Mongol-Tatar' horde. It was said that 'they have the strength of the lion, the cunning of the fox, the rapacity of the wolf and the ardour of a fighting-cock; when they attacked, they let out a chilling shriek.' They broke the once flourishing states of Central Asia, devastated them and were launched against the Russians, using their prisoners as slaves. In 1237 the khan attacked Ryazan, the prince of which begged the prince of Vladimir for help. 'They are your lands, defend them yourself', replied this prince. The prince of Ryazan was defeated, and Ryazan was ravaged and burnt, and its inhabitants either killed or enslaved.

> Then it was the turn of Vladimir to suffer this fate. But these victories for the khans were not easy, for the Russians defended themselves bravely. Then the Tatars moved westwards, but they had lost too much of their strength in the fighting with the Russians and the tide turned. The Russian people, by their bravery, saved the West from the Mongol-Tatar horde.

> If a man had no money, they took his child; if a man had no children they took his wife; if a man had no wife, they took him himself.

TEUTONIC KNIGHTS AND TATARS

The Mongol-Tatars had attacked from the east; unfortunately, Russia was now attacked by the Swedes and the Teutonic Knights from the west. The first to arrive were the Swedes whose ships came up the river Neva. They sent a message to Prince Alexander: 'If you are still able, defend yourself, we are on Russian soil.'

Alexander replied by defeating them on the Neva – hence the nickname Alexander Nevsky. 'Meanwhile the knights had also arrived in the Baltic lands. They compelled the Estonians and Letts to work for them, occupied Pskov and threatened Novgorod. Russia was in great danger.' The Russians prepared to defend their native soil. Merchants and workers united and abandoned their peaceable ways to meet the invaders. The peasants armed themselves with spiked clubs and hatchets. The refugees from Pskov rallied to them, as did the men of Vladimir who had had to face the Mongols. Alexander Nevsky met the enemy on the shores of the Shudsky lake. The knights advanced in a wedge-formation, heavily laden-down by iron breast-plates; even their horses were armoured. Nevsky allowed them to stave in his front lines, for his light cavalry were in position to ambush them. When they attacked, the heavy enemy horses slid around while responding to quick-silver light attacks; under their own weight they fell through the ice and were swallowed up in the frozen waters.

'This victory on the ice in 1242 stopped the German invaders, saved native Russian soil and helped the Baltic peoples in their struggle for liberation.' However, the Russian state was now being consolidated around Moscow, a formerly small principality which was now becoming 'the unifier of Russia'. It was beginning to show a certain restiveness towards the Mamai-khan. Prince Dmitry resolved to fight when the khan collected his forces on the Dniepr.

> His soldiers arrived, and crossed the Don without making a sound: to ensure silence Dmitry had the horse-shoes muffled by little pads of grass. When in the morning the Tatars saw the Russians coming through the morning mist they were panic-stricken. The Herculean Tamir rose out of their ranks and began to mock the Russians, shouting at them in a stentorian tone, 'Not one of you will dare to take me on.' But from the Russian camp there emerged a horseman, Peresvet, with a lance. They fell to, and both perished.

After this, the Russians fell back, but reinforcements came, and the Russians' vigour was renewed. The Mongols, who supposed that they had won, were forced to retreat; Mamai fled, and the Russians won the field. From this battle, Kulikovo, Dmitry took the nickname 'Donskoy'.

> Gradually the Tatar yoke was loosened. When Ivan III tried to rebel, the boyars still advised him to continue with submission, but the people protested and Ivan decided to stop paying tribute. When he faced the khan with an army, the Tatars avoided conflict and gave up the game; it was the end of the Tatar yoke.

'Tatar hordes', duplicity of rich boyars, and solidarity of Estonians, Letts and other Baltic peoples with their Russian brothers against the western invaders: such are the leitmotifs of this Soviet history, and the Poles, thereafter, replace the Germans as predators on Russian land.

THE EXPULSION OF THE POLES

The Muscovite state was being consolidated: Ivan III was proclaimed Tsar of all the Russias, and the Mari, Mordvinians and Karelians were united with the Russian people. Only Byelorussia and the Ukraine remained apart for they were under Polish and Lithuanian occupation. The great Polish land-owners still occupied the western part of Russia: the Ukraine and Byelorussia. They intervened in Russia and even managed to seize Moscow. Dmitry Pozharsky and, in Nizhny-Novgorod, Kozma Minin, rose against them, Minin appealing to the people to save Moscow, which was only liberated after it had been burned down.

'It was during this war that a peasant, Ivan Susanin, heroically sacrificed himself. Polish officers asked him the way to Kostroma. It was in the middle of winter, and Ivan tricked them into a tangled forest. He was beheaded, and so paid with his life for what he had done.' The 'Polish land-owners' did not manage to enslave Russia, though they took over the Ukraine and Byelorussia. 'They destroyed the schools, and forbade the local language;

they wanted the Ukrainians and Byelorussians to forget even the name of their native land. The princes and boyars in alliance with the Poles agreed to this expropriation and enslavement of the peasants who no longer had anything of their own.'

> One day, a peasant could not pay his taxes, which were too onerous. The land-owner ordered his cattle to be taken from the plough and sent over to him. The young peasant resisted. The land-owner took the law into his own hands and killed him there and then. The murdered peasant's widow mourned her husband. Dependent peasants were exploited to the uttermost by the kulaks, but what could they do? They did, however, have faith that one day all would be set right, and accounts would be settled.

THE LIBERATION OF THE UKRAINE

The peasants fled from the Ukraine and became Cossacks. Under their leadership, uprisings followed. The decisive fight for freedom for the Ukrainian people came in 1648, under the leadership of Bogdan Khmelnitsky. The Polish general who arrived to confront these peasant armies said boastingly that 'It is shameful for such a great army to have been mustered against such a small group of miserable peasants. A single regiment would be enough.' But Bogdan won the battle, and the Polish general was taken prisoner. The Russians helped in the victory by giving arms, corn and gun-powder, but the Poles came back in force and the war went on for another six years. In 1654 Bogdan Khmelnitsky, recognizing that he needed union with Russia, collected the Cossacks, peasants and urban poor and asked them: 'Do you want to carry on under the yoke of Polish land-owners or will you unite with your Russian brothers?' 'We will unite with our Russian brothers', the assembly answered; it was called *Rada* ('council'). 'Thus the union of the

Ukraine and Russia was decided, at Pereyaslavl, on 8 January 1654.'

DISCUSSION

Soviet children already have an abbreviated and inaccurate view of the union with the Ukraine. As Roger Portal has said, it is very much a history in strip-cartoon style. It takes no account at all of the existence of Ukrainian patriotism (or maybe even nationalism, though such terms did not then have the same meaning as now). History as taught to children presupposes only a single Old-Russian nationality which went on from the ninth to the twelfth century up to the agreement of Pereyaslavl (and beyond). But in fact there had been a gradually-increasing differentiation, for the Tatar conquests on the one side, and the Polish occupation on the other made the Ukraine into a separate territory with a character that was increasingly different as time went by. In Soviet eyes the Ukraine was a part of Russia which had to deal in the east with the Tatars and in the west with Poles and Lithuanians, not unlike the Russians themselves. They insist too far on Russian-Ukrainian solidarity, whereas the Ukrainian tradition stresses the individual character of the Ukrainian west, i.e. Galicia, and the utter absence of any intention of accepting the protection of Muscovy, which is portrayed as barbarian. It was clearly only necessity that compelled Khmelnitsky and the Ukrainians to seek Muscovy's help against the (unquestionably hated) Poles, and on this point all the traditions agree. It seems, even, that Muscovy had no conscious will to annex the Ukraine, at a time when Poles, Turks and even Swedes were wrangling over these lands. The Ukraine appeared to Moscow as semi-independent frontier marches, between Poland and the Turkish empire. Thus, in a sense, says Portal, Bogdan Khmelnitsky 'forced the hand of the Tsar to make him conclude a treaty between suzerain and vassal rather than between two equal states'.

In Ukrainian eyes, Hetman Khmelnitsky is only an 'ambitious traitor' who, to maintain his privileges, which the then circumstances challenged, sought Russian protection. Contrary to Russian legend, 'there never was any fraternal feeling between Russians and Ukrainians.' For the latter, the true national hero was Mazeppa, who was soon to rise, with Swedish help, against the Russians. Soviet children do not encounter him except as 'the traitor Mazeppa' who went over to the Swedes while 'the people rose at the Russians' side'. Here again is a half-truth, for though Mazeppa was not loved by his people, who did not understand the meanderings of his policies or his harshness as Hetman, none the less it was the independence of the Ukraine, and nothing else, that he wanted, as is shown by the treaty he signed with Charles XII of Sweden, even if defeat at Poltava turned the treaty into a vain hope.

THE GREAT PATRIOTIC WAR IN SOVIET EYES

The works of Ivanov, Israelian, Boltin and others form 'the vulgate' of Soviet historiography of the Second World War. I shall discuss this in strategic terms, rather than in terms of individual battles or even of the sufferings and sacrifices which the peoples of the USSR underwent through Nazi atrocities and the German invasion; with 17,000,000 deaths at least, the experience of the USSR has no counterpart elsewhere save Poland. Similarly, I shall not discuss the internal history of the war, with its transfers of whole peoples and its huge shifts of industry.

The Nazis attacked *by surprise*, says the Soviet version, at a time when, as a result of the Anglo-Franco-American appeasement policies, the USSR had only very tense relations with her neighbours, i.e. had to face very unfavourable military conditions. Of course, from the outset, mistrust prevailed in Anglo-American relations with the Soviet Union. As early as 18 July, Stalin asked the British to attempt a second front, during the brief period when all German forces had been committed in the east. But the British would envisage such a landing only once the Germans had been defeated in the Soviet Union – a possibility that they regarded, in any case, as incredible. Churchill hoped to defeat Germany by increasingly powerful aerial bombardment which would bleed her white. Soviet historiography insists on this theme again and again, to show that Churchill's strategy was aimed as much to exhaust the USSR (which was to be supported only in so far as her overthrow must be avoided) as to defeat the Fascists.

British bad faith towards the Soviet Union was displayed during the Moscow Conference of 1 October 1941, when Lord Beaverbrook announced the long delays that must be faced before Anglo-American military equipment could reach the USSR. The first contacts with the USA were equally full of mistrust. Many people in Washington argued that a Soviet victory would be 'worse' than a German one. However, Roosevelt, Marshall and others extended 'Lend-Lease' (though only covertly) and the Hopkins Mission took place. Its outcome was unimpressive, though at least positive, in that military deliveries did start, though at a ridiculous level and in such conditions ('chaos') that it was clear the Americans also did not believe in Soviet power; they too did not want to waste their matériel and were less concerned to strengthen the Russian army than to see it exhaust itself against Germany.

The Americans did, later, display rather more understanding of the USSR's problems. But to begin with their aim was more to take advantage of its weakness – for instance, in attempting to gain the concession of bases in Siberia in the event of war with Japan. General Deane, of the US military mission in Moscow, even wished to make this matter of aerodromes a test-case for Soviet good faith. The agreements with the Anglo-Americans were followed by other agreements, with Czechoslovakia, de Gaulle's Free French, and even Poland which, though laying down all manner of territorial preconditions, finally signed the treaty of 4 December 1941. The USSR, it is explained, took the lead in proposing to accept, in these contentious questions, the Allies' arbitration after the war, and showed, from 1941, a desire to create international courts of arbitration, whereas the Anglo-Americans insisted on the 'unequal' treaties (of 1919–21).

In another matter, too, the USSR showed how far advanced she was, for, on 3 July 1941, Stalin defended the right of self-determination, a principle that the Atlantic Charter took up on 14 August. Even then, there was a difference: the USSR, for its part, meant not only to assist the victims of Hitler-fascism towards Liberation, but also to help *all* peoples, including the colonial peoples, towards sovereign independence.

In the period from Pearl Harbor to the Allied landing in North Africa (December 1941–November 1942) the Washington Conference of late December 1941 showed that Churchill's defensive strategy, based on the Mediterranean, had the preference, as against strategies that involved direct help to the USSR, for instance in the form of a landing. This was the era of 'Mr Molotov's journeys'. Molotov did manage to extract from the Allies a 'declaration on the second front' and the signature of an Anglo-Soviet treaty on 26 May 1942. But Churchill was obviously advancing technical arguments to avoid fulfilling his promise; since 14 April he had had no intention of realizing American plans for the invasion of Europe. Pressure of public opinion did finally compel him into the Dieppe Landing, but it was a futile operation which acted as a pretext and an alibi in demonstrating the difficulties that any true second front would have to face. This preposterous adventure benefited only the Nazis, for it reassured them as to Allied intentions (and weakness, M. F.) and allowed them to turn all their energies against the USSR.

In the meantime, war had broken out in the Pacific – but not in the way the Japanese had hoped for. Since the Imperial Council of 2 July 1941, the Japanese leaders had adopted a policy of avoiding conflict with the USA, the better to concentrate against the USSR. During the summer and autumn of 1941, Japan feverishly prepared for an attack on Russia; and since the Germans were already advancing so fast, there were fears of 'missing the bus while the fruit was ripe for picking'. However, the Red Army resisted so well that troops did not have to be shifted from the Far East towards the German front, and so the Kankokuen Plan was abortive. First of all, it was put off to spring 1941, when the occupation of Siberia as far as Omsk was contemplated. But then it was postponed *sine die*, the negotiations with America having finally collapsed, and Pearl Harbor having launched the war in the Pacific.*

Germany constantly encouraged Japan to intervene as soon as it could against the USSR. To give it a bait, Germany concluded a convention on 18 January 1942, which, for it, was a climbdown, in that Japan was treated as an equal. The treaty laid down that neither state would make a separate peace, and the respective operational zones were precisely delineated – Japan took on everything east of 70 degrees longitude, including America, while Germany and Italy had everything west of that line, including both America and Africa. The Italian and German navies would move into Indian and Pacific waters if the main Allied effort went against Japan; and the Japanese navy would move to the Atlantic if that effort were directed against Germany and Italy. Perhaps Rommel's advance, in spring 1942, had something to do with this Japanese treaty.

In spite of Ribbentrop's appeals, Japan never did intervene

* It is true that the Japanese army had tested the formidable strength of Soviet armour in a battle in 1939 (Khanchin Gol). The army, at the time, was stuck fast in China, so that the navy could on its own advocate an attack towards warmer waters, where there were more raw materials in abundance, and where symbolic power could be won (M. F.).

against the USSR. At the time of Stalingrad, it declared it 'did not have the strength'. Then came Stalingrad, the 'turning-point', both in the Far East and in the West. It was a heroic battle, which forced Germany to direct nearly all of its air-strength against the Soviet Union, which explains both El Alamein and the case of the Allied landing in North Africa. It was a battle with vast international significance, for victory meant the creation of a true 'front' of all European and Asiatic resistance movements. This, we hear, caused the British and Americans to develop secret services, to thwart the progress of the fighting organizations, which were dominated by the communists.

Stalingrad also led to crisis in the Fascist camp. Goering, in Germany, appears to have had his first premonitions of disaster, and allowed Hohenlohe to make contact with Allen Dulles; then in Italy, Stalingrad was an alarm-bell; and even in Japan, it explains Yu-Kai-Sian's mission to Chungking, in February 1943. Germany's satellites were emboldened to make their first peace-moves. Hungary, Romania and Finland all followed the same tactic. They argued towards the western Powers – with whom they wished to treat – that the Central European states, in fighting the USSR, had been serving the vital interests of the West. They hoped to have Great Britain (where they found a willing ear) protect them against Soviet occupation, perhaps through the intervention of Turkey, which could 'fill the void' left by the retreating German army.

At Casablanca, in February 1943, these matters were certainly in Churchill's mind, and nothing concrete was decided as to the second front. Quite the contrary: at his instigation, the Sicilian expedition was substituted – a strategic 'absurdity' which, at bottom, was only a political compromise between the American idea of striking at the enemy's heart, through France, Sardinia or Rome, and the British scheme of nibbling at the enemy flanks while bleeding him white through aerial bombing. This plan would allow the West to forestall the Soviet advance into eastern and southern Europe. Churchill, who had already managed to assert priority for the Mediterranean over the Atlantic, thus gained a further success with the landing in Sicily. He stuck obstinately to his plan, firstly with an attack on Calabria which would let him invade Yugoslavia, and then with the march through to northern Italy, from which he could reach Vienna, his final goal, before the Russians could occupy strategic positions in Central Europe. If he did not succeed in this end, it was because America was gradually imposing her own war-plans, and they were shaped by altogether different strategic and political considerations.

Italy now surrendered: such was the result of the vast Soviet effort which had permitted Allied success in the Mediterranean. It was also a result of the Italian people's struggle for peace, and the consequent difficulties of Mussolini's government. The British at once reacted with hostility towards the Italian popular forces which sought to defeat Fascism: London and Washington ignored the Italian resistance, and strengthened Badoglio in order to forestall revolution. George VI expressed monarchical solidarity with 'the emperor of Ethiopia'.

If Stalingrad was the turning-point of the war, then 1944 saw disintegration of the Fascist Bloc. The immense Soviet advance determined this. Well before D-Day on 6 June, Finland, Romania and Hungary had attempted to make peace, and long before the various peoples, even the Germans, had begun to revolt against the Nazi-Fascist leaders. The Soviet account of Japanese efforts to leave the war is the complement of the version concerning the West. It seems that, from April 1944, the Japanese made systematic soundings towards Moscow, London, Washington and Chungking, all of which failed.

Finally, the Soviet presentation of the German and Japanese surrenders: Nazi troops, falling back under Soviet blows, attempted to push the British into a new Dunkirk, and launched the Ardennes counter-offensive, which failed. The Russian winter offensive, on the other hand, was a great success, and forced the Germans to transfer troops back to the east. At Yalta, Stalin's first request was for the Allies to stop this, but Churchill's first concern was to save Austria from Soviet invasion (Malta Conference). He did not dare reveal this to Stalin, but tried instead to win Roosevelt over to a plan of tripartite occupation of Central Europe. He did not get far.

At Yalta, the Big Three's greatest concern was the future of Germany: the West wished to break it up, but the USSR opposed such enslavement. A Partition Commission was appointed, though the USSR speedily announced that it saw the whole partition-plan merely as a means to put pressure on Germany. That the plan was abandoned was thus owing to the USSR. It did not solve the two vital questions, German demilitarization and democratization, and, pending a solution, Germany was to be split into zones of occupation; the only problem as regards boundaries was between the British and American zones. The decision was also taken to set up a Control Commission to co-ordinate occupation-policies.

The agreement worked more smoothly as regards the structure of the future peace. Procedural questions concerning the UN were settled amicably, although the problem of mandates had to be shelved, in view of Churchill's attitude, until the San Francisco Conference. On the other hand, there was an immediate proclamation of European liberties: each people was to regain independence, and the USSR, Great Britain and the USA would help them to set up provisional governments and democratic institutions. There was even agreement, in detail, in the cases of Poland and Yugoslavia, each of which had two governments. In the Polish question, the USSR proposed (and received agreement to) the establishment of a tripartite commission which would attempt to reconcile the two governments; over Yugoslavia, the Powers confined themselves to laying down methods for attaining this end.

The USSR meant 'to intervene as little as possible in the affairs of other countries'. Thus in China it refused to act as mediator between Chiang Kai-Shek and Mao Tse-Tung's communists, whereas the Americans had hoped with this ploy to save their imperialist position. The USSR, for its part, only wished to fight the Japanese invaders by making a pact with the Chinese government. Stalin undertook to declare war on Japan within only a few weeks of the end of the German war – at Yalta, the western Powers had strongly favoured this rapid intervention in the Japanese war, because they foresaw its lasting for some time and they also hoped to divert the USSR from European affairs.

Whatever the Allies' differences of opinion, the conference of Yalta was very positive in its outcome. It laid down the groundwork for a democratic peace, which could only be achieved through collaboration with the USSR. It also marked the highpoint of the alliance of 'the Big Three'. However, when it came to settling the Polish affair, the British sabotaged the Yalta agreement such that the USSR was compelled to sign a pact of friendship with the Lublin government (21 April 1945). The British went on from there to violate the Yalta spirit in several ways.

There were various stages in this hardening of attitude towards the USSR. There was, first of all, the welcome given by the British to German attempts at a separate peace, which would have let both Powers turn against the USSR. It was only public opinion in Great Britain and the USA which prevented such a separate peace and a reversal of alliances. There was also the unclear outcome of such a reversal of alliances, given that Soviet help was needed to defeat Japan. Next came San Francisco, where Vandenberg and Dulles boasted that they could establish a charter for the United Nations on their own, 'whether the USSR likes it or not'. An effort was made, through increasing use of procedural devices, to reduce the Soviet Union's role in the future Security Council. At San Francisco, nevertheless, the USSR managed to assert the principle of a natural evolution of each people towards independence, which was a blow to imperialism.

The British and Americans stepped up their provocative and hostile activities towards the USSR. They terminated 'Lend-Lease' and told their forces to store captured German *matériel* for possible return to the *Wehrmacht* in the event of the Soviet offensive's succeeding too soon. Even as early as 28 May, only twenty days after the German surrender, Churchill was envisaging a war with the USSR, as he confided to J. Davis. 'It is easy to see why, at Potsdam, the USSR behaved so mistrustfully.'

Truman arrived at Potsdam with proposals that ran counter to what had been jointly agreed at Yalta. While claiming to help set up 'free' elections in Romania and Bulgaria, the Americans, under Truman, were really trying to reestablish the institutions earlier associated with imperialism. The democratic governments which had been set up in Bucharest and Sofia had in fact succeeded in their object, and they appeared 'totalitarian' only to commentators who knew nothing of Balkan political conditions. Besides, at Yalta, there had been no question of joint intervention to establish provisional governments unless Fascism showed signs of resistance, which did not apply either to Romania or to Bulgaria. The West had no business there, and the firm hand used by the USSR successfully thwarted the West's designs.

The West was also beaten when it tried to partition or abolish Germany. The USSR opposed all such 'reactionary' measures. On the other hand, it did agree to collaborate in establishing a lasting peace, once a constructive attitude to the future was required. It was therefore quite unequivocal as regards Japan, now that it was in a position to keep the promises to which the Anglo-Saxons were firmly attached, however destructive their own bombing of Hiroshima and Nagasaki proved to be. Hence the Soviet declaration of war on 9 August, which forced the Japanese into unconditional surrender, given that this intervention, and the Sino-Soviet treaty, deprived them of all

hope of a separate peace, whether with the Americans (negotiations at Berne and Stockholm), the Soviet Union (the Mirota
discussions) or Chiang Kai-Shek's Chinese (the Liao-Vink
mission).

CRITICAL OBSERVATIONS

The Soviets can thus provide a completely coherent picture of
the Second World War. They can logically demonstrate how, at
each stage of the fighting, the 'imperialist camp', led firstly by
Churchill and then by the Dulles–Truman tandem, did everything possible to ensure that victory over Germany and Japan
would also be a defeat for the USSR; and some circles had no
compunction in giving the struggle against communist domination priority over that against Fascism. There is undeniably
some truth in this.

But the element of truth can certainly not be tested within the
given framework alone. At many points in the Soviet account,
readers will be taken aback. The Soviets gladly enumerate the
various efforts at a separate peace that were made behind their
backs. But what of the German-Soviet discussions at Stockholm
in June 1943? There are more serious omissions, not to mention
distortions. Over the peace-negotiations with Romania, no mention is made of the Anglo-American bombings of Bucharest;
over de Gaulle's visit to Moscow, nothing is said as to the two
Powers' disagreement over the Polish government, nor is there a
word on the USSR's objection to France's having an occupation-
zone in Germany or a place in the Reparations Council. In the
bibliography, itself very brief, it is astonishing to see no reference to the accounts of Dedijer, Ripka, Bor-Komorowski, Chiang
Kai-Shek, Stilwell, etc. Lenin, by contrast, receives twelve men-
tions, though Stalin, like Khrushchev, only two. There is almost
nothing on the Italian campaign, except for a reference to the
workers' rising against Fascism. It is surprising to find no

acknowledgement of the scale of Yugoslav resistance, or the Soviet disagreements with Tito in 1944–5; but then there is also nothing on the problem of the Greek resistance in December 1944 either. Relations with Czechoslovakia are presented as an unsullied idyll (no adequate discussion of the Ruthenian question); and relations with China are very skimpily covered. More generally, the communist parties appear only to be given honourable mention and called leaders of the resistance-movements; nothing is said of the contradictions which complicated their relations with Moscow or – a related issue – the degree to which their attitudes were, to some extent, forced upon them by the Anglo-Soviet 'agreement' of October 1944 or the decisions reached at Yalta. Similarly, the anti-Comintern Pact is stressed, but not the fact that the Comintern itself was dissolved in June 1943.

Other problems which cannot be avoided are nevertheless presented in a peculiar way. This occurs with the German question. A reading of the western accounts, as M. G. Castellan has shown, demonstrates that until 26 March 1945 Stalin was in agreement with the principle of partitioning Germany; at the foreign ministers' meeting of October 1943 he had given an enthusiastic welcome to the Cordell Hull plan. It was only with the victorious advance of the Red Army not long before Potsdam that the USSR began to oppose partition.

According to Soviet accounts, the USSR had never favoured it. When they discuss the conference of October 1943, at which Stalin showed delighted agreement, they do not mention the question of partition at all. Thus when they expound what happened at Yalta (4–11 February 1945), where it was agreed to establish a Partition Commission, they mention the Commission's existence only to add that on 26 March 1945 the USSR saw the Allied plan for partition only as a 'way of putting pressure on Germany'. Finally, when they deal with the German problem as it came up at the Potsdam Conference in July 1945, they stress that the USSR had always been uncompromising to the idea of partition.

WHAT PERESTROIKA FOR THE KNOWLEDGE OF HISTORY?

In the USSR, the Communist Party based its legitimacy on History, and historians had the task of showing that there was a conformity between the decisions taken by the rulers and the unfolding of History, that their policies were 'just' (see pp. 170–74). From the moment the Party was rejected and discredited, History as it had been taught hitherto shared its fate.

In point of fact, History had already come to grief before the Party: to begin with, this discredit had been attached to those who had been involved in the history of the USSR itself; but by a process of contamination it affected all historical knowledge as a whole, even if this disavowal was to a large extent unjustified.

This rejection is explained by the fact that the historians of this country were indeed the last to tell the truth about its immediate or recent past: the novelists, most often dissidents, had preceded them and been the first to speak: about the gulag (Solzhenitsyn), collectivization (Bykov), the turmoil undergone by the scientific world (Kron), while Shatrov wondered whether the October Revolution had answered the aspirations of society and Grossmann drew a comparison between the Nazi and Soviet regimes, a sacrilegious question which was nonetheless a real historian's question. Thus it was the writers or the cinema directors who analysed the lived experience of past or present history, whether of the Second World War (Tarkovksy's *Ivan's Childhood*, 1962) or of the climate of tyranny that reigned during the Stalin period (*Repentance*, by Abouladze, 1984).

The authenticity of these works lies in the way they gave the Russians back their past, a past that had been confiscated and manipulated in preceding periods, when certain events had been consigned to oblivion. By virtue of this, in history, witness took over from analysis and became an experience of the truth; the memory of the citizens was appealed to, so as to reconstitute a censored history, and also prevent the reproduction of the dramas that the past had experienced (the Memorial movement); others (within the Pamyat movement) reevaluated what the Revolution had destroyed or condemned, going so far as to glorify the period of Nicholas II, forgetting that the gibbets that had spread everywhere at that time had been called 'Stolypin's neckties', and the last Romanov the 'bloody tsar'.

Having lost its bearings in this way, the teaching of history has tried to modify its stock of knowledge, and correct the errors of the past. Several changes have been seen since 1985:

- The reintroduction into the pantheon of personalities to be rehabilitated such as Bukharin, Trotsky, etc. And by merely reversing evaluations from negative to positive, this procedure has perpetuated the habits of the past, since it developed in tandem with political change. But after Stalinism, it was the turn of Leninism to be questioned and the moment came when the whole Bolshevik pantheon risked being placed under the spotlight; by 'rehabilitating' Mensheviks such as Martov, or condemning one or other personality, you do not escape from a situation in which the meaning of history remains associated with an ideology.

- The updating of forbidden, concealed areas was not limited to taking into account the witness of survivors. The archives have been opened, sometimes under pressure from abroad (for Katyn) or from the inhabitants of republics that are now independent (secret treaties with Hitler, famines in the

Ukraine, the deportation of the Tatars, etc.), sometimes on the initiative of historians (the collusion of Nazis and Ukrainians in the massacre of the Jews). It should be noted, however, that the absence of archives does not account for the calumnies uttered by official history against historical personalities such as Trotsky or others. It was not being banned from consulting the archives that was the fundamental cause of a subversion of historical truth in the USSR.

- The breakup of historical discourse was not limited to the juxtaposition of disparate views of the past, a traditionalist interpretation and a reformed or reformist view; what we see is a multiplication of sites on which this history can be centred, each nation or republic questioning both the Marxist vision and the Russian-Eurocentric vision of history: the same applies to the Tatars, the Kazakhs, etc.

- The questioning of determinism and the Marxist interpretation of History – with the periodization of its great phases – leads to a kind of vacuum: today, the direction and meaning of events is held in abeyance; thus the Soviets turn to other countries, to the French *Annales* school in particular, to gain a new lease of life and find their way to a de-ideologized and autonomous practice.

In these conditions, the teaching of History is in part left in abeyance, as people await the publication of new textbooks; but the idea that there might be several different ones is a cause of surprise: could there, then, be several diagnoses of history?

APPENDIX
THE TABLE OF CONTENTS OF A TEXTBOOK OF WORLD HISTORY 1640–1870, DESIGNED FOR THE EIGHTH CLASS*

A PRE-PERESTROIKA EDITION

The world in the early modern era

1 From the beginnings of social organization to class-society
2 The unevenness of development in continents and nations

Part 1 The early modern era

CH. 1 THE BOURGEOIS REVOLUTION IN SEVENTEENTH-CENTURY ENGLAND AND THE INDUSTRIAL TRANSFORMATION IN ENGLAND

1 The causes of the revolution
2 Beginnings of the revolution; Civil War
3 Parliament and the army against the crown; rising of the bourgeoisie against the popular masses
4 The consequences and significance of the bourgeois revolution in England
5 Factory manufacturing
6 Proletariat and bourgeoisie; two aspects of industrial change

* This table of contents reflects a Marxist periodization of history and is of great interest for the perspective it offers. The early modern era begins with the rise of Great Britain and the proletariat makes an appearance even in the seventeenth century. This view is more useful than the traditional approach in western historiography, predominance of Spain, followed by predominance of France under Louis XIV, and then by predominance of Great Britain after 1714. The Soviet perspective makes it easier to understand the succession of revolutions and independence movements: 1689, 1774, 1789, 1830, 1848, 1871 and 1917.

CH. 16 THE OUTCOME OF THE FIRST PERIOD OF MODERN AND
CONTEMPORARY HISTORY: THE STRENGTHENING OF
CAPITALISM, 1640–1870

9

HISTORY: THE SAFEGUARD OF NATIONAL IDENTITY IN ARMENIA

ARMENIA: A BRIEF CHRONOLOGY*

9th–7th C. BC	Civilization of Urartu.
c. 550 BC	Conquered by Cyrus, Armenia becomes a satrapy of the Persian empire.
331 BC	Conquered by Alexander.
330 BC	Under the Seleucids, successors of Alexander, independent Armenian kingdoms come into existence.
215 BC	Reconquered by the Arsacides of Iran.
189 BC	Birth of the Armenian state, Ardaches I.
95–55 BC	Tigranes I, the Great.
66 BC	Treaty with Pompey; Armenia becomes a Roman dependency.

* Armenian names are subject to the vagaries of transcription. The versions used here are reasonably standard. (*Translator's note.*)

AD 70	Nero has Tiridates (of the Arsacid dynasty) crowned king of Armenia.
224	Collapse of the Arsacids of Persia.
301	Gregory the Bringer of Light; conversion of Dertad III to Christianity; Armenia, the first Christian nation in history.
451	War against Persia; battle of Avarair; Armenia is able to remain Christian.
491	Schism in the Armenian church.
536	Uprising against Byzantium.
645–852	Arab domination.
885	The Bagratids, independence regained: foundation of the Ani.
1048–71	Conquest of Armenia by the Seljuk Turks. End of independence.
1081–1375	Armenian Kingdom of Cilicia.
1236	Alliance between Cilicia and the Mongols.
1512	First books printed in Armenian.
1555	First partitioning of Armenia between Turkey and Persia.
1677	Conference of Echmiadzin for the liberation of Armenia.
1699	Israel Ori appeals to the tsar.
1794	First Armenian newspaper: *Azdarar*.
1804–13	Russo-Persian War.
1806–12	Russo-Turkish War.
1828	Second Russo-Persian War: 'Union of Eastern Armenia and Russia'. The Russians liberate Erivan from Persian occupation.
1862	Uprising of the heroes of Zitoun.
1877–78	Russo-Turkish War and Peace of San Stefano. Kars, Ardahan and Batumi reunited with Russia.
1895	First great pogroms of Armenians in Turkey.

	Birth of great socialist and nationalist Armenian groups: Dashnaks, Specifist, Social-Democrat.
1904	Sassoun uprising.
1915	Genocide of Armenians in Turkey.
November 1917	Chahoumian, Commissar for the Caucasus: establishment of the Transcaucasian Republic.
28 May 1918	Independence for Armenia; the Dashnak party takes power.
November 1919	Kemal crushes the national Armenian homeland in Cilicia.
January 1920	The Treaty of Sèvres recognizes the existence of an Armenian state; establishment of a Moscow–Ankara axis.
May 1920	The American Senate rejects a mandate over Armenia.
September 1920	Atatürk invades the Republic of Armenia; Peace of Alexandropol.
November 1920	Ordjonikidze intervenes in Armenia: reconquest or liberation?
1921	Fall of the Dashnak regime; installation of an Armenian Bolshevik government in Erivan.
1923	Treaty of Lausanne: there is no more talk of Armenia.

In a Russian children's textbook, the history of Armenia figures only with a few observations, hardly differentiating it from Georgian or Azerbaijani history: Armenia experiences the same stages of feudalism, passing the same historical landmarks, and the singularity of its Christianity – its antiquity, for instance – is barely noticed. Treated as it is in the Marxist way, and therefore reduced to common character, the distinctiveness of the Armenian nation dissolves. In one fourth-class textbook, Armenian history appears only twice – firstly, with the location of a tumulus near Erivan, and then with the Armenians' appeal to the Russians for help in freeing the country from Persian occupation. At one point, there is an allusion to 'the peoples of the Caucasus' but they are not named: 'they put up heroic resistance to the first wave of Mongol invasions.' In all, very little is said.

In the schools of Soviet Armenia there is of course much more about Armenian history. Here, there are two traditions – that taught in Russian, and that passed on in Armenian, where popular memory and tradition have a greater role. However, this latter is declining, since it offers little opportunity for career-advancement. It is therefore the family which remains the sanctuary of the collective memory, since, even in the diaspora, all Armenian children inherit it, for instance through the *ashoughs*, or minstrels, who are well-known in every Armenian community.

Nowadays, Armenia's old territory is divided between Turkey, Iran and the Soviet Union. A reading of the *History of our Ancestors* published in Venice by the Mekhitarist Fathers (Armenian Benedictines settled in that city since 1717) shows that preservation of the past is the nation's constant concern. The Armenians' view of their history is, as will be seen, pure and simple: there are good men, bad men, heroes and traitors. Armenia, several times defeated and conquered, has glorified her history with the sacred crown of martyrdom. She was looted, persecuted and partitioned, especially by the Turks, and was struck off the list of states; her history tended, in compensation, to become a set of golden legends, of giants and herculean heroes breaking the backs of lions and striking bulls to death: it is difficult to imagine how such a people could ever have been defeated, let alone extinguished. The Mekhitarist Fathers' book presents some of the great calamities with such dexterity and melancholy that you cannot easily tell when Armenia was effectively independent, and when she came under foreign rule. You have constantly to remind yourself that Armenia became independent for the first time between 189 and 66 BC (the Roman conquest) and underwent several periods of foreign rule before freeing herself from the Moslems in 885; the Turks then ended Armenian independence in 1048, and although the kingdom of Little Armenia subsisted in Cilicia from 1081 to 1375, it was conquered by the Ottomans. Armenia once more had a fleeting moment of independence between 28 May 1918 and November 1920.

The émigré children's textbook ends up with a map of Greater Armenia, which, centuries ago, stretched from the Caspian to Anatolia. In the words of the poet, 'We exist, we shall exist, and we shall multiply' (Baruyr Sevrak); or even – as is shown in the name of the chief political movement – 'we shall be reborn.' It is illustrative, therefore, to compare the émigrés' history with that taught in Soviet Armenia and with the general 'vulgate' version.

THE SONS OF HAIK

Like humanity itself, Armenia starts with an ancestor, the hero Haik or Haig: 'a fine figure of a man, with soft eyes and gentle features, handsome and with curly hair.' This beginning is attributed to 'the historian', i.e. Moses of Choreme who, in the fifth century AD, when Armenia lost her independence to the Persians but still had religious freedom, wrote the first great history of the Armenian people. Even in the fifth century the Armenians were thus trying to preserve their history, and it is this tradition which is carried on by an historical work composed fifteen centuries later.

In the beginning,

> When the Tower of Babel was built and all languages were mixed together, Haik, with his children and servants, together nearly 300 people, went towards the north. There he overcame the giant Pel who reigned in the Assyrian plains, and settled in

a beautiful region, with impenetrable forests, which was the lush green country of Armenia. The neighbouring peoples constantly raided, and so Haik's sons and grandsons, amongst them Aram, launched attacks to the east where the Medes, 'ancestors of the Kurds' lived. Aram defeated these enemies, drove them back to their capital of Armavir, and there hung them from the city walls. He became so powerful that the country was named after him, 'Armenia'. . . . Aram's son was so handsome that Princess Semiramis, who reigned in Assyria, wished to marry him. He refused, being already married, and she ordered her soldiers to kidnap him. But he was killed in this war, and the inconsolable Semiramis had his body exposed for the Gods to bring him back to life. It did not happen.

Another legendary hero was Vahaga who defeated Darius, the king of the Persians, and drove him out of Armenia.

He also made war on a giant king, Barsham, who reigned in Syria. The two gods rose up into the sky, and there was a giant battle. Vahaga struck at the famous giant and cut off his head, and then, with the head under his arm, came down to the barns, seized some sacks of straw and carried them off through the heavens to Armenia. Since then, at night, you can see in the sky a constellation which Armenians call 'the trail of the flying straw.'

The king of the Medes, another giant king, wanted to enlarge his kingdom and conquer Armenia, but he feared its king, Tigranes.

He dreamt of a woman who gave birth to three sons, each seated on an animal: one on a panther, another on a lion, and the third, Tigranes, on a dragon, who attacked. To be rid of this, he cunningly married his sister, but the sister told her brother of her husband's crime. One day, the giant invited Tigranes to a hunting party, but Tigranes came with an army. The giant also had one, and there was a fight, in which Tigranes plunged his sword into the giant's chest, giving him his just deserts.

Next comes Vagharshag, another great king who was of the Parthian Arshaguni dynasty. After his death, the Armenians fell 'for a short time' under Persian domination, though they were pagans and sun-worshippers; after which Alexander the Great crushed the Persians and introduced Greek culture to Armenia. The 'short time' lasted, in fact, for four centuries. 'Around 190 King Artaxes founded a great dynasty and decreed independence "from the Euphrates to the Caspian" in a magnificent ceremony that announced to foreigners that they would no longer profit from the treasures of our land.'

In this account, legend and reality are intertwined right up to the period when the historical facts became known. Reference to the Bible can place Armenian history within the Christian context, for they had a reciprocal relationship; Armenia, containing both Eden and Noah's Ark, has a privileged place within the Bible. The other details, largely taken from Moses of Choreme ('the Herodotus of Armenia') are, however, suspect. For instance, Darius, far from being expelled, conquered Armenia, as is shown in the Behistun inscription (only his first expedition was successfully resisted). We also know that latterly Armenia was a faithful satrapy which sent a contingent to Xerxes' aid against the Greeks, and then helped Darius III against Alexander. In these three centuries, from the mid-seventh century to Alexander's time, Armenia was only independent after Alexander's death, when the Diadochi fought for the succession: she was free from 330 to 215, was retaken by the Seleucids between 215 and 190, and only regained her independence under Artaxes, from 190 to 66.

Soviet Armenian children have a less epic view of these events, for they have more elaborate knowledge, even though it skips over the long period of Armenian dependence: it appears only as a 'stage in the formation of the Armenian people'. Moreover, the Armenians' autochthonous character is presupposed, whereas most Armenian historians place the 'arrival' of the Armenians within the framework of Indo-European invasions around the eighth century BC.

> The Armenians are one of the oldest peoples in the world; it is *well known* that Armenian tribes inhabited the various mountain regions of the area from the second millennium. During the Urartu period, these tribes maintained their autonomy ... and during the decadent period, their links were strengthened. ... The Urartu kingdom fell to the Medes but the Armenians rose in resistance. Cyaxares, king of the Medes (625–585) told them: 'Why are you rebelling?' 'I am fighting for liberty because I prefer liberty above all, and want to bequeath it to my children.' Then the Persians, who had defeated the Medes, imposed their rule over Armenia.

In the Soviet book, this period is identified as 'having contributed to the unification of the Armenian population.' Thus the whole of the Persian period is telescoped and the loyalty shown by the Armenians towards the Achaemenids is concealed. The only allusion to this dependence is that no longer were there foreigners, under Artaxes, who could profit from the 'treasures of our land.'

TIGRANES THE GREAT

The territorial unity of independent Armenia was finally accomplished under Tigranes I, 'the Great', 'who established an empire from the Caucasus to the Euphrates and the Mediterranean.' Tigranes I had been held hostage as a child by the

Parthians and swore hatred for his former jailors just as did his neighbour and ally, Mithridates, for the Romans. He defeated the Parthians and the Syrian Seleucids, moved a whole population into his capital, transfiguring it utterly, and he divided the empire into 120 provinces. He was the great Hellenizer, but also saw himself as heir of 'the King of Kings' and the apogee of this Armenian empire came around 70 BC when Mithridates, defeated by the Romans, sought its protection. Tigranes I took over from him, fought Lucullus, but had to surrender to Pompey and return most of the provinces he had conquered, together with an indemnity of over 50,000 talents.

> Tigranes took off his royal mantle, keeping only the circlet and royal diadem, and then presented himself to the Roman camp on horseback to surrender his tiers and diadem to the pro-consul. Pompey bade the old king stand up and gave him his insignia, according to him the title friend and ally of the Roman people [i.e. vassal].

Young Armenians are not told of this pathetic surrender, which will remind Frenchmen of Vercingetorix's surrender to Julius Caesar. They only hear that 'having grown old, Tigranes made peace with the Romans and became their ally'; or else it is said that he was betrayed by his people. There are in fact two conflicting versions of these events, which form the first grafting of Armenia onto the West: in the émigré tradition, Tigranes I appears as a great and 'peaceful' king, without reference to the countries he conquered. True, 'his empire stretched from the Caucasus to the Euphrates. . . . He laid the foundations of a great fortified city, a new capital that was greater and more beautiful than any before, which he named Tigranakert, after himself.' However, 'all the prisoners of war, Assyrians and Jews, worked under the direction of Greek architects and constructed a wonderful city.'

There is something curious here. In the émigré textbooks, Jews and Assyrians figure among the different kinds of prisoners that were taken: for the fact is that Tigranes was a great conqueror of nations. The children of Soviet Armenia are told that these slaves were Greek, and that it was they who, in response to Lucullus' promises of freedom, opened the doors of the capital to the Roman troops. 'But the Romans did not keep their promise, and pillaged the city's treasures.' The Erivan version is hostile to the Hellenic, western orientation of Tigranes, and stresses his role in unifying the Armenians as much as his ambition or his Hellenic leanings: 'the soldiers and the Greeks exploited the local population who worked as slaves. In the countryside, the farmers were free men who made up the armed forces.' The peace of 66 BC marked a 'great turning-point in history', the moment when independence was definitively lost.

THE TRANSFIGURATION OF DEFEAT

This initial loss of independence was diluted through a family alliance; and the second loss is telescoped in such a way that a disastrous event is transformed into an ultimate victory.

In 55 BC Ardavazd, the son of Dikran, a poet and thinker, succeeded to the throne. The Parthians declared war on Rome, the army of which was led by Crassus. Ardavazd, as friend and ally of the Romans, gathered an army of 30,000 men and advised Crassus to start the war in Armenia, not in Syria, which was a desert, favourable to the Parthians' cavalry. Crassus would not listen to this advice, and accused our king of treachery. [Since Crassus did not follow the advice, he was open to attack from the north and so Ardavazd retained his 30,000 men (M.F.)] Crassus was beaten, and the Parthians beheaded him. Ardavazd, annoyed at the Romans' attitude, made peace with the Parthians, and gave his sister in marriage to the heir to the

> Parthian throne; before the ceremony began, Crassus' head
> was carried onto the stage of the royal theatre of Ardashad and
> the people celebrated their victory and their new alliance.

Armenia now fell alternately under the Arsacids and Roman domination. She became a vassal-state, playing a difficult role between two empires. Relations with Rome became tense again when Ardavazd II, a prisoner of Mark Anthony, was put to death by Cleopatra, whom he had refused to recognize as his sovereign. In reprisal, all Romans in Armenia were massacred, at the order of Ardavazd's son, Artaxes II.

In the first century AD after Corbulonus' campaign, Nero set Tiridates on the Armenian throne, but the country was still a vassal, and in 161, and again in 216, the Armenian nobles rose against Antoninus Pius and Caracalla. The Arsacid dynasty's collapse in 224, and further troubles with Rome, led to a new era in which Armenia was converted to Christianity and eventually became associated with Byzantium.

THE FIRST CHRISTIAN NATION IN HISTORY

In adopting the Christian religon at the end of the third century, Armenia became the first Christian nation ever; and that is the Armenians' great pride. The story of the conversion of Dertad (Tiridates III) is well-known to all children of the diaspora.

> The fourth century was the age of Dertad III, 'the Great'. He
> tried his strength in the circus, substituting himself for Diocle-
> tian in man-to-man combat and overcoming Herch, king of the
> Goths, who had proposed to the old emperor that they should
> fight in single combat, and so decide the outcome of their war.
> Dertad disguised himself as Diocletian, took some powerful
> weaponry and slew the robust Herch. He meant to offer up his
> thanks to the goddess, Anahit, and everyone placed flowers

and green branches before her statue. 'You too must place flowers, Gregory', said Dertad. 'No, I will not make offering to a statue', said Gregory, 'for I am a Christian.' Dertad subjected him to a number of punishments and threw him into a deep ditch, the Khor Virab. . . . Just then, a band of young virgins arrived in Armenia, fleeing from Rome. Dertad learned that one of them was a girl of great beauty, Hripsim; Dertad tried to make her marry him, but she would not, so he used force; but, in the struggle, she overcame him and managed to escape from the palace. These young girls had consecrated their lives to God, and Dertad had them executed, but he sickened with remorse, and went mad. His sister had a dream, and told him that only Gregory could cure him. He was then dragged out of the ditch where he had languished for fifteen years, cured the king, and preached the Gospel. Dertad was soon converted, together with the whole nation. Armenia became the first Christian state, in 314. Gregory, who had brought enlightenment to the country, was named 'Bringer of Light.'

A VICTORY IN DEFEAT: AVARAIR, 451

After 428, Armenia was under Persian domination, and the King of Kings tried to impose the cult of Mazda. He had an ally in the governor, the treacherous Sassag, although the nobles, the army and the clergy were at one in proclaiming their determination to remain loyal provided they were allowed to retain the faith, which they meant to defend to the death. War began, and the Christians were led by Vartan the Red (or Vardan) 'who symbolized the faith and freedom of the whole Armenian people'. The priest, Giewont, kept up the army's morale, though later he was to die a martyr's death.

At the battle of Avarair, the Armenians had only 60,000 soldiers against 300,000 Persians with elephants, horses and camels.

> Vardan Mamigonian had placed his army on three different
> fronts. At the vital moment of the battle, Vassak of Suniam
> went over to the enemy, and so weakened one of the fronts;
> Vardan went there and, like a lion, struck out in all direc-
> tions, repelling and overthrowing men, horses, elephants.
> Night fell ... an arrow pierced his heart.... The fighting
> went on for many more years, until the enemy, though
> stronger in number, recognized Armenians' right to religious
> liberty (451).

It was the first time that such an agreement was struck in the East.

The Byzantines also tried to put down the Armenian church, especially in the reign of Emperor Maurice (around 600). He captured Sempad Bazmahagd, a young and strong nobleman, whose vigour astounded the inhabitants of Constantinople.

> He was sent into the arena and was put against a brown bear;
> but he seized hold of it and smashed its head. Then a ram-
> paging bull was let loose, and next a lion with a long mane; but
> Sempad seized it by the muzzle and broke its jaw. Dripping
> with sweat he sat astride the beast. The people demanded that
> he be pardoned, and Maurice exiled him to North Africa.

THE ERIVAN VERSION: OMISSIONS FROM THE OFFICIAL STORY

These accounts are corroborated by the historical tradition, but an essential is missing, the schism of the Armenian church. This explains the isolation of the Armenians in the face of the Sassanids and Emperor Maurice. The schism occurred when the Armenian church decided to remain faithful to the monophysite pronouncements of the Council of Nicaea, according to which the God in Jesus absorbed the Man, which ran counter to the new doctrines of the Council of Chalcedon in 451, by which the two natures of Christ were to be separated.

The break which followed, in 491, gave the Armenian church its particular character. This brought upon it the hatred of the 'Orthodox' church in Byzantium, for it, unlike the Armenian church, was identified with the state and so had a powerful secular arm. The consequences were considerable: for Byzantium's evangelizing mission led to Armenia's seeking allies, later on, even in Islamic territory.

Soviet Armenians taught in Russian know nothing of this. No mention is made of Gregory, the Bringer of Light, and in their history book the spread of Christianity in Armenia rates only a paragraph, even then without evaluation of the event's significance and import.

> With the development of slavery and feudal relations, paganism no longer corresponded to the needs of the ruling class. Christianity, once proclaimed religion of state, fulfilled this function. From this period, a powerful clergy was established, concentrating within its hands the land and wealth of the pagan church, and so became one of the fundamental elements in an exploitative society of the feudal type.

This is a catch-all passage which, even, in its own way, copies the lines meant for Russian children studying their own country's Christianization: 'Paganism was useless to the power of the prince. . . . Christianity supported the feudal power over the peasants and strengthened the princes' power.' In contrast to the Russian example, however, it is not said in Armenia that Christianity was imposed by force. On the contrary, 'the wars of liberation from the fifth to the ninth centuries were often caused by the Sassanids' and then the Arabs' desire to convert the Armenians to their faith.' The great battle of Avarair is thus described with the same detail as in the tradition, though the consequences of the battle, the Armenians' freedom to follow Christianity, are hardly mentioned at all. 'Thanks to these wars, where Armenia was often linked with Georgia', says the Erivan version, 'she kept her autonomy and stopped the Persian Sassanids from realizing their assimilationist policies . . . so they were free to develop their economy and culture' (sic). Still, whereas Armenian writing, the invention of the alphabet and the development of Armenian literature are all described at great length, the religious function of this literature and its role in conserving the eastern-Christian religious writings are not mentioned at all, although Armenians take pride in having been the first and greatest translators of the Bible, and Armenia's national identity is widely associated with religious identity.

We can therefore appreciate what it meant when the Soviet regime in 1975 with great pomp and ceremony allowed a statue to be set up at Erivan to the hero of Avarair. The ceremony was attended by the First Secretary of the Armenian Communist Party, together with the prime minister, the mayor of the town and a huge crowd, commemorating this Christian victory. According to *Hairenike Tzain*, an Erivan weekly, the mayor paid tribute to the 'heroes who died so that Armenia could keep her character'. The secretary of the Armenian trade unions, *Zeituntzian*, added that 'there are certain names that, for ever, symbolize our country: Mashdats, culture, Komitas, music, Vardan Mamigonian, freedom.' The first two were priests, and the third was canonized. But among the notables who attended there was only one Russian, Anisikov, the second secretary of the Armenian Communist Party, his eyes were half-shut.

THE RESURRECTION AND DEATH OF THE ARMENIAN STATE

Under Sassanid domination the feudal system was reinforced and Armenia henceforth consisted of principalities governed by great noble families – Mamigonian, Artzuni, Bagration, etc. They preferred, not the great centralizing power of Byzantium, but the limited autonomy promised them by the Arsacids' successors. When Arab invasion began, given the absence of the hoped-for assistance from Byzantium, this kind of relationship was maintained with the new occupants; the Armenians were also made to promise the emirs to supply 15,000 soldiers per annum on condition only that they should not be used against Byzantium. Two whole centuries of Arab occupation (645–852) passed in this way, but they receive only a brief mention in a work published by the Mekhitarist Fathers, and hardly more than that in the Soviet version. The Soviet one does, however, examine the great rebellions of 697–705 and 773, the first of which ended in a blood-bath. 'The Arabs had assembled the whole Armenian nobility in the cathedral of Nakhichevan on pretext of taking a census; and massacred them all. The second uprising, fomented by the Mamigonians, was also crushed with the collaboration of other families, especially the Artzuni and Bagratids'. The third insurrection, fomented by the Bagratids (Bagrations) worked. 'This dynasty', writes Pasdermadjian, 'had grown up in the shadow of the Arab caliphs, just as did the Moscow princes under the Golden Horde.' Before staging their rebellion, they had taken care to eliminate rivals.

In 862 Ashod the Victorious was recognized by Baghdad as Prince of Princes in Armenia. However, certain families, such as the Artzuni, opposed the new dynasty and the new state broke into several rival principalities in its turn. Kars had been the capital of the Bagratids, but Ashod the Pious built a new capital, a superb city named Ani. 'It was 3,000 metres round, and gradually took in almost a million people, most of whom lived beyond the walls though, during wars, they took refuge inside the city.'

The end of Ani and the Bagratids belongs among the great tragedies of history. During the first invasion by the Seljuk Turks,

King Sempad, realizing the inevitable outcome, bequeathed his kingdom as a gift to the Byzantine emperor. Armenia was therefore to be protected, as a Christian land. His successor, Gakig II (1042–5) did not recognize the will, however, judged it illegitimate and took over the country. The emperor Constantine Monomachus demanded the town of Ani, but Gakig refused to surrender it. Profiting from the Turkish invasion, the Armenians began to fight Byzantium. . . . The emperor sent 100,000 men to take Ani, but

> the inhabitants, led by Bahlavuni, put up furious resistance. Armenian élite troops charged out of the city walls and spread panic in the Greek army; then, with the help of disloyal Hellenophile landlords, Constantine invited Gakig II to Constantinople and sent him to exile. The Hellenophile landlords of Ani gave the keys of their city to the emperor and so brought to an end the existence of the great kingdom of the Pakraduni.

The Soviet text presents the facts in the same way, and ignores, like the émigré version, the intervention of the Katholicos Petrus who directed the occupation of Armenia and so obtained his end, an attempted conversion to Orthodoxy. 'Without their king, the Armenians lost courage', says the Soviet work, 'and were quite lost when they had to face a new attack by the Seljuks.' Once the country had become a mere Byzantine province, it could no longer play its part as bastion of Christendom.

After a rebuff at Ani, the Turks moved towards the principality of Kars which was still independent: 'the Vanandetzi came out to meet them with 5,000 horse, and battle took place. The Armenians tried to force encirclement, but failed and had heavy loss.'

> Among the Armenians there was a great general, Tatul Vanandetzi, who, in the fight, seriously wounded the son of Emir

Assuran. Tatul was captured and carried off to Dughril, who told him, 'If the son of my dear friend Assuran recovers, then you will be pardoned. If not, you will be sacrificed.' Tatul answered, 'If it was I who struck him, he will have no chance of survival; if it was someone else, then perhaps he will live.' After some days, the emir's son died, and Dughril had Tatul's right arm cut off. He offered it to his friend, Assuran, and said, 'At least you know that your son was not slain by a weak hand.'

A new invasion came several years later, under Alp Arslan. It culminated in a terrible massacre, though the memory is spared to Soviet-Armenian children.

The assailants had a knife in each hand and a third in the mouth; the inhabitants were mown down like grass. Blood flowed like a torrent through the streets of Ani; thousands and thousands of people perished by the sword and those who took cover in the churches finally succumbed to the ruins of the buildings which were burned down.

Matthew of Edessa remembered the complaints of the Armenians against Byzantium, which had shown such contempt for military strength and martial virtues. Once Armenia had fallen, Romanus IV did try to repel the invaders and liberate the lands taken by the Turks, but he was crushed in battle at Manzikert (1071) which marked, once and for all, the end of Armenian liberty.

In European perspective, history remembers the fall of Constantinople in 1453 as a fundamental event. From the Armenian angle, and in Arab or Persian eyes as well, the start of Turkish dominion is at Manzikert. The 'betrayal' by Byzantium, which 'attacked' Armenia instead of defending her, and the 'crime' of the Hellenophiles who opened Ani's gates to Basil constitute grievances shared by all Armenians, Soviet ones included.

History in European eyes – Ranke, Rambaud, Spengler etc. – also sees Byzantium as committing the worst imaginable 'blunder' in putting down Armenia which, if free, would have been the stoutest bulwark against the Turks.

OMISSIONS IN THE ARMENIAN TRADITION

Here, too, there are gaps – how do we explain the 'treachery'? Neither the Soviets nor the émigré Armenians mention that the very emperor to whom Sempad gave up during the Seljuk attack was himself an Armenian – Basil. He was called 'the Macedonian' because he was born in Macedonia, but he was of Armenian origin, like the clan which brought him to power. The Armenians who had been transplanted to Thrace and Macedonia in and after Maurice's time played a powerful role in Byzantium, and had founded the dynasty of the Basils late in the tenth century. It includes Leo V of the Artzuni family and Basil II, called 'the Bulgar-Slayer' because he stopped the threat from the Bulgars. 'He had the eyes of 15,000 prisoners put out, leaving only 150 who, though they had lost one eye, at least could see enough to lead the victims back to the tsar, Samuel, who, on beholding their plight, was shocked to death.'

The 'treason' of the Hellenophile Armenians has therefore to be reconstituted in another context. These Byzantine emperors were themselves Armenians, and perceived that at Ani there reigned an Armenian of their clan, and not of another. It was thus that Vast-Sarkis was to replace Gagkik II, after which the Hellenophile Armenians, i.e. the supporters of Vast-Sarkis, attached Armenia to Byzantium, forcibly introducing the Orthodox rite. These divisions among the Armenians, which had already had tragic consequences for the national lands in preceding centuries, had a mortal effect on the nation's destiny. For its own part, the Armenian population – especially in the countryside – opposed the Byzantine Armenians and many of them participated in peasant uprisings against the landlords who 'collaborated', and against Byzantium. The greatest of these uprisings occurred in the Tondrak region in the tenth century.

When the Armenian state had been beaten and destroyed, the nation divided; one part was ruled by Byzantium, and developed within the empire, with a growing economic role both in the empire and abroad (the Crimea, Poland, etc.). This was the start of the great adventure of the Armenian merchants. Another part of the nation remained within the ancestral lands. It submitted resentfully to the yoke of the conquerors. A third part, in which landlords and peasants united, would not submit, and decided to transfer the Fatherland to a free territory. This was a new Anabasis, the extraordinary exodus of Armenians who became invaders and conquerors and, *manu militari*, set up a kingdom that was independent both of the Arabs and of the Byzantines. They set up 500 leagues away, in Cilicia, creating 'Little Armenia', the kingdom that helped the First Crusade, and they were associated with the Vatican and the West; they carried on the standard of Armenian liberty for three centuries (1080–1375) and then themselves succumbed.

> The Armenians remained without a government or a state for many years. Sometimes, like Vulcan, the Armenians shook the heavy chains of their slavery, sometimes they fought back, and at certain moments they even managed to struggle free. At Gharabagh, there were even Armenian Meliks who lived in semi-independence under Persia.

These few lines are all that there is on these centuries of martyrdom and oppression under successive or joint oppression by Arabs, Turks, Mongols, Persians or Turkmeni. What history has not set out in black and white has been preserved in oral tradition, which turns the most tragic moments into glorious episodes, such as the story of 'King Kakig and his greatest treasure, his daughter, Dzovinar'.

> She was so beautiful that she seemed to be telling the stars to go to sleep, for she outshone them. . . . One day when the caliph of Baghdad had massacred and destroyed all he could . . . Kakig's cause seemed quite hopeless against an army ten times the size of his own. . . . In the evening, Dzovinar decided to have a walk on the ramparts. There was a full moon, but as soon as the princess appeared the moon stopped shining. Sennacherib, the caliph of Baghdad, was dumbstruck at all this, left his tent, looked up and saw the princess. From then on, nothing else mattered to him. . . . He sent a message to Kakig, promising to withdraw his forces if Kakig gave him his daughter; Kakig hesitated, but Dzovinar wasted not a second; she accepted, provided the caliph agreed not to touch her for the first forty days. Sennacherib agreed. . . . On the forty-first day, Dzovinar knew she was going to have a child: she had conceived from the source-water she had drunk on Blav mountain. The caliph was furious with jealousy when Dzovinar, through her mouth, gave birth to two male children. . . . Soon, these two men became giants, and protected the poor who came in droves to their house. Together they built a town, a vast city that was to be impregnable, and it was called Sassun.

Another allegory, this time on the Mongol conquests, was the old legend of the church with the pigeons:

> Stage by stage, Tamerlane and his horde arrived in Armenia and gobbled it up. A large part of the population was massacred; and those whose lives were spared were taken prisoner and dragged along with the vast army of the crippled Tamerlane, who was delighted at his achievements. He came to the shores of Lake Sevann, and gave his troops a brief rest. At a

nearby small church, an old monk, Father Ohan, begged for mercy; but he could not stand the presence of the accursed Tamerlane, and, with his white locks and beard flowing in the wind, he walked on the limpid waters of the lake. 'I don't believe it; I must be dreaming', said the conqueror, but, when he called, the old monk came back just as he had gone. 'Holy man', said Tamerlane, 'what do you want?' The monk replied, 'the freedom of my people'. 'Very well,' said Tamerlane, 'I shall liberate all those who can squeeze into your church.' He gave the order . . . some of the prisoners were led into the church . . . and they went by the thousand, ten thousand and hundred thousand. Still, the church had not been filled up, and Tamerlane was dumbstruck, though he let them go on into the building. Soon, not a single captive stood outside the church, and Tamerlane's lieutenants went into it. They found only the old Father, kneeling in prayer before the holy altar. God had granted his prayer. All of the prisoners who had been led into the church had been transformed into white pigeons, and they had flown out, free, through the open window towards the mountains where they had been born.

Yet it was in these very centuries that the ancestral lands of Armenia were destroyed and their population executed or enslaved.

A SIGNIFICANT OMISSION: THE ARMENIAN MERCHANT

This did not happen to the exiled part of the people. But there is a strange omission, in this dramatic story, in both the émigré and the Erivan versions, and it is an omission of great importance – any reference to the Armenian merchants, money, or the commerce that enriched the Armenians of the diaspora and their church, which was the sanctuary of the nation and the preserver of its culture: it is almost as if Armenian history looks with shame at its own good fortune and money. In these bloody centuries, the status of the Armenian church was recognized in return for cash-payments to Constantinople; the civil status of the Armenian colonies was also recognized, both by the first sultans as a counter-weight to the Orthodox church and by the shahs of Persia; they benefitted from a commercial network that stretched from Amsterdam to the Philippines, with depots at Constantinople, Smyrna and especially Isfahan, in the Zulfaya quarter, the opulence of which was described by Tavernier in the seventeenth century, under Shah Abbas. Fernand Braudel has wondered whether, outside their own national territory, the Armenians 'were not too adaptable for their own good', i.e. whether their success did not make them forget the tragic fate of their ancestral home.

Sophie Mappa shows a similar problem in the nineteenth century amongst the diaspora Greeks who, especially at Alexandria, lived quite differently from the Greeks of Hellas. In the nineteenth century these Greeks held privileges and riches from the Ottoman empire; to control the Turkish empire from within seemed to them a better means to bring about the triumph of Hellenism. The Armenians' case was not the same except perhaps in the Byzantine empire, but it is still a problem of the same order in that it poses, uniquely, as Sophie Mappa has shown, the question as to the link between national identity and territory, and so to some degree reintroduces the Marxist theory of nationality.

THE NATIONAL RENAISSANCE

In Armenia itself, the native land, some embers were never quite extinguished. According to the tradition maintained by the church, renewal of the fight for independence started with Bishop (Katholikos) Hagop IV. 'In 1678, he joined the semi-independent Meliks of Persian Armenia and appealed to Russia, although Peter the Great preferred to negotiate with the Turks.' A second, and a third, time the bishop appealed to the Christian princes' solidarity, especially to Georgia, which had also been formed under the Bagratids. Only Holy Russia responded, for Pashkevitch's army liberated Persian Armenia, Archbishop Nerses and 10,000 Armenians taking part in the fight, with 10,000 Russian soldiers. 'Nicholas I did not grant the promised independence, but made Armenia the small autonomous province of Erivan, with an emblem representing Noah's Ark, Dikran's Crown and Mount Massis.'

In fact, with the ukaz of 21 March 1828 Nicholas I was proclaimed king of Armenia, which allowed Pashkevitch to exile Archbishop Nerses: a configuration that suggested what was to come in the relationship of Russia and Armenia. Still, the tsar had freed half of Armenia from the yoke of a Moslem sovereign, and for those Armenians who were even worse persecuted, under the Turks, Russia became a refuge.

From then on, the tsars became recognized defenders of Armenian rights within the Ottoman empire; from the Congress of Berlin to the First World War they tried, though in vain, to guarantee the fulfilment of the clause of the Treaty of San Stefano relating to Armenian liberties. However, in the diaspora, in Turkish Armenia, and in Russian Armenia, nationalist and revolutionary parties appeared, which prepared for struggle to free Turkish Armenia and to unify the whole nation, which, one day, they hoped to see free. First came the Armeningan Party, in 1885, founded on the model of the Carbonari; then came the Henchagian and Dashnaksutiun (Dashnaks) who were the most active. Soviet Armenian children also hear, beyond this list of 'bourgeois' parties, of the long struggle of Armenians within the Baku social-democratic movement, for much is made of Shaumyan and Lenin.

The Armenians, following the Serbs, Greeks and Bulgars,

could once more dream of independence. In Turkish Armenia itself, in parts of Turkey itself where Armenians had grouped together – Cilicia, Taurus, etc. – 'revolts had broken out against the Ottomans' abuses.' One of the most famous of these happened through 'the heroes of Zeitun' in 1862: the inhabitants of this village, who had long been exposed to ill-treatment, on their own defeated the troops of the pasha of Marash, and, through Napoleon III's intervention, they gained a full-scale treaty from the sultan. It was a great set-back for the central government, and the victory of the heroes of Zeitun (an eyrie, high in Cilicia) had an extraordinary effect, for it revealed to Europe the existence of an Armenian nation, and its struggle for freedom, whereas hitherto the Armenians had simply been seen as a people of traders.

GENOCIDE AND ITS ORIGINS

This new recognition came together with new revolutionary movements, the constitution of 'self-defence' groups and then the spread of Dashnak terrorism, as shown in the armed attack on the Ottoman Bank in Istanbul, which was the 'gala première' of terrorism (1896). This allowed the sultan to talk in terms of an Armenian plot, and, by playing on this, to bring into motion the whole machinery of repression and terror. The Armenian massacres played the same role as pogroms in Russia, with the Kurds acting as *provocateurs* or thugs. Some people saw the emigration of young Armenians (in so far as this was still possible) as the means to salvation and perhaps even, through the new vigour that this would demand for the older Armenians, a way of ensuring their survival. Elia Kazan's *America, America* describes with unflinching boldness the difficult and often sordid itinerary of this new diaspora. Stavos, its hero, is a Greek, but he could just as well have been an Armenian.

Yves Ternon, in a recent work, has clearly shown that the great massacres of 1895, which shook the conscience of Europe, were carefully planned and organized by Sultan Abdul Hamid. The process of Armenian genocide was silently but evidently under way. The West felt it coming, and the Young Turk revolutionaries condemned the covert crimes being fomented by the regime, even though it was these same Young Turks, twenty years later, who set out to perpetrate the first genocide of the twentieth century.

> During the First World War, the Young Turks organized a great massacre, designed to wipe out the entire Armenian population. The massacre and transportation were carried out at Talaat Pasha's order. The men were conscripted, and then led into the mountains and valleys, where they were shot. The rest of the population was deported, their houses, lands and goods being confiscated. The people were looted on the way, and children were murdered before their mothers' eyes, while young girls were seized, and the others were forced to march, starving and dying of thirst, into the desert of Der-El Zor. Those who managed to survive the journey were massacred on the spot; caves were filled with their bodies, and their bones can still be seen there. Thus came about an unprecedented and unrivalled racial massacre. The civilized nations of Christian Europe allowed this to happen. Every year, on 24 April, the Armenian people gather with fervour to remember these martyrs of fatherland and faith.

The Soviet text hardly differs in substance from that of the Mekhitarist Fathers. It notes 'a circular of 15 April, resolving to liquidate the Armenians, to reduce this foreign element and expel it to the Arabian desert'. It describes 'the burning of homes, the mass-drownings, the horrors of the forced march to Der-El Zor and the final agony'. Like the Mekhitarist work, it stresses the vigour of Armenian resistance, at Van especially, where groups for self-defence were set up, even though their very existence simply served as a pretext for the massacres.

This genocide came as the culmination of a long history and had its precursors in 1895, 1896 and 1908. However, for centuries past, the Ottomans had limited themselves to mild persecution of the Armenians, to satisfy the exactions of the Kurds. This situation changed when Armenians became conscious of their national rights and when the Greeks and Bulgarians set the example of independence; it changed still more when the Russians appeared as Christian Big Brothers, and as advocates of the Armenian cause, ever ready to condemn the Porte's doings.

The change of power in 1908 and the advent of the Young Turks seemed to inaugurate a new era. The new leaders of the Turks seemed to favour the rights of nations: they preached absolute equality for all citizens of the empire, and declared their intention of starting with secularization. Such intentions explain why the Armenian revolutionary parties, the Dashnaks in particular, declared solidarity with the plans of their brothers in revolution, the Young Turks. These lay and revolutionary ideas seem closer to their own than the ideas of the tsarist aristocracy who, in Alexander III's time, advanced a programme of Russification in Armenia. The tsar persecuted the Dashnaks, and they noted how, in the past, 'the Russian option' had only produced disappointment and disillusion, even, in Turkish Armenia, further persecution.

The Dashnaks were prisoners of their own revolutionary phraseology and logic. They were convinced that the victory of socialism would end national conflict, and they disarmed popular vigilance by associating with the Young Turks, in the supposition that each partner would overthrow the detested old system in his own way. In Constantinople the Armenian hierarchy and eminent citizens approved of this union. In view of Greek and Bulgarian attitudes since independence, the Sublime Porte was now happy to name Armenia 'the faithful nationality'. In 1914 a few months before war broke out, an international mission was even permitted to enter Turkey to look into the workings of the Armenian guarantees that dated from the peace of San Stefano in 1878.

But even now, the fates were at work. In 1908, at the time of the Cilician massacres, the new government, fearing unpopularity, had not dared to attack the perpetrators and so run counter to popular sentiment: it had allowed the Armenians to be massacred and then shifted the responsibility onto the old regime. It felt that its very existence would be at stake if it gave equality to the Constantinople Greeks, the Arabs and the Armenians, and so made an about-turn. For federation and equality of communities, it substituted integration, i.e. assimilation. The regeneration of the Ottoman empire was to come through glorification of the Turkish people and its return to greatness. The World War allowed this hope, in the shape of the 'Turanian' cause, a myth that enabled appeals to be made for revolt against the tsar by Crimean Turks, Tatars and Turkmeni in Russia. In such a context, Armenia, which stood straight in the path of Turkish regeneration, had to disappear.

The Young Turks asked if the Dashnaks would participate in the Transcaucasian uprising against Russia; the Dashnaks replied that they would remain loyal, and would respond to tsarist appeals. From then on they were trapped, and the Armenians' fate was sealed. A 'final solution' to the Armenian problem was one that had been in people's minds for some time; it was applied just after the Turkish defeat at Sarikamish. Seventy thousand Armenians, seeing what was to happen, deserted and fled to the Russians after the battle; at Van, to forestall an alleged Armenian revolt, a Turkish army of 130,000 invested the town, which put up its own defence and was delivered by the vanguard of the Russian army, itself composed mainly of Armenians. 'The Van uprising' was a pretext for the subsequent massacre, deportation or murder of over a million

Armenians and genocide affected virtually all Armenians in Turkey.

The complete silence of the Turks on this matter is without parallel in history. For the past sixty-five years no official voice has made any sort of acknowledgement, such as Chancellor Brandt made in Germany in condemnation of his fellow-citizens' massacre of the Jews, or in the USA by President Johnson to disavow the crimes committed against American Blacks. Even Turkish historiography is silent. In the highly-learned *Cambridge History of Islam*, which devoted 170 pages to Turkey and the Ottoman empire, there is, in the section written by Turkish historians, no mention, let alone analysis, of the Armenian massacres. Such silence only perpetuates the martyr-nation's resentment.

'THE ERIVAN SPRING'

As to the recovery of independence after the victory of Sardara-bad over the Turks, the children's and adults' books are both very discreet.

> 28 May 1918 is a historic date: after 500 years of servitude . . . we had a small but independent Armenia. . . . The red, blue and orange flag flew at Erivan. . . . When this small Armenia began to progress, Kemal's Turkey attacked it, in 1920. The Armenian army resisted, but it could not put up a front against the Turks for long, for they also had the aid of foreign powers. The Armenians sought peace. The frontiers were again cut back. It was at this time, on 29 November 1920, that the communist army made its entry into Erivan and took power there. Armenia became a part of the Soviet state, and today Erivan is one of the most beautiful towns in the Soviet Union. . . . For the last fifty-five years, the flag of Soviet Armenia has been the red flag, to which a blue band was added in 1954.

The Soviet version of this stresses the 'anti-Soviet' character of the Transcaucasian republic which was established in April 1918 after the peace of Brest-Litovsk:

> It declared itself independent and was separated officially from Soviet Russia.... But no agreement was possible between Georgia, Armenia and Azerbaijan: the German-Turkish invaders were applying the principle of 'divide and rule'. On 26 May, the Transcaucasian republic was dissolved; bourgeois governments were established in the three countries.

Thus the historic date of 28 May can be omitted from the Soviet texts.

> The Dashnak government, in its two-and-a-half years of impotence, brought the country and people to ruin. It followed the hated policies of tsarism and the Provisional Government, in the exclusive interests of the bourgeoisie, the kulaks and the land-owners.... According to Mikoyan, under the Dashnaks, Armenia was in a pitiable state, for she was wild and abandoned.

The Bolsheviks won ground under the leadership of Ordzhonikidze, Mikoyan and Kirov.

> The imperialists, on the one hand, incited the Turks to attack Armenia, and on the other they encouraged the Dashnaks to rely on them.... When Armenian troops were beaten by the Turks in 1920, and appealed to the Entente powers, these powers forgot their promises and failed to help ... the Dashnaks none the less refused the help of the Soviets several times.... It was a terrible war: the Turks lost 56,000 dead, 60,000 wounded and 32,000 casualties of sickness and disease.... But on 26 November the Dashnaks were forced to

accept a very harsh peace, which was a further misfortune for Armenia. The Dashnak regime was in fact losing all credibility and all Armenia was falling into dependence on Turkey . . . the national territory was reduced to only 20,000 square kilometres, without Kars or Ardahan, and Alexandropol: Armenia had the right to maintain only 1,500 soldiers, eight guns and 20 machine guns. . . . The negotiations of Alexandropol were therefore an eternal shame for the Dashnaks. . . . Dissatisfaction with them being at its height, . . . the only way to save Armenian liberty was the establishment of Soviet power there. . . . The mass uprising of 20 November 1920, under the leadership of a military-revolutionary committee under Kasjan, brought down the Dashnaks and set up the Soviet Republic of Armenia. . . . Dashnak adventurers tried to regain power . . . but were speedily defeated.

These two exposés form an enigma, and some of the clues are missing. Lenin's Decree on Nationality, in November 1917, did promise self-determination to Armenia, though to Turkish Armenia, and her alone. At Brest-Litovsk, in March 1918, the Turks recognized the independence of Armenia, though only of Russian Armenia, and her alone. Still, she was to be partitioned and cut up. Turkish troops, in pursuit of the pan-Turanian dream, marched on Erivan and Baku. Constantinople would not accept the Transcaucasian republic which had been set up in October, and had concluded the peace; the Turks would recognize only its separate members; Georgia was not concerned, and became independent; Azerbaijan was an object of Turkish plans at Armenia's expense; and Armenia was the only one to fight and so gain independence on 28 May 1918. In spite of Sardarabad on 4 June, she had to conclude a treaty, ceding land.

After the Allied victory, the defeat of Turkey and the armistice of Mudros, the fight began again, and in May 1919 Armenia proclaimed the reunification of her entire territory, ex-Turkish

Armenia, including Cilicia, being part of this. However, an axis between Ankara and Moscow was formed against foreign intervention in Russia and the dismemberment of the Turkish empire for the benefit of the imperialist powers. Between these lay Armenia, which relied on the Allies to execute the clauses of the Treaty of Sèvres and especially the arbitration of President Wilson, which – verbally – guaranteed the quasi-unity of the country.

Atatürk at once attacked Armenia, before the Allies could give her even minimal aid; Great Britain was buzy seizing the Arab areas of the old Ottoman empire, France was quietly engaged in taking the 'sphere' due to her by virtue of the Sykes-Picot agreement, and she also failed to give the help she had promised to the Armenians of Cilicia, and the United States simply escaped into isolationism. Yet the Turkish invasion was a deadly threat to the Armenian Republic. After the disastrous peace of Alexandropol, Soviet intervention appeared not so much as a political move against the Dashnaks, but as an effort to recover Russian Armenia, a chance to snatch it before the Turks could take it. The exhausted Armenians had little choice but to accept the Soviet option which at least offered survival. It was preferable to a precarious existence as a rump Armenia threatened by the Kemalist reconquest.

Once the immediate danger had passed, a large part of the populace rose against the Bolsheviks who, contrary to their promises, threw the Dashnaks from power. But the majority of these Bolsheviks were themselves former 'specifists' or old Mensheviks and Dashnaks, who had repudiated their faith, and now saw, in the manner of the famous king in the West, that Erivan was worth a mass. The second Soviet intervention put into power Armenians who, though they arrived in the baggage-waggons of the Russian army, appeared as liberators.

THE SECOND SOVIETIZATION

With the second Sovietization, Armenia's fate seemed sealed. To rebuild this mutilated province involved several hundreds of thousands of orphans, women, refugee children from the Turkish side, and all the survivors of genocide. It also involved an exhausted population, which the Dashnak nationalists had had to keep alive without aid, although the people had sunk to the deepest depths of misery ever known in Armenia.

The process of Sovietization developed quietly and gradually. Armenia, having had its own foreign war, came into the Soviet system only at the time of NEP. It is true that, for the old Dashnaks, who were persecuted and broken like all political parties in the USSR, NEP was not a period of détente. However, for the peasantry, which accounted for 81 per cent of the population, détente ruled. The great persecutions did not occur until after collectivization, for the Armenians were especially attached to their land and their small plots, and the rural community was associated not with the whole village but with the family, the nucleus of Armenian identity.

Soviet textbooks eagerly stress the loyalty and patriotism of the Armenians towards the USSR in the Second World War. In fact, the 1940s and 1950s were a period in which the greatest number of Armenians made their way into the apparatus of the Soviet state – army, Politburo, media etc. – and the Armenianization of institutions and the resurrection of the Armenian patrimony assisted in the consolidation of this loyalty towards Moscow. It had very long roots.

A PARADOX

Nevertheless, the partition of Armenia today is paradoxical. Its territorial heart is Ani, formerly Turkish Armenia, which is still under the Turks although, since the genocide, it no longer contains any Armenians. In Soviet Armenia, under the Soviet aegis, the Armenians have revived their old culture and now revere the cultural patrimony of their ancient nation. But this land hardly corresponds at all to old Armenia; it only incorporates its most marginal eastern fringes, which in the past were mainly inhabited by Kurds and Persians, who themselves had been massacred or had disappeared in the tragic years 1918–21. Even before 1918, the heart of the Armenian nation did not beat in Erivan, which at that time was only a small provincial town, nor in Kars or Ardahan, which were smothered by Ottoman tyranny, but in the great communities of the Armenian diaspora, Tiflis, Baku or Batum, in Russia.

Part of this bourgeoisie took power in Armenia itself, as we have seen, from the beginning of 1921, though it was in turn liquidated by the Stalinist purges. Another group experienced the regime outside Armenia by penetrating the state apparatus and rising to the highest positions in it. These Armenians of the Russian diaspora had nothing in common with their ancestral homeland unless perhaps they were required to govern it. When the Russification of institutions started again, after Khrushchev's fall, the Armenians were once more tempted towards emigration out of the USSR rather than towards a return to the homeland, which was a rural, provincial place without attractions to them. Even in Soviet Armenia, people wanted to emigrate.

The external diaspora had its attractions. An extremely lively national sentiment survived there; the Armenian communities in the USA, France or Australia are among the most homogeneous of the ethnic groups found in these countries. As in the eighteenth century, religion and patriotism can be easily adapted to the comforts of the good life in exile, far – very far – from the mountains of Armenia. Uneasy consciousness of the non-existence of a free state of their own merely nourishes a passionate Armenian committment to history, culture and the lost

Fatherland. To sing of its misfortunes and tragedies has a therapeutic effect.

There are, however, souls who take history and its demands at face value, and try to avenge their ancestors. The newspapers, from time to time, announce their deeds when, in moments of exultation, they kill a Turk. They are renewing the tradition of Armenian 'terrorists' of the nineteenth century; that tradition also lives on in the Palestinian *Feddayin*, who are directly descended from the 'Assassins', and they supply an uncomfortable reminder to the diaspora Armenians, however anxious they are for respectability; as Christians, they wish to be part of the West, but such actions also emphasize that, after all, Armenia also belongs to the East.

10

HISTORY IN PROFILE: POLAND

POLAND: A BRIEF CHRONOLOGY

960–992	Around Gniezno and the dynasty of the Piast gathers the embryo of a Polish state, vassal to Otho I.
966	Conversion of Milszko I to Christianity, who places his kingdom under the protection of the Holy See.
992–1025	Boleslaw the Brave increases his territory to the west at the expense of Emperor Henry II (Pomerania, Silesia, Lusatia, etc.), and to the east by occupying Kiev temporarily. He is crowned first king of Poland.
11th C.	Reaction of the nobility and conflicts with the emperor; the king is usually supported by the Papacy, Gregory VII in particular. The Poles contribute to the conversion of the Pomeranians.
1138	Boleslaw III divides Poland between his sons, which initiates a period of conflicts.

1226	Against the pagan Lithuanians, the Duke of Mazovia appeals to the Knights of the Teutonic Order; they occupy Prussia and threaten the independence of the Poles.
1241	Mongol invasion, sack of Cracow.
12th–13th C.	The Lesser Nobility (*Szlachta*) appeals to German colonizers.
second half of 13th C.	Cities receive Charters of Freedom and adopt the Germanic Law of Magdeburg (Torun, Poznan, Cracow, etc.).
1320	Reconstitution of Polish unity under Ladislas I.
1330–70	Casimir III the Great compensates these losses by the annexion, on the east, of Galicia, Volkynie, Podolia, formerly part of Kievan Russia.
1386	Edwige, daughter of Casimir III, marries Jagiello, Grand Prince of Lithuania, elected king of Poland and Lithuania under the name Ladislas II; Poland extends from Poznan to Smolensk.
1410	Ladislas II crushes the Teutonic Knights at the battle of Tannenberg, or Grunwald.
second half of 15th C.	By the statutes of Nieszawa (1454) and the Constitution *Nihil Novi*, royal authority is controlled by its Nobility (the *szlachta*).
1543	Death of Copernicus.
1569	'Indissoluble union' of Lithuania and Poland.
Mid-16th C.	Zenith of Cracow and of intellectual life.
1587	The *Pacta conventa* increasingly limit the powers of Jagiello's successors.
1587–1632	Sigismund III, a fervent Catholic, puts an end to the period of religious tolerance.
1596	Synod of Brest-Litovsk; creation for the Ukraine of the Uniate Church of the Greek rite, but attached to Rome.
1610	The 'Time of Troubles' in Russia; Ladislas, son of

	Sigismund of Poland, is proclaimed tsar of Russia.
1648	Revolt of the Cossacks against the Poles.
1651	Defeated by John Casimir, Bogdan Khmelnitsky surrenders to Russia.
1652	Establishment of the *Liberum Veto*. Exercising it will paralyse the Polish state.
1656	Swedish invasion, struggle for control of the Baltic Sea. Heroic resistance of the monastery of Czestochowa.
1660–67	Treaties of Oliva and Androuszow: Poland abandons Livonia to Sweden and the Ukraine to Russia.
1683	Jan Sobieski liberates Vienna from the Turkish threat.
1696–1795	Poland vulnerable to its four neighbours: Prussia, Sweden, Russia, Austria.
1772	First partitioning of Poland, reduced by a third of its territory.
1791	Constitution of 1791, inspired by J.-J. Rousseau.
1793	Second partitioning of Poland.
1794	Uprising of Kościuszko; crushed by the Russians; massacres of Praga.
1795	Third partitioning and disappearance of the Polish state: 45 per cent to Russia, 19 per cent to Prussia, 35 per cent to Austria.
1807	Resurrection of the Duchy of Warsaw, thanks to Napoleon I and the Polish Legion of Dembowksi.
1815	Return to the situation of 1795.
1830	Warsaw uprising, crushed by the Russians: 'Order reigns in Warsaw'.
1831	Polish intelligentsia goes into exile in the West: Mickiewicz, Chopin, etc.

1846	Insurrection of Mieroslavski in Prussian Poland, and Dembowski in Austrian Poland: this inaugurates 'The Springtime of Peoples' (1848).
1863	Uprising of Russian Poland, crushed with the help of Prussia.
1916	The Germans create a fictitious independent Poland.
1917	Lenin recognizes the right of the Poles to self-determination (they are under German control).
1919	Independence of Poland, Pilsudski government.
1919–20	Polish-Soviet War, German-Polish conflict in Silesia.
May 1926	Putsch by General Pilsudski.
1938	Refusal of Polish government to allow Soviet troops passage in the event of war between France and Nazi Germany.
23 August 1939	German-Soviet pact.
1 September 1939	German invasion.
October 1939	The Soviets occupy the eastern part of Poland. Establishment of a Polish government in London.
1943	Uprising in the Warsaw ghetto. The discovery of the graves at Katyn leads the London government to decide to break with Moscow.
December 1943	Moscow co-operates in the formation of a National Popular Council which sets up headquarters in Lublin. The army of the interior will recognize only Bor, Head of the Army taking orders from London.
1 August 1944	Warsaw insurrection.

31 December 1944	Entry of the Soviets and the troops of the Lublin Committee into Warsaw.
1945	The Yalta agreements define the future frontiers of Poland.
1947	Establishment of a government for the democratic 'bloc' presided over by a socialist, Cyrankiewicz.
1949	Poland aligned with the USSR: Sovietization: internment of the communist Gomulka following the Tito affair; the (Soviet) Marshal Rokossovski is appointed minister of national defence; internment of Cardinal Wyszynski.
1956	Poznan uprising, return of Gomulka: the 'Polish October'; abandoning of forced collectivization; liberation of Cardinal Wyszynski; measures of tolerance towards the church.
March 1968	Student demonstrations in Warsaw, harshly repressed by police; Gierek replaces Gomulka.
1970–80	Economic deterioration and bureaucratic control lead to Gdansk strikes and the establishment of 'free' trade unions.
1981–89	Miltary coup d'état. Repression of *Solidarnocz*.

In Poland, the clock of political history stops in 1945 and the subsequent era hardly figures at all in history taught to children. True, this decree does not simply concern education. Until *Man of Marble*, films concerned with the present day rarely received any form of endorsement, subsidy or encouragement. This no doubt explains, in part, why the Polish cinema has found refuge in the past, which serves to reveal the present, i.e. in which there is a demonstrable clash of passions.

The result is that it can be difficult to teach the most recent past. 'The children's parents have already, in part, lived through the course of events which we handle in the eighth class', says Józef Olszewski in a lecture on education, 'For them it is not really history at all. . . . Children will already have heard about the past from the radio, the television, or the home. . . . It is our task to enrich, complete and correct what they are told at home.' That is obvious enough. There are several co-existing visions of the past – official history, and private history, heard at home. There is also history as seen in the cinema, which transfigures the others, for the cinema, with its special art, can express everything without saying anything. In *Kanal*, the Warsaw insurgents are seen waiting, hidden in the sewers, vainly, for the Red Army to attack the Nazis and so come to the Poles' rescue. In the distance you can hear gunfire, but when the Poles emerge they are cut to pieces by German machine-guns. The viewer simply knows that the Soviets have waited for them all to be killed before arriving; and yet this message cannot be demonstrated, since it is not explicit, and the film ends at that point, so that nothing could be cut by the censor.

It is not easy to tell the history of Poland under the suspicious scrutiny of the Soviets, behind which the Poles see the old Russia, or under the anxious and uneasy 'collaborating' Polish Party.

As regards earlier periods, there are other differences. The official version is more or less tributary to the Marxist tradition, and clashes with the national version popularized in novels, drama and poetry, especially that of Mickiewicz; productions of *Forefathers' Eve* (1833) dramatized the Polish nation's misfortunes under the Russian boot, and have several times been censored. The sophistication of the Polish historical school has also sometimes made the task of official history difficult. True, the state has sometimes profited from this sophistication. After 1945 the historians, called upon to legitimize Poland's right to Silesia, could not use the written sources that had been purposely destroyed by the Germans – these archives might have shown that Slav settlements west of the Oder (and in Pomerania which, in Slavonic, means 'near the sea') were very old, and predated the German settlement. Polish historians hit upon an idea of using new sources altogether for the study of history, the records of material life, whether old traces of the shape of fields, or types of agricultural implements discovered in long-lost villages. In this way they entirely altered our ways of looking at evidence and so they greatly promoted both archaeology and history. They served their own nation well, but were also pioneers in a strengthening of local history, which they used not, as elsewhere in the world, merely for monographic purposes, but to reveal points of general history. They were thus able to circumvent official directives such as that of 1958 which 'for the history of Poland' required 'an especial concentration on the northern and western regions', not, in other words, the eastern areas that the Soviet Union had seized. With all the censorship and mirror-games, history in Poland must be looked at with special spectacles.

In a series of lectures and articles on education and history Józef Olszewski defined history's goal for schoolteachers: 'The aim of history teaching is to create good citizens' so it becomes important 'to choose suitable subject-matter' and to 'awaken admiration for the heroes of past ages, such as Leonardo da Vinci, Copernicus, Christopher Columbus, Einstein, or Fleming. The ultimate aim is to show the relationship between individual and society . . . and make children see that good citizens should work for the public good and act in the interests of society as a whole.' It is therefore vital to 'praise the revolutionary movements and national struggles that occurred in Poland and the rest of the world'. In particular 'it is vital to emphasize the exemplary roles played by some figures in the past, whether soldiers, leaders or historical heroes . . . and to stimulate children's imagination and engage their emotions . . . so that they can appreciate the motivation of these heroes.' Using textbook material as illustration, this Party educationalist puts forward some instances, from the earliest times to now.

THE STRUGGLE FOR GREEK INDEPENDENCE

Aim: To awaken a patriotic sentiment by extolling the spirit of sacrifice and of heroism against the Persians.

Lesson plan: Mention the Olympic Games; being strong and healthy, the Greeks had a feeling for national well-being, and the unity of Greece.

Create emotional tension in the class and ask the question:

'What answer would you have given to Darius when he demanded the Greeks' subjection?'

All will then reply: 'declare war on the Persians' . . .

'Even when there are 10,000 against 15,000?'

Unanimous shout: 'Yes. . . . For the Greeks think that they are brighter and better trained than the Persians, thanks to the Olympic Games, and so they will win!'

Then you should ask:

'Do you know of any other wars for independence fought against an enemy superior in number?'

'Yes, when the Nazis invaded Poland.'

SECOND EXAMPLE: THE STRUGGLE OF BOLESLAW THE BRAVE AGAINST THE GERMANS (992–1025)

Aim: To show the heroism of the Poles in defending their country against foreign invasion, and to awaken a patriotic sentiment among the children; to prepare them to work for everything that national defence requires.

Material: Cardboard, a model siege-engine, magazine articles on this period, for example those in *Plomyk Spark*, and *Swiat mtodych* (*Youth World*).

Plan: Set questions on the development of relations between

Germany and Poland under Mieszko I. Show how the Germans always aimed to conquer Slav territory.

Question: Why did Boleslaw fight this war?

Answer: Because he had foresight and wanted to forestall an attack by the emperor Henry II.

Question: But if the emperor had many more soldiers at his disposal, how do we explain the Polish victory?

Answer: When one defends one's fatherland, one always finds the heart to fight.

Read an extract from Dietmar on the endurance of the Poles during this war.

THIRD EXAMPLE: THE BATTLE OF GRUNWALD IN 1410

Aim: To awaken a feeling of national pride by an analysis of this victory which gained liberty and peace and broke the power of the Teutonic Knights.

Material: Map of Poland, Lithuania, etc.

The painting by J. Matejki, *The Battle of Grunwald*

Portraits of Jagiello and Witold.

Extracts from H. Sienkiewicz's novel, *The Teutonic Knights*, etc.

Analysis: Show that what was new was the common struggle of all the Slav peoples, Poles, Lithuanians, Czechs and Russians, against the Teutonic Knights.

Example for the summary: Poland and Lithuania defended themselves against extermination, for the Teutonic Knights wanted to destroy and annihilate them. The Knights feared the union between Lithuanians and Poles. In the battle, the most important part was taken by the Poles, but other Slavic peoples also had a large share.

FOURTH EXAMPLE: NICHOLAS COPERNICUS, A GREAT POLISH SCHOLAR

Aim: To awaken a feeling of pride in the scope of a scholar's work, to show its significance, and the importance of science in the life of individuals.

Materials: Map of Poland in the sixteenth and seventeenth centuries, portrait of Copernicus, set of slides, etc.

Lesson: Summarize the work of Copernicus, show its importance and how he changed the view of his contemporaries on the celestial spheres; show how, without Copernicus, it would have been impossible to go into space.

Analyse the hostile attitude of the church and how it is to be explained. Stress the role of the Jesuits, and the Inquisition; show a picture of an auto-da-fé in which a priest burns some books (cf. p. 55 of the sixth-form textbook).

Remind the class that Copernicus was a great patriot, and that he fought for the defence of his country.

FIFTH EXAMPLE: THE PEOPLE'S STRUGGLE UNDER THE LEADERSHIP OF S. CZARNIECKI AGAINST THE SWEDISH INVASION, 1655–1660.

Aim: To show the importance of the theme, popular patriotism; to stress the people's attachment to independence whereas the *Szlachta* and magnates think only of their interests.

Materials: A map of Europe and Poland in the seventeenth century. Portraits of Stefan Czarniecki and John Casimir, and sketches showing the struggles of the Polish against the Swedes; the film: *In the Swedish Time*, songs of the period, etc.

Show the hatred that was felt towards the invaders, the destruction that was brought about by the Swedes, and analyse the contentious policies of Charles-Gustav and John Casimir.

SIXTH EXAMPLE: THE PEASANTS REVOLT OF PIOTR SCIEGIENNY

Aim: To awaken a sentiment of love towards a heroic son of the Polish nation who devoted his life to his people.

Materials: A map of Poland at the time of the partition. The portrait of Piotr Sciegienny. A description of peasant life. Mlynarski's book on Piotr Sciegienny.

Meaning of the lesson: Description of the situation after the uprising of November 1830.

Why was Piotr beaten, who were his allies and his enemies?

Of what did his patriotism consist?

One pupil replies: 'He organized an uprising in the cause of liberty and justice; he was punished in tsarist prisons for his activities.'

This lesson gives the children an example of heroic action *in spite* of the resistance of the *Szlachta* and magnates, who stifled the liberty of the Polish people.

SEVENTH EXAMPLE: EDWARD DEMBOWSKI

Aim of the lesson: To evoke a patriotic sentiment in the children through the example of Edward Dembowski's self-sacrificing devotion in the liberal, social and educational struggles of the Polish people.

Materials: Portrait of Edward Dembowski. Extracts from his letters, discussing the social oppression of the Polish masses. Map of the partitions of Poland. W. Anczyc's poems, *The Messenger.*

Lesson plan: The teacher asks questions to explain 'who' were the messengers. The children answer, remembering the names of Piotr Sciegienny, Konarski, etc. both executed as messengers [it is not said that they were both of them priests (M. F.)]

Describe Dembowski's house, the gentry lordship of his

father, the conflicts and tensions between Edward and his parents: he blames them for the wrongs done to the peasants.

The children will stress that Dembowski was questioned by the police for his activities against the rich and the partitioning state (the Prussians, the Austrians and the Russians). One pupil says: 'The ordinary people gave him their help.' Another says: 'Dembowski fought for social justice and the liberty of the Fatherland; so that the landlords would no longer live off the sweat of the poor.'

Conclude with the part played by the Poles in the first proletarian struggles, and link this up with the lesson on the Paris Commune and the activity of Poles during it. This needs considerable emotion.

Ludwik Warynski, founder of The Proletariat, is also the subject of another lesson aiming to encourage sympathy for this ardent fighter in the 'social cause.' Here the recommendation is to remind children of the causes of industrial development within Europe, the activity of the working-class leaders, Karl Marx and Friedrich Engels, and to recall once more the part played by the Poles in the struggles of the Paris Commune at the beginning of the period of industrialization in Poland. Here teachers should show 'that the struggles of men like Warynski aroused the hatred of industrialists and other exploiters, and that at his trial, the tsar and the bourgeoisie were in alliance against the people.' Children must be helped to understand these problems. He predicted that one day the revolution would take its revenge, and the people would end up by breaking their chains of bondage.

Lenin, the subject of the next lesson, 'is difficult to approach, because the children have heard him talked about but know little about him.' In order to arouse admiration for this great leader of the working classes, Józef Olszewski suggests reading the poetry of Mayakovsky, extracts from Krupskaya's My Life with Lenin, and short biographies of Lenin. He would suggest stressing certain points: the fact that Lenin always felt the wrongs that were done to the people, that his life had been entirely devoted to the revolution, that in his whole existence he delighted in the past and love of the people, that he took part in the formation of the socialist state and that he was openly in favour of Polish independence.

After another lesson on the Nazi invasion of 1939, the final example is dedicated to popular resistance to the German occupation under the leadership of the PPR (Polish Workers' Party). The aim of this lesson is to 'arouse sentiments of hatred towards the enemy and admiration and love of liberty and social justice. A map of Poland, photographs of the PPR leaders and those of the ZWM (Youth-Fighters League) are used to illustrate the lesson: photographs of P. Fonder, M. Nowotko, M. Fornalska, J. Krasicki (all members of the "Advance Committee" dropped by parachute into occupied Poland in December 1941 by the Soviets). It is essential to stress the Nazi occupation's policies, the terrible crime they involved and the cruelty of their measures against the Polish people, which they wanted to destroy right down to the very roots of its culture, in the occupied territories.'

It is best to describe that anti-Nazi resistance with stress on the distinction between the organizations connected to London, which propagated the theory of the 'two enemies' [the Nazis and the Soviets (M.F.)] and those with a revolutionary character which appealed to all-out resistance against the Nazis.

To recreate the atmosphere of the times 'you should play the music of the People's Guard, and show the children the heroism of those who died by telling them for example, the story of the heroic death of Savicka.'

The book ends with this quotation: 'We are bringing up our children in order to make them into good patriots,' said

Gomulka in April 1960; 'and this patriotism must be free from the poisoned miasma of nationalism and chauvinism. It must flow from the ideal of socialism itself, the ideal aims at the friendship of peoples', etc., etc.*

NO POLISH–RUSSIAN CONFLICT

The thirteen chosen examples amount to a caricature of the official history, for their chief features are extensions of the official line, although quite true to it.

Conflict with Russia (and then the USSR) is completely skipped over, and the origins of the old Polish hatred for their neighbours are missed out. The German alone, and even the Swede, appears as the butcher of Poland. Not only is no mention made of the partition of Poland as a historical example for children; there is also no mention of the great uprisings against Russia, even though these determined the course of Polish history after the later eighteenth century. Quite the contrary: two of these examples show 'friendship' between Poles and Russians. This feature is important enough for it to be worth checking against the accounts presented in the textbooks. A useful test-case is the rising of 1795.

As regards the Kościuszko rising against the Russians, and the Third Partition that ended Polish independence in 1795, the tradition is that the capture of Warsaw by the Russian commander, Suvorov, was followed by the destruction of the suburb of Praga and the massacre of its inhabitants. The classic, and still

---

* The quotation is from Gomulka, secretary of the Polish Communist Party at the time of the publication of the book. The readers should know that in a later edition, another similar quotation from Gierek was substituted for this one. When the work of a great Soviet historian on the *Popular Uprisings in France between 1623 and 1648* was translated into French, I myself was present at the extraordinary scene in 1963, when the author hurriedly substituted, at proof stage, quotations from Khrushchev for those of Stalin.

quite accurate, account of this in the textbook of 1968 runs: 'Suvorov's forces arrived on 2 November (1795) in Praga. On the 4th, after a bloody assault on the city, during which Jasinski was killed, he took Praga and massacred the inhabitants. The king ordered the citizens to surrender.'

The new version, in a sixth-form textbook of 1976, reads: 'Suvorov, the commander-in-chief of the tsarist army, arrived at Praga and within two days had successfully assaulted the city itself. General Jasinski, who commanded the insurrection in Lithuania, was killed in the defence of Praga, and shortly afterwards Warsaw surrendered. The insurrection was over.' There is no longer any mention of the massacre of Praga's inhabitants. However, there is a further surprise. The suburb of Praga does appear in a later edition, of 1979; but not in allusion to the Russians' massacre in 1795, but rather with reference to the 'repression of the workers' carried out in Praga by Marshal Pilsudski on 12 May 1926 in the course of his rebellion: 'The fighting lasted for three days, with over 400 dead and 1,000 wounded.' Such, then, is history as taught in Poland: not only is the massacre of 1795 forgotten but the memory associated with the name 'Praga' is diverted towards an event in the 1920s.

But in any case, the reduction itself is deceptive and damaging. The fight against Pilsudski's putsch cannot be summarized as a workers' revolt, its initial success and subsequent defeat, for among the dead of 1926 there were also officers and men who remained loyal to the Wojciechowski regime, and in any case Praga's role was not outstanding.

At the other end of the history of partitioned Poland, there is no mention of the German-Soviet pact of 1939, the fifth partition (in effect), when the country's eastern part was invaded and later annexed by the Soviets. To the Ukrainians and Byelorussians who made up the majority in these parts, Molotov announced in 1940 that 'Nothing Polish will survive.' The region was immediately Sovietized, and Catholicism was forbidden, which shocked even the Polish communists. The process of de-Polonization began with the deportation and massacre of officers of the old army. Some died at Katyn, and others disappeared in the northern wastes; others still escaped this weird anabasis, found their way to beyond the Caspian, and thence passed to Persia, from where they were able to join the British in Egypt.

Only the historical works of the émigré Poles make any mention of these problems. Moreover, presentation of the conflicts which arose between the London-based and the Moscow-based resistance movements varies considerably as does the record of grievances against Soviet troops that the rebels of Warsaw could demonstrate – the same rebels who, in *Kanal*, could point to the long delay, from July 1944 to January 1945, in the Soviet liberation of Warsaw. The Soviet view is that the uprising took place too early, in the wrong way, and only to establish an anti-Soviet government in Warsaw before the Red Army arrived. That is certainly right: the Poles wanted to set up an authority independent of all foreign interference, whether Soviet or not, and Stalin, wishing to forestall this, described this independent form of government as 'anti-Soviet'. That the uprising was premature is possible and even likely, but it is also true that Moscow refused to let Polish aircraft from London use runways that the Red Army controlled, at less than an hour's flight from Warsaw, so that the Allies could hardly give more than slight help to the Warsaw rebels.

The problem of the two resistance movements and governments, in London and Lublin, still haunts the Polish historical memory. Several hundred books and articles have been written on the subject, and there have been over fifty films dealing with the two resistance movements, the resistance in general, and the Second World War (by far the greatest proportion in any country in relation to the total output of films). They also examine the country's sufferings under German occupation, which was nowhere worse than in Poland, and the extraordinary resistance of the Poles, who led Europe in tenacity, solidarity and the length of their struggle. Only geographical factors account for the Polish resistance's doing less damage to the occupants than the Yugoslav; for the Polish resistance was the most desperate of all.

As I have noted above, school textbooks often mention this struggle against the Germans. Inversely, as a logical counterpart, Polish historians (this time, of every leaning) omit to say why Poles were so resented by Russians. This goes back to the expansionism of the *Szlachta* nobility which, in the sixteenth century, saw the eastern borderlands as a natural field for empire. Just as the Russians in that era moved outward to Siberia, or the Spanish nobles to America, so this movement was a consequence of the general impoverishment of the European nobility: this suggestion, by the Polish historian Marian Malowist, has been supported by the work of W. Czaplinski, for even in the sixteenth century contemporaries remarked on the similarity of the overseas conquests and the eastern expansion. Polish lords occupied and looted Moscow, installed a garrison in the Kremlin, sought to dominate Russia in the reign of King Sigismund (which coincided with the 'Time of Troubles' in the east) and oppressed the Ukrainians who rose in revolt in 1647. They wanted independence; however, if they had to have a Polish or Russian master, they would choose Russia. Children's textbooks in Russia certainly never fail to point out this choice, whereas Polish works on this subject omit mention of the option taken by Bogdan Khmelnitsky and his assembled peasants. These works only say that the Ukrainians 'allied with the Tatars and the Russians against the Poles'.

This expansionism brought the Poles towards the east, and in Lithuania, where they encountered and fought the Russians for the first time in 1507. The pendulum swung back in the sixteenth century, and the tsars conquered Courland and Livonia and won over the Ukrainians. Thereafter, Russian power grew and grew, and its expansion to the west could hardly be stopped. Poland herself was wedged in: Russia, her strength renewed by Peter the Great, lay to the east; Sweden, aiming to control the Baltic, threatened from the north; the Turkish empire to the south-east and a constantly-growing Prussia to the west completed this pattern. Poland's tragic fate was marked by geography, and she had to suffer concerted attacks from her enemies. Of them all, Russia and Germany were the most predatory and in the east Poland, step by step, lost all of her most cherished possessions. The memory of Great Poland survives, as does that of the three partitions; so, under foreign rule, the dream of reconquest went on, and came to brutal life when independence was recovered in 1918.

On the events of 1918–20 the official history is singularly succinct, this time in both Poland and the USSR. Generally, it keeps close to the military events, noting the Polish army's occupation of Kiev and Minsk, the Soviet counter-offensive which reached Warsaw itself, and the peace of Riga in 1921. The blame for this conflict is shifted onto foreign intervention, since the British and French 'manipulated' Poland into attacking the USSR. On the Polish side there is, however, no mention of the alliance with Petlyura, which was intended to detach the Ukraine from Soviet Russia and bring to life an independent Ukraine that would be more or less dominated by Poland. There is also no mention of the military reversal and the Soviet advance on Warsaw, the Third International, its appeal to Polish workers to rise against their government or the setting-up of a communist government at Bialystok, under Marchlewski, Kon and Dzierzyński (the 'Revkom').

Neither in Poland nor in the USSR is there any reference to Tukhachevski's proclamations, which were meant to start, in Poland, a revolution brought in and imposed from without, and there is silence as to the political and military failure of this first attempt at Sovietization of Poland. Only Radek foresaw this failure, to the fury of Lenin and Trotsky, for he knew that in Poland, hatred of the Russians would be a more powerful force than love of Soviets. Not only are such things not told to children, but in the USSR every effort is made to conceal all trace of them. In Soviet libraries, the passage in Klara Zetkin's *Lenin Remembered* where she discusses these events and Radek's warnings has disappeared. The same happened to Tukhachevski's *Pokhod na Vislu* (1923).

Overall, Polish children do not seem to learn of the Comintern, or Soviet-Polish relations from 1919 to 1939, or even the existence of Polish communists. Study does begin with the origins of all this – the 'working-class movement' from 'the Paris Commune to the Second International and Lenin', but after that there is something of a black-out. No mention is made of the schism in the Communist Party when Comintern instructed the Polish communists to support Pilsudski, nor is there any allusion to Comintern's dissolution of the Polish Communist Party in 1938, and finally there is utter silence as to its founders' and members' martyrdom, for they, refugees in Moscow, were executed in the Purges: Lenski, Warski, Durubal and countless others were killed as old associates of Radek. The only ones to receive mention are those who went to Spain and died for the republic there.

FURTHER DISTORTIONS IN THE OFFICIAL VERSION

As noted above, the passages on the Swedish invasion, on Piotr Sciegienny, Dembowski and some others clearly state the problem of class struggle as laid down in the Marxist 'Vulgate'. The nobles and the rich have always a wicked part to play, and they betray the Fatherland. However, this line can only be maintained through a wild distortion of Polish history which offends the sensibilities of all who know, or used to know, that it is a travesty of the facts. The account given of Dembowski is characteristic. The 'recommendations' conceal what was said in earlier textbooks, for that did not agree with 'the meaning of the argument'. The account of Piotr Sciegienny carefully hid the fact that he, the great organizer of peasant revolts, was a priest; there is no mention of his carrying everywhere he went a letter from Gregory XVI in 'a little golden book', in which he recorded sermons ostensibly concerned exclusively with religious matters, but in reality calling for revolt.

There is a further well-known distortion. In Poland, everyone knows that when the nobles organized a general uprising in Austrian Galicia, the peasants believed that they did so to prevent a decree abolishing serfdom, which the nobles would not tolerate. In fact this false information was the work of the imperial bureaucracy which managed to turn peasants against nobles. To thwart these manoeuvres, Dembowski also proclaimed the abolition of serfdom, but too late, for the peasants did rise and were 'the only people in the empire to resist the abolition of serfdom'. They helped the emperor of Austria to crush the Cracow rebellion, and the insurgents were defeated at Gdów. In spite of this, Dembowski did not give up, for he felt he could persuade the peasants to join the patriotic side. On 27 February 1846, a procession left Cracow with crosses and banners waving in the wind, and priests at its head; Dembowski was its leader. The Habsburg infantry was alerted by peasants, laid an ambush, and opened fire. Dembowski was among the first to fall. All of this appeared in the textbook of 1968, but these matters cease to be 'links in the argument' for Józef Olszewski, for they do not work in the 'desired sense'. The truth of this is that the revolutionary nobles were murdered because of peasants' denouncing them to the authorities.

That today the Polish church, whose stand is certainly highly conservative, is able to act as liberator and so pose as the only moral force opposing the state, is in itself a sign of the regime's unpopularity and of the lack of trust that its leaders inspire.

The government, faced with its own weakness, has ceased to fight rebellion and the clergy, and has even reversed the relationship of church and state that exists in the USSR. The state tries to win round the bishops, and to control them, colonize them and play on the church's inveterate love of order so that the clergy can become a 'transmission-belt' for the government, rather in the manner of the old trade unions. For its part the church has sought to uphold its own highly-regarded position in society and has strenuously opposed any movement towards modernism, whether over the status of women or over abortion, which would have made the church seem to be imitating the regime. In fact the church has adopted a conservative stance which in the old days was tinged with militant anti-Semitism – a feature that, at times, the Communist Party has itself adopted in turn. Józef Olszewski says nothing as to the Jews, whereas liberal tradition happily recognized the importance of their part in Polish history.*

It is true that in other aspects this conservatism is the successor of an earlier tradition. As early as the Middle Ages, to block the rising monarch, it was the only church in Europe not to sanctify any monarch at all: hence Poland never knew the

* As in the rest of Catholic Europe, anti-Semitism is nourished from infancy by the teachings of the church. Since the horrors undergone by the Jews and the Warsaw ghetto uprising of 1943, there has been a considerable debate as to whether Polish resistance fighters helped Jews. Officially, this aid is said to have been impressive, the ghetto uprising even being seen as part of Polish resistance. The Jews deny any help, given the Poles' visceral anti-Semitism. According to Michal Borwicz, who has read documents buried by the Jews before they were killed, there was some form of effective help; but the resistance men were known, were conscious of Poles' feelings towards Jews and took care not to let the aid be known, for it might have made the cause unpopular. The fact remains that in Poland the resistance people shot people who denounced Jews.

phenomenon of Divine Right, and has only hero-kings, not God-kings. In the era of Partition, from 1795 to 1918, the church was the incarnation of national unity, for it was the only institution common to all three parts of the country. It had a powerful role in cultural and patriotic conservatism, resisting all modernization, as a threat to 'the very existence of the nation'. The church had also to remain loyal to the papacy, which was expected to protect Polish Catholics, although the Vatican had already condemned several uprisings against the established order, i.e. the system established by the Holy Alliance.

The links of church and nation were strengthened during these periods of repression. They became corroded when Poland regained her independence, as could be seen in the situation before 1790 and again between 1919 and 1939. The relationship between church and nation has been subtly analysed by K. Pomian, and of course it is not officially discussed in the school textbooks. The question of Christianity is of course raised, but this affects its place, not its role, which appears only in a negative way: thus Copernicus made his discoveries despite church censorship; the pope condemned the rebels of 1830, etc. Almost nothing is said of the church's record in toleration, which is unique in Europe, in the sixteenth century, the era of religious wars; that such toleration was the obvious cause of Poland's Golden Age is virtually unimaginable in these pages.

Above all, in this official history an essential characteristic of Polish history is missed out completely, the fact that Catholicism grafted Poland onto the West, which gave the Poles a strong link with Rome that set them apart from all other eastern European peoples except the Croats. In an *Essay on the History of Education in Poland*, in 1810, Hugo Kollatai discussed the link between the first stages of civilization and the introduction of Christianity: 'The Latin rite showed us the well-established model of the West.' As Marian Serejski says, there is in Poland a deeply-embedded idea that civilization comes mainly from the West. This is a vital fact which explains the historic, and still-considerable place taken by classical history in Poland – which is quite unlike the case in others of the people's democracies.

A NEW SITUATION SINCE 1990

Reading Stefan Meller, who has a good knowledge of the history of textbooks in Poland, we find that a movement in favour of the revision of history was set up, illegally, in the wake of the coup d'état of 13 December 1981; it led to the appearance of a clandestine edition of the history of Poland from 1918 to 1980, liberal in hue, written by Andrzej Albert, the pseudonym of Wojciech Roskowski. At the same time, the regime had approved the distribution of a work which referred to the Molotov–Ribbentrop pact and the matryrdom suffered by Poles in the USSR, in short which limited itself to corrections and filling in the 'blanks'.

Today, several textbooks are in circulation or are being prepared, from those which, in support of the past, are nationalist or Polish-centred, to those which strive for a certain objectivity.

11

A NOTE ON THE HISTORY OF CHINA

The *Manual for Secondary-School Teaching* published in 1958 by the Shanghai Centre for Education asserts that history should have a very important role in education because it has to 'establish the place of the proletariat in Chinese children's consciousness', 'show that the people is the motor of history' and 'that Marxism is the only means by which the laws of historical development can be grasped'. Children 'have to absorb the idea that capitalism will inevitably be destroyed and that socialism is superior'. Description 'must be lively so that the child can feel and resent what his parents had to endure and understand why they fought back'. Children should also be told why history is taught: for, to build socialism, Marx and Lenin based their work on study of the past.

Throughout history, teachers should seek to inculcate four qualities in particular:

1 Patriotism. It should be emphasized that, though China was oppressed for so long, she managed to create her own culture. The Chinese people have nothing to be ashamed of, and can take pride in having emancipated themselves from the past. It is vital to combat the tendency that some intellectuals have of seeking models in the West rather than in China.

2 Internationalism. It should not be a hollow, vain concept; the links between various peoples and their common interests should be shown. The concept of internationalism can show what nationalism means, what constitutes 'a just war', 'an oppressed people', etc.

3 Socialist morality. This will triumph 'if we uproot the poisonous weeds left by the West and capitalism; class morality is the true morality, that of the labouring masses.'

4 Education by work and recognition of the value of labour. The teacher should at each stage of historical development describe the life and work of the masses, 'for today there is still a certain condescension towards manual labour'.

These 'instructions' form the preface to the historical manual published at Shanghai. They easily reveal how determined the leaders are to make historical analysis dependent on ideology, a characteristic that is even more clearly present in China than in the USSR. This preface also shows one of the difficulties of history in China, that of reconciling China's own past with the Marxist model or, more exactly, finding in China's history not merely some vague parallel with the Marxist models, but the models themselves. These words were written during the Great Leap Forward, when China was freeing herself from the Soviet model, and it is significant that patriotism counts as the chief virtue, the class struggle coming second. The historian

Liu Shieh even wrote, 'the class struggle is a useful tool, and must be employed for the understanding of modern history, but for earlier history do we have to apply it in an automatic way?'

The history taught to Chinese is different in Peking and in Taipei. The young Shen Pai-Hua, born in Formosa in 1955, had to learn the list of the fifteen principal dynasties off by heart — Chou, Ch'in, Tang, Sung, Ming etc. — once he reached the age of nine, whereas the young Chinese of Shanghai have to learn all about various peasant wars as the chief motive-force of history. There is a similar contrast with heroes and villains. In Peking, Genghis Khan is no longer the cruel conqueror, but the unifier of the Mongols and Chinese, spreading the triumphs of oriental science and the glories of Chinese civilization (the magnetic compass, gunpowder, printing) to the West. On the other hand the saintly Confucius, teacher of 20,000,000 pupils, who preached civility, respect for parents and for elders, is, in Peking, morally responsible for all the misfortunes of China. In Peking, history is no longer a mirror of the past, but part of the Chinese people's inexorable march towards socialism.

HISTORY, FROM THE DOCTRINES OF SUN YAT-SEN TO THOSE OF MAO

In China, as in Japan, and much more than in other countries, there has only been a proper educational policy as regards history since the beginning of the twentieth century. In China, it can be dated precisely from the revolution of 1911.

At that time, long before Maoism, the idea of a unified system of education was thought 'desirable' but 'impossible to effect'. At least there was agreement between publishers and writers as to the application of principles that brought Sun Yat-Sen to power. Morality and civic instruction were to go hand in hand with the teaching of history, and a ministerial instruction of 1912 laid down the qualities to be emphasized in the teaching of history to schools and in higher education: a spirit of loyalty, fraternalism and altruism, courage, respect for others, and industriousness – i.e. a Confucian disposition. History and geography were designed to serve analysis of Chinese dependence on the outside world and to explain her then condition. The civic sense thus took priority over moral principles, and books were meant mainly to create citizens (Kuo-Min); inevitably there was a reaction in favour of Confucius in the era of Yuan Shi-Kai and the War Lords. In this way, for both the Kuo-Min-Tang and Chiang Kai-Shek, the eradication of Confucius seemed to be a necessity. The Maoists of the Cultural Revolution who wanted this eradication were not as original as was supposed, although, in the meantime, the regime of Chiang and Taiwan had become more and more detached from Mao and his socialist vision; there had been forty years of foreign and civil war in China.

In the lower school classes at the beginning of this century, not only was the outside world not mentioned, since only China was discussed, but history and geography were not even taught as individual subjects; they were approached through reading-books and morality tales. This is still the case in communist China and so we may briefly compare the textbooks of the 1960s and 1970s in Taiwan and Peking.

THE TAIWAN VERSION

Pride in Chinese history is certainly the first thing to be taught to Taiwanese children. Only later, in the third, and especially the fourth, form (i.e. around the age of twelve) do they learn that the two Chinas have been separate since 1949. 'China, China, the country that we love, there is no country in the world that is greater than you.' China has 'the most gifted race in the world. . . . The reason for this is that 3,000 years ago, when the other peoples of the earth were still savages, our country was already developed, and her culture and organization were based on writing and written rules. . . . China invented paper, silk, the compass, printing, etc.' Taiwan as such is not mentioned, save as 'a magnificent treasure island, as the ancient legends of China said.'

Defence of the Fatherland is a duty associated with the defence of family or mother. Confucianism comes to the fore in a story illustrating this theme. Once, a chief of state was kidnapped; the young Yueh-Fei wanted to join the army and fight for his cause, and defend the threatened country. But he realized that his filial duty required him to stay behind and protect his old mother, and so he hesitated, until his mother herself begged him to leave, saying that, if the country falls, 'what will become of the family? You must see where the great danger lies, and defend us all from it.' In another story, Wang-Chi died while defending his country against another and more powerful one: is this supposed to be Peking China? Probably, for the older children are always clearly being told that continental China should one day be reconquered: 'We all think that way here.' The need for this is shown through the story of a child who visited the graves of the seventy-two martyrs: they had been executed by the communists, and the sight of the graves arouses hatred for the communists and respect for the heroes. Other stories support the idea that the country has declined since the communists took over: economic misery, particularly, prevails, as can be seen in the picture of an old man, kneeling, tied to a tree and being whipped by communist soldiers. Later on, a further story tells the story of a poor man who drowns himself because he cannot pay the heavy taxes. The communists fish his body out of the water and cut off it the weight of the sum he should have paid. His enraged widow shrieks: 'Beasts, when our army comes, it'll be the end of you.'

THE PEKING VERSION

In People's China, the books for young children are even more politicized. They also use instances from today which introduce characters with whom the children can identify – a grand-mother, an old uncle who works in the rural commune, the cousin in industry, etc. One of them is captured by the enemy, but, on the point of death, he announces with pride, 'My only sorrow is that I can no longer serve the Party.' In another story, a mother lets herself be burned alive rather than reveal secrets of the Communist Party to the Kuo-Min-Tang. Most of these stories recall the harshness of life at this time, 'when misery and poverty made our skins go yellow, and the capitalists constantly exploited the worker.' The essential message is to enrage readers at the inhumanity of this period, the humiliations inflicted by foreigners ('Forbidden to dogs and Chinamen') and to express gratitude for the makers of the new society.

There are also essential messengers. Liu Shao-Chi, to whom a soldier gives his blanket during a cold winter's night, waits for the soldier to go back to sleep and then carefully replaces the blanket on the suffering soldier. Mao himself, even more than Lenin, is a sort of Robin Hood, Tarzan and Fra Diavolo. Did he somehow never feel hungry? A peasant offers him eggs; Mao jumps onto his horse and gallops furiously to the nearest hospital to give them to starving children. He is the great hero: saviour, sage, and servant of the people.

THE MARXIST VERSION OF CHINESE HISTORY: ITS MAIN CONCERNS

Albert Feuerwerker has examined 'the Marxist disguise' of Chinese history. He has shown that its approach and revisionism affect matters such that the present can be revalued and the communists' authority legitimized.

To give priority to peasant revolts corresponds to the theoretical revolutions both of Marx and Mao: Marx's, in the sense that the masses, not just the leaders, are the motive-force of history, and Mao's, in that peasants are substituted for proletarians as agents to achieve the socialist revolution. Thus, history is embodied in the peasantry's struggle against feudalism and imperialism: Mao's analysis was correct, his victory the outcome. The movement of history occurs as dynasties are overthrown by peasant struggles, and the periodization of history in China is dominated by the two chief revolts, extending from the Chou dynasty (1027 BC) to our own times. This argument only postpones a central problem – the vast period in between still has to be analysed and the alternation of progress and stagnation has to be shown. This will be discussed below.

In any case, the whole question raises a further difficulty, that of the birth of capitalism in China. Did feudal society in China evolve and what would it have become without the intervention of foreigners? Mao said, 'It would have become capitalist even without foreign intervention', and he took care to separate the history of China from the Russian or western models. The historian Shang-Hu has shown, accordingly, that by the Ming era (fourteenth–seventeenth centuries) there already existed in China a small-scale capitalism that had manufacturing, some division of labour and a search for foreign markets. There was also apparently a tradition of 'bourgeois thought' embodied in the Dream of the Red Room. The fall of the Ming can thus be explained as the outcome of an alliance of this bourgeoisie and the peasantry under Li Tsu-Cheng, with China rapidly developing towards an industrial revolution, stopped only by the arrival of the imperialists. The role of China as Europe's victim is thus maintained, and so historians can explain why feudalism lasted so far into the nineteenth century. The Opium Wars, in their way, then become anti-feudal and anti-imperialist; however the capitalists' position was not predominant before the nineteenth century, so the lead in the democratic movement was taken by the proletariat.

The history of imperialist aggression in China, and the obstacles that the Powers put up against China's becoming a truly independent nation, similarly require an adjustment in the 'vulgate'. It is easy to show that the frustration of the Chinese revolutions occurred because foreigners were so powerful, but the difficulty comes in demonstrating that China was ever ready for change: 'the connection of internal and external events has to be demonstrated'.

Accordingly, the significance of events may change according to whether the criteria chosen for periodization are the great revolutionary waves of the 'chief contradictions', or 'fundamental contradictions' of modern Chinese society: imperialism against China, people against feudalism, bourgeoisie against proletariat. In the first case, the Boxer Rising becomes a simple manoeuvre for the imperial government to be rid of foreigners; in the second, it becomes a response by the court to a very real threat to the dynasty's existence, and is to be explained as a powerful popular movement against imperialism.

Such analyses are abstract and subject to variations that follow the course of history itself. They are often also confused, precisely because they aim both to analyse the past and to make it accord with Mao's thought, i.e. the existing government. It is this feature that explains the peculiar instability of history in China, the fact that 'everywhere people complain that there is no basic book, no overall history of China.' This lack of stability can be seen if we compare the analyses of the same great peasant revolt supplied by Shanghai and Taipei textbooks.

THE PEKING VERSION: THE CH'IN EMPIRE (221–206 BC): FEUDAL, CENTRALIZED, DESPOTIC

The emperor Ch'in Huang-Ti stepped up the pace of reform. As uniter of the country, he took the title 'Huang-Ti', or celestial emperor, for he had the presumptuous belief that the dynasty would last forever. The emperor had supreme power. He did discuss everything with ministers, but it was he alone who took decisions, even though the ministers were irremovable. The peasants owned the land and the government began to register them, with name, age, sex and amount of land held. It was from this source that the state worked out taxes, conscription and *corvées*.

The empire was divided into thirty-six provinces and these, in turn, into districts. Government functionaries were responsible for collecting taxes and raising armies, and were themselves supervised by other officials, appointed directly by the emperor, who had power to dismiss them. The system of fiefs that had flourished since Chou times was thus replaced by a system of governorships.

The emperor spent his time in compiling state registers so that he knew exactly what was happening. He took several steps to reinforce the empire's unity. In the era of the warrior kings, each region had its own separate laws, currency and customs, but the emperor united them all, and took as his model the customs of the Ch'in in Shansi. He similarly codified the system of writing, destroyed the walls that had separated the different regions, linked up irrigation networks and had several roads built to connect places with the capital. To fore-stall rebellion, the government expelled 200,000 highly-placed adherents of the old dynasties, or made them live in the capital. At the same time, all weapons in the country were collected and melted down into bells and into twelve gigantic statues. These measures were intended to break the power of the nobles, and this transition from a system of fiefs to one of governorships provoked reaction. Those who opposed these measures used ancient books to attack them. The emperor, at the suggestion of his minister, Li-Si, decided to burn them all, except those on medicine, agriculture and astrology. In this way, the opposition no longer had books to support their arguments.

The emperor gained land for his state by sending Meng Ch'an on an expedition against the barbarians of the north, the Hsiung-Nu, who were pushed back over the To-Fong; other generals were sent south, pacified the natives of the Kwang-Si and penetrated the centre of Vietnam. These new provinces acquired proper governors; convicts had their sentences quashed and were sent to these parts to intermingle with their people, and to introduce metallurgy and efficient agriculture. Gradually, the level of output of these areas rose; and there was also great progress in the west, in Szechuan, where people lived from fruit cultivation.

The emperor thus extended his frontiers, and, now, millions of people were already working in the land that is now our country. They had a common form of writing, a common culture, and an economy which, thanks to the unification of the means of transport, was marked by division of labour. China at this time became the greatest empire in the world.

THE CH'IN TYRANNY IN THE PEKING VERSION

The people bore all the burden of *corvées*, taxes and conscription. Men worked hard, but still went hungry, and women wove, but still had nothing to wear. The number of men sent off to war on the borders was constantly increased; hundreds of thousands of people – over 700,000 – were employed in building palaces and tombs, but since they were not enough, thousands of free citizens were conscripted as well. The situation grew worse when Ch'in was succeeded by his son. Many people could tolerate it no longer, and hanged themselves from the trees. The slightest dereliction made them 'criminals', and the slightest misdemeanour earned the harshest of punishments. If a man transgressed, the state might execute his family, and if the family resisted, the whole village could be executed.

During the last years of the reign, prisoners and 'criminals' in convoy were blocking the roads. Each year, thousands of cases had to be tried and dealt with; people found it more and more difficult to bear the tyranny, and hated the government.

The old nobles of the recently-destroyed military monarchies were eager to recover their autonomy and independence, and people tried every means to escape the state's tyranny. An uprising became inevitable.

It was the first great popular uprising of Chinese history. The peasants were led by Cheng-Sheng and Wu-Kwang, in 209, when the emperor's son went campaigning. The revolt broke out when 900 peasants were working at forced labour. A great rain-fall blocked the road for them, and they could not continue; the whole convoy could not carry out its task according to the timetable, and the workers knew that, if it was late, they would be killed: each man felt execution hanging over him. Cheng-Sheng and Wu-Kwang, who headed the convoy, decided to revolt. They murdered the government functionaries escorting them on the task, summoned the 900 convicts and offered them hope instead of marching on to a certain death. They became generals of the peasants, and organized an army; as they spread out over the countryside, they soon won over the peasants of all parts of the land; the old nobles and scholars at once joined in; there were revolts in each of the provinces, and soon half of the country had risen.

The people's army moved towards the heart of the empire, and the further it advanced, the more peasants joined it. When it came to within a few miles of the capital, it had 1,000 chariots and several hundred thousand men – this high tide of rebellion occurring within two months of the initial uprising. The government panicked, and turned its own prisoners into soldiers to fight the rebels. Cheng-Sheng himself was, sadly, killed by conspirators, and Wu-Kwang died in battle.

They were succeeded by Liu-Pang and Hsiang-Hu, and it was they who won the final victory. The capital, together with the dynasty, fell. Soon after the emperor's fall, Liu-Pang proclaimed the abolition of all the inhumane Ch'in laws, and won the people's unanimous support, although he and Hsiang-Hu then wrangled as to which should inherit the throne. Hsiang-Hu was beaten, and killed himself, and in 202 Liu-Pang became emperor, founding the Han dynasty, with his capital as Sian.

These events are treated rather differently in the school-books of the Republic of China, at Taipei.

THE TAIWAN VERSION OF CH'IN SHI HUANG-TI'S INTERNAL POLITICS

With the destruction of the six former rival states (the warlord kingdoms) Ch'in Shi Huang-Ti founded a united empire such as had never previously existed. He saw this as a tremendous achievement, for which the title of king no longer sufficed, and so he declared himself emperor and imagined that he could rule as such for ever. To improve the government and to fore-stall rebellion, he was very active. He suppressed the old fiefs and substituted for them a new system of governorships, div-iding the country into thirty-six provinces which were then sub-divided into districts, cantons, *ting* and villages. None of the new functionaries was appointed for life, and all could be dismissed at any time; all power lay in the hands of the emperor.

He wished the newly formed empire to be united and made uniform, so he constructed a universal system of weights, measures, currency and writing. The effect of these measures was that, culturally and politically, China became one great indissoluble organism; this was of decisive significance for generations to come.

He confiscated the weaponry of the various kingdoms and had it melted down and made into bells, and into twelve giant statues of solid gold, which were placed in his palace. One hundred and twenty thousand former nobles were deported to the capital, where it was easier to supervise them. This new stability caused the court to flourish. He created a vast system of roads, the two chief ones leading out from Ksieng-Yang, one to the east and the old Ti and Shantung kingdoms, and the other towards the south, and the kingdoms of Wu and Chou, and Tian-Nang. If there were rebellions in these areas, it would therefore be easier to restore order.

The expedition to subdue the Hsiung-Nu and the southern barbarians

Ever since the time of the warlord kings, the Hsiung-Nu had been the scourge of the petty northern kings. The emperor sent Meng-Ti to fight them and recover the lands they had seized. At the same time, to repel foreign invasions, he linked up all the sections of the Great Wall, which from that time on was famous throughout Chinese history. At this time, too, all the known lands beyond were attached to China – in the east, as far as Korea, in the south, present-day Vietnam, in the west, Kwang-Si and in the north the mountains of Inchan: the future map of China had been drawn.

The end of the empire

All of these measures were taken in response to the needs of the hour, but they were an important contribution to the formation of the Chinese state. All other measures were, however, tyrannical, and were universally condemned.

To control public opinion, the emperor resolved at the suggestion of his minister Li-Si to burn all the existing books of the time except those on medicine and water-divining: they were all consumed over twenty-three days, which, given our ancient patrimony, was an irreparable loss. To show that he would not tolerate dissension, he had nearly 400 Confucian and Taoist scholars buried alive. His eldest son, Fu-Su, criticized him for these excesses and was exiled to the north as inspector of the army.

The emperor exploited his people without mercy, for he stepped up the *corvées* and taxes, and made life intolerable. Three hundred thousand men were sent off to fight in the north, and 500,000 in the south. To build the Great Wall and the roads, palaces and tombs, he employed the forced labour of huge numbers of peasants: merely to construct his own palace and tomb involved 700,000 people. All his enterprises were undertaken through the blood and sweat of the people, and sometimes even their lives. Their hardships became increasingly intolerable, and the slightest opportunity might mean the dynasty's end. The opportunity came during the reign of the second Ch'in emperor and his minister, Zhao-Kao. He had been ruling for thirty-seven years, had been touring the country and had contracted an illness. His son, Fu-Su, was in the north, and only his young son, Hu-Hai continued to follow him. The emperor had his ministers write to order Fu-Su to return to the capital to succeed to the throne, but he died before the letter was finished, and his ministers, anxious to keep power, sent a letter which falsely ordered the son to kill himself, in his father's name. Then they placed the young Hu-Hai on the throne.

Hu-Hai was inexperienced and had not his father's grasp. He was even more cruel and despotic; he continued the building that his father had started, and raised a huge number of horses and animals, and so needed a vast amount of fodder, which was confiscated within a radius of 300 *Li*. People starved to death, and could stand it no more. A revolutionary movement was born.

Cheng-Sheng and Wu-Kwang were the first to rebel and they were helped by nearly all the soldiers of a whole region. The nobles of all the former six kingdoms supported the rebels so as to restore their former sovereigns. The most famous among these were Liu-Pang and Hsiang-Hu, who each commanded part of the army. Zhao-Kao had not told the emperor that the revolt had occurred, and when Liu-Pang's army came to the capital, the emperor bitterly reproached him. Zhao-Kao killed the emperor, and replaced him with a cousin, who was named king, not emperor. Shortly afterwards, when Liu-Pang entered the capital, the new king surrendered, but he too was killed when Hsiang-Hu burned down the Great Palace and looted its treasures. Then Hsiang-Hu retired towards the eastern part of the country. There was a conflict between the two conquerors which ended in Liu-Pang's victory. It was the beginning of the Han dynasty.

THE DIFFERENCES

The odd thing about these versions is their similarity. The structure of the accounts is the same, and so are the sub-divisons; only two anecdotes are different. However, the Peking book does not specify that the persecutions were aimed at the adherents of Confucianism and Taoism – to which there is a clear modern parallel.

The Marxist element is only present in appearance, in the chapter-headings. There are chapters entitled 'From slavery to feudalism' and, later on, 'The Ch'in empire, a centralized and tyrannical feudal state'. The despotism, here and in the Taipei book, is obvious enough, but the feudal side is much harder to see. The impression given is rather that the Ch'in state harshly attacked feudalism in the shape of the warlord-kings and that the centralization turned China into a bureaucratic state. It would appear that feudalism was collapsing or at least had begun to decline, whereas ideology maintains that it lasted a good deal longer. Instead of having it end with the Han dynasty, which is implicit in the Taipei textbook, the Peking version makes it start then. To this typically historicist account of the facts, Marxist historians in China have added a more sociological analysis of the peasant revolts. The facts can therefore be 'subsumed'.

HISTORY: SQUARING THE CIRCLE

Marxist historians therefore distinguish several types of peasant war. The first type is the simple, inconsequential revolt, of which there were thousands in Chinese history. The Cheng-Sheng uprising, in 209 BC, figures in a second category which is called 'defeated mass-movements', and that also applies to the revolt of Chang-Chueh in AD 184. These movements were organized ones, but they were rapidly beaten. A further type is the peasant war contaminated by the ruling classes, and so turned into movements for change of dynasty, such as the revolt against Wang-Weng, the Sui and the Mongols. Then there are long-term peasant movements, lasting for several centuries, such as the Szechuan upheavals. Finally, come the general and almost permanent peasant movements, which defend the interests of the peasantry and have an egalitarian ideology – thus the risings at the end of the Tang dynasty, the Taiping, etc.

Chinese historians have similarly classified the rebel chieftains. There is, first of all, the isolated hero, such as the noble Hsiang-Hu who did not in any way participate in the life of the masses; then comes the leader of the mass movement, who had his own goal, quite different from that of his peasant followers; there are also leaders who differ from the peasantry but none the less contributed to their organization, such as Li-Mi in 616 and Chung-Siang in 1120. Liu-Pang, whose role we have already noted, belongs to a further category of leaders, who helped the masses to organize but had their own objectives as well, and subsequently turned out to be representatives of feudalism. There is a final category of peasant leaders who fought feudalism in the peasant's name. Such are the Taiping leaders.

The trouble here, as has been seen, is that these movements

always evolve in such a way that 'those who failed are seen as brigands, while those who succeed are acclaimed.' In these conditions, it is difficult to identify 'historical progress', unless the failures are taken as contributions to advancement – here, the labour movement in the West before 1917 is used as an instance – and unless a king can be called 'progressive' even though by definition he will have crushed the peasants and exploited them. This means that Marxist historians must identify emperors who 'cause' historical progress in spite of their class-dictated activities.

James P. Harrison, who has studied this interpretation of peasant wars in Chinese history, concludes that there are two predominant attitudes. Sometimes, given that feudalism is said to have lasted throughout these thousands of years, it is divided into periods, according to various dynasties which all undergo the same evolution: ending in an alternation of the modes of production, so that Marxism and the cyclical view of history go hand in hand. Most historians resolve the problem differently: they assert that there was progress in the evolution of peasant wars, in the sense that they moved on from being a simple fight against a particular feudal noble or dynasty and become, even in the mid-Tang era, a struggle against the feudal system itself. Thus the first wars caused progress in production for they opposed the *corvée* and excessive seigneurial dues; then feudalism entered upon a period of decline and the peasants attacked its very foundations, the rules of land tenure and the basic inequalities.

This picture of the past is difficult to sustain, and holds up only in so far as Mao's thought and vision of history were predominant enough to support it. If another version of this history is worked out once Mao's 'errors' have been condemned, there will be an inevitable problem. How can the determinist vision of history, which is supposed to legitimize the present regime, be reconciled with the regime's own policies, which continually appeal to voluntarism and encounter so many acts of resistance among the people?

12

HISTORY IN JAPAN: A CODE OR AN IDEOLOGY?

JAPAN: A BRIEF CHRONOLOGY

660 BC	Mythical date of the foundation of the Empire by Jimmu.
4th C. AD	Legendary adventures of Yamato no Takeru.
5th–6th C.	Foundation and crisis of the state of Yamato.
Mid-6th C.	Introduction of Buddhism.
604	The Regent Shotoku promulgates a code establishing a bureaucracy.
607	First Japanese embassy to China.
7th–8th C.	Consolidation of the bureaucratic monarchy.
710–720	Compilation of the chronicles on the legendary past of Japan.
752	At the temple of Todai, a ceremony unites Shintoism and Buddhism.
Mid-8th C.	Formation of social classes: the court aristocracy, the monastic clergy, the peasants and the intermediary class of warriors (*bushi*).

794	Foundation of Kyoto.
9th C.	Submission of the 'peoples of the North'.
9th–10th C.	The Fujiwara clan monopolizes functions at the Imperial Court.
901	Exile of Sugawara no Mishizane who was thwarting them.
End of 11th C.	The 'retired' emperors attempt to emancipate themselves from the tutelage of the Fujiwara.
12th C.	Conflicts of interest between the warrior clans Minamato, Taira, etc.
1189	Suicide of Yoshitsune who had triumphed over the Taira.
1192	Minamoto Yoritomo founds the regime of warriors (Bakufu) of which he is the Shogun.
1221	Vain attempt of the emperors to regain power.
1274–1281	Repulsion of the Mongol invasions.
13th C.	Zen, a new Buddhist sect, spreads especially among the warriors.
1333–36	Restoration of imperial power, the so-called 'Kemmu' Restoration.
Second half of 14th C.	Southern Court versus Northern Court.
15th C.	Rapid economic development; patronage of Yoshimasa who builds the Silver Pavilion.
1467–77	New feudal wars, the so-called Onin Wars; elimination of the great clans.
End of 15th C., beginning of 16th C.	Peasant revolts, maritime expansion and spread of far-reaching piracy; development of cities.
1543	First contact with the Portuguese, who introduce firearms.
1549	Francis-Xavier in Japan; within thirty years, there are 150,000 Christians.

Second half of 16th C.	Toyotomi Hideyoshi reunites the country by force, and disarms the peasants.
1615	Tokugawa Ieyasu imposes his law following protracted inter-clan wars; he founds the Bakufu of Edo (1615–1853).
1600–40	Policy of progressively closing Japan to foreigners; Christianity forbidden. Neo-Confucianism becomes the official philosophy.
1660	Birth of a historical school favourable to the restoration of the emperor.
1701	Episode of the 47 Ronin.
c.1750	Rise in the price of rice, peasant revolts.
First half of 19th C.	Spread of peasant revolts.
1853	Arrival of Admiral Perry (USA).
1858	Signature of the Unequal Treaties.
1868	Meiji Restoration; the Shogun surrenders his powers.
1877	Satsuma rebellion; suicide of Saigo Takamori.
1889	Promulgation of the Meiji Constitution. Policy of modernization and westernization of Japan.
1894–95	Military victory of Japan over China, treaty of Shimonoseki.
1902	Treaty of Anglo-Japanese alliance.
1904–05	Russo-Japanese War; victory of Japan.
1914	Japan participates in the First World War.
1923	Washington Conference: limits Japanese naval armaments.
1930 onwards	Militarization of the regime.
1931	The Manchuria 'incident', 'Manchukuo' detached from China.
1937	Invasion of China.

1941	Pearl Harbor, Japan enters the war: fall of Singapore.
1945	Use of kamikazes, suicide-planes arousing the spirit of sacrifice. Atomic bombs dropped on Japan. Japan capitulates.
1946	Emperor Hirohito renounces his divine descent.
1952	San Francisco Peace Treaty (excluding the USSR).
1960 onwards	Leftist and anti-American protests.
1970	Hara-kiri of Mishima Yukio, after his failure to obtain a restoration of imperial power.
1972 onwards	Rapid expansion of Japanese exports.

Question: It is often said that our country is superior to others, and so deserves respect. On what is this judgement based?

Answer: That is a very good question, but to answer it briefly is impossible; I can only give you the ingredients for an answer. We all know that our monarchs descend from the gods, and have ruled over us, in hundreds, without a break. In China and other foreign lands even a simple subject can kill his master and proclaim himself emperor and king. Similarly, a king can be induced to abdicate, and if he refuses, he can be compelled; otherwise, emperors can be replaced by more modest figures. Such cases are strikingly obvious in other countries' history, but not in Japan, where nothing of this sort has ever taken place since the earliest times. Here, the status of the ruler and his subjects is fixed for eternity.

What is curious in these words, which identify history and myth, is of course that everything is quite untrue. The Fujiwara replaced their predecessors by force; two courts co-existed at the end of the fourteenth century; successful and unsuccessful efforts at usurpation are the very body of Japanese history.

However, the function of education is not to reveal what actually happened:

> its aim is to encourage patriotism, to identify the people with the doings of the emperor. . . . Our children must be taught the continuity of Japanese history, the glorious achievements of the emperors and the actions of their loyal subjects . . . so that they can know the phases of the country's past . . . and learn what a privilege it is to be Japanese.

THE AIMS OF EDUCATION

Japan is not the only country where the aims of education are so openly declared. In France, the constitution of 1791 expected 'education to bear a spirit of fraternity among citizens and to bind them to constitution, country and laws.' Napoleon, later on, was even more explicit: 'the duty of schools is to teach Catholicism and loyalty towards the emperor, and to produce citizens devoted to church, state and family.' More such instances could be quoted. Even so, there are few countries where, as in the France of the Third Republic, the goal was attained of making school textbooks, in Karasawa Tomitaro's words, 'the foundation of the nation' (1960).

The position adopted by the Japanese state is similar. Debates over school textbooks are necessarily violent, as they were in France under the Third Republic; indeed, they are more violent, to judge from what happened after the publication of a book by Ienaga Saburo, whom the government asked to make changes and deletions with thirty-eight additions, because he had not found any 'justification' for Japanese intervention in the war in 1941. The violence of the debate is above all explained by the fact that school textbooks have been nationalized since 1903, are few in number – perhaps ten, according to Wray – and are also standardized so that the plurality associated with democracy is non-existent. Besides, history, at primary school and in the popular memory, is linked with other disciplines: morality, geography, and study of language. Together, these four form the *kokutai*, i.e. the required version of the nation, its character and its past.

The text quoted comes from a book of morality written at the beginning of the twentieth century. The same ideas, formulated differently, come up in books on language or geography. Here they are, in a history-book version.

> In accordance with the wishes of the goddess Amaterasu, Japan must have only one imperial line of descent from the beginning to the end of time. The emperor cannot be overthrown or the dynasty interrupted. The nation must be fused in a common will around the family of state and be united in the ideas of filial piety and loyalty. This structure is peculiar to Japan and unique in the world. It makes Japan a country cherished by the gods. In all other countries the absence of *kokutai* produces crises, revolutions, periods of decadence and phases when the state is questioned, i.e. with radical ideologies. Such ideologies, in Japan's case, would be an aberration. Throughout the world rulers are usually to be seen as models of wisdom, virtue and power, qualities that are beyond their capacity. That is why they fall, and why the masses take over and rule. In Japan, it is different. The emperor, who descends from the gods, is venerated by the people, who know that he is the only true sovereign and cannot therefore share power. The country may undergo evolution, but not revolution. The restoration of the Meiji is a good example of this: the return of imperial power meant also a step forward in modernization.

This nation is seen as an enormous family, founded by the emperor, who is to be obeyed as a father, since the descendants of the sovereign family constitute the Japanese nation. The emperor's subjects are united with him by a mythical blood-tie, a moral attachment and a filial duty. Thereby, history becomes a definition of the various types of relationship that subjects have with their sovereigns. It is a moralizing history, based on Confucius's categories – loyalty, obedience, abnegation, stories of princes and 'great men'.

In reality, this vision of history, as in other countries, has undergone variations, especially since the end of the Second World War. Still, at least in primary education, it has remained substantially unaltered and has been strengthened by other disciplines, such as morality and geography. For many years the study of history was compulsory only in the primary schools; hence the text below is a primary-school one, demonstrating a universally-experienced education. The chosen text is that most widely-used on the eve of war, and was therefore the book best-known to the Japanese now aged from forty to seventy, i.e. the active and dominant sections of society. It does of course present the most traditional version of Japanese history: great changes have taken place since 1945 (to be examined below) but this is by far the most popular, or rather, the most firmly-entrenched version.

As regards the origins of Japanese history, it produces the kokutai ideology, which did undergo reappraisal at the beginning of the twentieth century, but returned subsequently (from roughly 1923 to 1945), which is itself a problem to be discussed in due course. It is interesting to examine some aspects of this history, dealing with the early stages of Japan (Yamato), the age of the Codes, of bureaucratic monarchy, and the Japanese Middle Ages.

HISTORY AND LEGEND

After Emperor Jimmu had taken the throne, imperial power was gradually extended throughout Yamato (the old name for

Japan). But in provinces far from the capital, there were still many evil-doers who oppressed the people. In the reign of the twelfth emperor, Keiko, the Kumaso, who lived in the south of Kyu-Shu, rebelled, and the emperor sent his son O-Usuno to put them down. His was a nature of energy and great strength, though he was only sixteen. The head of the Kumaso, Kawakami-no-Takeru, never imagined that O-Usuno would come, and he spent his time drinking *sake* in frivolous company. Prince O-Usuno let down his hair, looked like a young girl, and so managed to approach Takeru; he unsheathed his sabre and pierced Takeru's chest. 'What strength!' said the dying Takeru, in surprise. 'You are the strongest warrior in Japan. Take the name "Yamato-no-Takeru"' ('the bravest of Yamato'). At that, he died. . . . Then, when the Ezo revolted, the emperor sent his son to defeat them. O-Usuno was overjoyed at this task, and went, first of all, to gather his strength at the sanctuary of Kodai-Jingu in Ise, where he was given the Sword that Gathers the Clouds, and then made off towards the east. . . . When he reached his destination, he was deceived by the evil-doers of this region, who invited him to a stag-hunt in a vast plain. The traitors set fire to the grass so as to harm the prince. But he took out his divine sabre, scythed the grass around him and swept it away. . . . The evil-doers fell back and collapsed in the flames they had caused. Thereafter, the sabre was called 'the Sabre that cuts Grass'. . . . The Ezo were abashed at such strength, and gave in. But the prince, once back in the capital, fell ill and died. He was of a noble character, and always shared warriors' sufferings; since earliest youth he took no rest, and it was at the very moment when he was about to ascend the throne – for, through him, the country had become calm – that he died.

This story introduces the first of the legendary heroes of Japanese history. Ivan Morris, in *The Nobility of Failure*, described and analysed the tragic existence of this story's main characters: Yamato no Takeru is a composite character who, in *The Annals of Japan*, goes back 'to the century of enigma', the fourth century AD.

This document, written for children, omits an episode in the prince's boyhood. In response to his father, Emperor Keiko, who wondered why his elder brother was not at the imperial table – regular attendance at meals being a sign of loyalty – he punished his brother by murdering him in the lavatory. . . . 'Horrified at his son's brutal and bold nature', the emperor sent him off to fight the Kumaso, 'where he would find an outlet for his zeal'. The textbook also omits an act of disloyalty committed by Yamato no Takeru. In a reprisal raid against rebels, he swore an oath of friendship with their chief, made a sword out of wood, proposed jokingly to exchange swords for a duel, and then quickly took advantage of the exchange to kill the chief. He then celebrated his victory by writing a poem in which he mocked at 'the rebel of the wooden sword.'

Despite these omissions, and some others, the story of Yamato no Takeru has retained its structure and original significance: the hero who fulfils his duty towards the emperor and falls before attaining his goal, which, at the point of death, is to succeed his father. 'Is it because my father desires my premature death that he continually sends me off to fight?' he cries, showing the tragic destiny of the hero, the sense of a life devoted to total obedience and loyalty towards the sovereign. Back home, he dies, consumed by illness and melancholy, alone with his destiny. He is to disappear, without having reigned or even seen his father to tell him that the final mission had succeeded. 'Then', says legend, 'he turned into a white bird, which came out of the grave and flew away.'

THE MORAL OF HISTORY

Pierre-François Souyri has remarked that in Japanese history books, for the whole period before the Meiji, chapter headings use only the names of 'good' characters, whose moral qualities the books underline. People seen as incompetent, despotic or treacherous do not have the right to such honour, even when the telling of their deeds takes up a good part of the chapter. For instance, after the 'good' reign of the regent Shotoku Tayishi, who governed the country intelligently and established the first relations with China (592–622), the era of the Soga, a despotic clan, is not mentioned except with reference to the men who defeated the clan, the crown prince and the Soga's rivals, who resorted to murder to be rid of them: 'Nakatomi no Kamatari became the emperor Tengi. He visited his friend Kamatari who was dying; it was a sign of great honour and conferred on the family the name Fujiwara.'

The capital was modelled on the Chinese example. This 'Nara' period was prosperous, and the capital was embellished with splendid works of art. There were good monks such as Gyoki, who built temples and canals, and bad monks such as Dokyo, who was hungry for power and wished to replace the emperor. Meanwhile, 'the sister of Kioyomara, a faithful servant, was moved by sentiments of devotion and charity and so gave her life to the education of foundlings.'

The emperor Kammu moved his capital to Kyoto, which had a magnificent setting, and was bigger than Nara. Kyoto, then called Keian-Kyo, was laid out like a chess-board, after the example of the great Chinese capitals. The court entrusted Tamuramaro, who was appointed shogun, with the task of pacifying the Ezo (794). In this period the monk Saicho founded the great monastery of the Tendai sect.

In the ninth and tenth centuries, the Fujiwara clan took all power at court by monopolizing the offices and functions. The emperors tried to free themselves from Fujiwara authority.

> The fifty-ninth emperor, Uda, tried every means to confine the growing power of the Fujiwara, and relied particularly on Sugawara no Mishizane to weaken them. Mishizane was from a family of scholars. Since earliest youth, he had been a passionate student and even at the age of eleven or twelve he had composed poems and astonished everyone. He became a very learned man. Then, being good and just, he took court service and became the confidant of the emperor.

It was Sugawara no Mishizane's task to end the clan's monopoly of power. In fact, as we shall see, he failed. None the less, he had an important role. He refused the ambassadorship that the emperor offered him, saying that in view of the present decline of the Tang it was no longer necessary to pay them homage. Consequently, we can date the moment when Japan became completely autonomous from her powerful neighbour from the time of Sugawara no Mishizane. In fact this was more true in cultural than political terms, for Sugawara also masterminded the promotion of Japanese writing, which was dissociated, even as a scholarly language, from Chinese, the language in which all literary works had been composed.

This political aspect of Sugawara's life, which might be regarded as having the utmost importance, is not even mentioned in the historical book: instead, it stresses the exceptional nature of the ties linking Sugawara no Mishizane and the emperor – his fidelity even in disgrace and injustice, and his ancestors' poetry – for these are the characteristics that posterity remembers and that account for the revered memory of Sugawara.

THE FUNCTION AND REALITY OF HISTORICAL COMMENT ON THE MIDDLE AGES

This work of edification featured one of the figures noted for his devotion to the emperor. The story of prince Yamato no Takeru leads to another similar story. It is all as if historical commentary is meant to be only a description of acts of loyalty and devotion, the moral problems that these posed, and an indication of the right paths to follow, in which Confucian morality is inter-mingled with the chronicle of the past. The sense of duty took tragic form in Yamato no Takeru: he had killed his brother and accepted his own sacrifice. The story of Sugawara no Mishizane vaunted the virtues of meditation and austere, poetic sacrifice, despite the ingratitude of rulers. The stories on the Minamoto clan's rise to power and the shattering rebellion of the Taira are also mentioned in moral terms, to supply different instances of characters distinguished either by filial piety or by devotion to the emperor.

THE PRINCIPLE OF LEGITIMACY AND HISTORICAL ALLIANCES

The virtues of courage, loyalty, abnegation and determination are those most revered; conversely, selfishness, ostentatiousness and greed are the vices held up to obloquy. Clearly, neither the vices nor the virtues are attributed altogether accidentally. It is a matter not just of morality, but rather of the very legitimacy of the imperial power, which must be secured.

Imperial power had continually weakened since the age of the Codes in the later seventh century. The weakening accelerated in the Fujiwara era, when power was transferred from the emperor to the court aristocracy, and the decline went on when the military nobility, the *bushi* – Minamoto, Taira, etc. – took over. The *Bakafu*, who opposed the knights' regime, forged an interpretation of history by which legitimacy in Japan would mean a return to the old system, i.e. power should be given back to an effective bureaucracy, supervised by the emperor. This idea almost succeeded in the period of the 'withdrawn' emperors of the eleventh century; it did succeed, but only for a moment, following the 'Kemmu Restoration' of 1333–36.

These chapters deal only with such problems, and the rest of the book is the same. They do not bother with other aspects of Japanese life, such as the cultural apogee under the Fujiwara: the book is only concerned with matters of legitimacy. The same applies to later periods. In the fifteenth century, for instance, the age of 'the great warrior' is glorified, as also happens in film, for Kurosawa, for instance, devoted one of his masterpieces, *Kagemusha* (*The Shadow Warrior*) to Takeda Shingen. Even so, neither the economic advance of this era, nor maritime expansion (in particular, the success of long-range piracy) nor the advances of the horticultural art, nor the creation of Nô theatre, are mentioned, except in so far as their existence reinforced the legitimacy of the sovereign, at other periods. There is no mention even of the northern court, rivalling the southern one: that would be to question the principle of *kokutai*. The West has also experienced such tampering with historical truth – for instance, when the Holy See concealed the existence of antipopes.

These characteristics are found far less often in modern works, especially in illustrated books where the drawings, by their nature, require wider coverage of Japanese architecture, art, customs and other aspects of daily life.

None the less, traces of the old remain, even now, as can be seen in the history books, the aim of which is to show that the imperial restoration of 1868 was welcome, and a renewal of Japan after 700 years of warrior-regime: it was wanted by everyone, and when the emperor Meiji arrived in Tokyo the people, all along the road, venerated the procession and wept for 'gratitude and joy'. Not a word is said here of the 180 or so

popular upheavals that were officially recorded after the restoration, between 1868 and 1874. This restoration had been
'desired by the gods' and so was legitimate: since it maintained
peace and furthered progress, it also represented the Confucian
theory of the 'divine Mandate'. History as taught to children was
designed not only to foster loyalty and self-sacrifice, but also to
equate the rulers with divinity.

THE BREACH

Most of these excerpts show a continual need to glorify certain
values that have remained constant in the presentation of Japanese history in children's and young adults' textbooks. Loyalty
towards the emperor is seen as vitally important for the national
will, and the emperor is not only the symbol of state but also its
essence – i.e. the belief in Japan's superiority (which geography
books also glorify) and, for the recent centuries of Japanese
history, the certainty that modernization is good, provided that
the particular characteristics of Japanese civilization are
respected. It would however be incorrect to believe that these are
the only values to be reinforced. They are of course the basis of
these stories of the most distant past; but for later periods, from
the era of feudalism onwards, they are joined or replaced by
other value-systems, with which they have been in conflict ever
since the great revolution of 1868, and which show two con-
trasting aspects of Japanese history, one or other of which,
according to circumstances, has prevailed. We owe to H. J. Wray
an account of this evolution.

The first of these movements, formed at the turn of the century, links purely Japanese values with those of the West. The
movement prevailed until after the victory over Russia, when it
receded before a return to specifically Japanese virtues. From
1918 to 1933 the two systems balanced out, though the second
prevailed, to explosive effect, during the Second World War. The

first movement came to the fore again after 1950 and still prevails today. Where do they still clash, and how do they fit in with the still-existing *kokutai*?

The main characteristic of the new ideas that emerged around 1900, and nowadays prevail, is their glorification of individual merit, which rates as highly as birth and seniority of age. The underlying idea is that only an individualistic society can be inventive and truly modern. The foreigners mentioned as examples are Benjamin Franklin and D'Aguesseau, who calculated how not to waste time in daily life. The English doctor, Jenner, is cited for vaccinating his fellow-citizens against smallpox despite the reigning scepticism and hostility towards him. Such courage is 'real', we are told, i.e. there exist virtues other than the martial one of the military, who do not have a monopoly of patriotism and public service. Other foreign instances are Edison and Columbus, who 'overcame their poverty' and all the other obstacles of established society.

An idea thus emerges that national progress depends on individuals' progress for the whole of society's good; that the past is no longer to serve as an example for comparison, since, in it, there reigned inequality, arrogance, injustice and *Samurai* brutality.

The stress on western ideas is balanced by an omission of Asia which appears only in negative terms: Japan alone is a country with a proper constitution and a parliament. She is recognized by the West as a modern country. Since the start of the twentieth century, Great Britain has been the inspiring example, for she combined political democracy with economic efficiency. Before 1950, Germany was similarly highly-regarded, for her hygiene, high technological development, industry and army. America is admired for her vast cities, wealth and productive capacity. Up to 1950 France hardly came into the picture – 'she was once a highly cultured country but has now declined, although her cloth, wine and monuments deserve respect.'

THE REACTION AGAINST RESPECT FOR THE WEST

Although society was glorified on account of its members' achievements, there was a critical element. To see what this criticism portended, you need only compare the preface of a book published in 1903 which states that 'Everyone must improve himself' with that of a book of 1910 or 1942, where citizens are no longer individual factors: 'Our country is an enormous family, and just as our children owe us respect, so we owe respect to the emperor.' This is a constant feature, as I have suggested, but there are changes in its implications – filial devotion towards the emperor becomes glorification of the state which, together with the emperor, is seen as more important than society. Loyalty, patriotism, veneration of ancestors are no longer dissociated; the cultural heritage supplants innovation; no longer is social progress even mentioned. Above all, the sea and war are stressed, especially between 1937 and 1945. The Japanese become 'the children of the sea' and martial virtues, the Bushido, are vaunted as never before.

Among foreign examples there figures Darwin, with 'the survival of the fittest'. Akira Iriye wrote that 'We must make our way alone, for we have no friends.' He went on:

> Advance, advance, never retreat/Your ageing father has this one hope/That you serve the country faithfully/And give his house the honour of filial virtue/Take care of yourself, says your mother/She has only one wish/Take care of your health in the army/So that if you die it will be for Japan.

Women, hitherto unmentioned, thus suddenly make an appearance, though only to glorify the warrior.

> A sailor is weeping. He is rebuked by an officer, and shows a letter from his mother to say she is ashamed her son has not

yet fought: 'I cannot look my neighbours in the face,' she says. The officer apologizes, and remarks that today's wars do not let men die as they would like.

There is strong reaction against any hint of criticism. 'Japan does not have to try to be a great country: she is one.' She figures as one of the great powers of the world, and in the past she was also great. The age of the Tokugawa, until then considered as obscurantist, becomes a brilliant historical period, with scholars and mathematicians such as Seki who are equal to the greatest scholars of the West. The foreigner no longer merits praise: Shanghai is 'noisy', London 'congested', Cairo 'torrid'. Darwinism does make its appearance, doubtless because it seems to justify the rise of Japan, though also for casting doubt on the Christian view of man, so that two problems are dealt with at one stroke. Christianity is even accused of every vice, including the anarchy that reigned in the Sengoku era just before the rise of the Tokugawa. Germany becomes the most admired European power for although 'like Japan she has no colonies, she became powerful.' The heroes of history are men such as Yoshida Shoin, the champion of loyalty at the time of Perry, Toyotomi Hideyoshi, Admiral Togo and especially General Nogi.

He had lost his two sons in the Russo-Japanese War, and committed suicide, together with his wife, when the signal was given for the emperor's burial-service to start. As a child he was a weakling, and vulnerable, but he overcame all of his natural handicaps, took icecold baths, walked from Tokyo to Osaka at the age of ten, never complained about his food and constantly went to meditate at the graves of the forty-seven Ronin who gave their lives for their country.

During the war, these attitudes became extreme and the values of the West were no longer simply questioned but were explicitly repudiated. With the 'invasion' of Asia by America and Europe, anything that might vindicate it was forbidden – even the Bible, and Toynbee's *Study of History* as well as Karl Marx and Bertrand Russell. There was systematic silence as to western countries. Japan was 'created by the gods, ruled by them, and is protected by them.' She owes everything to her own efforts, and from abroad only threats and challenges have come. Foreigners have only humiliated Japan, and there have been many occasions in history when Japan has lost opportunities because of frustration by Europe and America – thus the Treaty of Shimonoseki in 1895, when foreign arbitration prevented Japan from capitalizing her victory over China; then in 1905, when the USA similarly prevented Japan from exploiting her victory at Tsushima, when she defeated Russia in 'the greatest naval battle of all time' (the Peace of Portsmouth); finally in 1923, when the Washington Conference placed a limitation on the Japanese navy.

This rejection of the West now appeared as an essential theme, and Ashikaga Yoshimitsu, who became a tributary of China, was now seen as a traitor – collaboration between Japan and China must not involve such a relationship, for they are countries with a similar structure 'and all rice-producing countries should help each other.' To appreciate this, 'compare the tolerant policy of Japan towards China at the beginning of this century and the authoritarian ways of the Russians in Soviet Mongolia.' Japanese aggression in China thus becomes a humanitarian act and of course precedents are found in which still more ancestors come to light in a heroic role. First, Yamada Nagasama, who founded a Japanese city in 1620 and protected the Thai king from all kinds of threat; then Hamada Yahyoe, a brave sea-captain who expelled the Portuguese and Dutch from Taiwan, 'for they had gone so far as to check Japanese cargoes and levy taxes on them'; and finally Hideyoshi, who had always counted as a hero but who now becomes even more heroic as founder of Japanese influence in Korea. Japan, as custodian of Asia, and Europe as the eternal aggressor; such was the history taught during the war. For good measure, we even hear that the Chinese constructed a Great Wall so as to protect themselves in advance from the Russians.

THE TRIVIALIZATION OF HISTORY

After the atom bomb and the fall of Japan in 1945, the books were again changed in content. When America intervened and supervised the country, books were purged of passages glorifying kokutai, militarism, martial and nationalist virtues On the other hand, democracy and parliament were held up as ideals. Since then, the books no longer start with the goddess Amaterasu, but rather with prehistoric man and the Iron Age. Sovereign and state appear only with the Codes (late seventh century) and no reference is made to the foundation myths, even though they survive here and there as stories. They are of course fixed in popular consciousness because of other ways of chronicling, whether Nô theatre, stories, Shinto practices and traditions, or, especially, the cinema. All of these, in their way, ensure the survival of kokutai.

In the 1960s, democratic, socialist and even Marxist ideologies gained the upper hand. Attention was paid as in China to the peasant revolts of the pre-Meiji era, and later to the strikes and labour movement, while the same kind of repression as occurred in Germany has ensured that the causes of the Second World War and the war itself are simply summarized and, even today, have two pages out of 168 in one book.

Since 1962 traditional elements have contested this reevaluation of history and the dismantling of kokutai. Their position is difficult to maintain, since it was these traditional forces that collaborated most eagerly with the Americans, whereas the Left mobilized opinion against 'the occupier'. The Left could not be accused of treason, as happened between 1930 and 1945; instead, authors of school-books have been attacked for 'ideologizing' history, i.e. shifting it to the Left. The traditional elements seem to think that history was neutral when it relied on myth and served to legitimate the state.

Feuding has gone on ever since between the supporters of these various views of history. But the historians, though divided among themselves, are gradually pushing on towards the objectivization of historical knowledge, and have insisted more and more on quantitative analysis of economic progress, typology of social conflicts, and, as well, the individuality of Japanese civilization.

13

DECONSTRUCTING 'WHITE HISTORY': THE USA

The overthrow of old dynasties, the rise of new ones, and the most important revolutions have had quite trivial consequences compared with those of the discovery of America. . . . The consequences of the greatest victories have not, generally, brought happiness to humanity, or an improvement in the human condition: rather the reverse, whereas the discovery of America had beneficial results, though not uniformly. In South America we know how many centuries have passed since the Conquest. . . . It is, however, only too obvious that progress, the extension of literature and the arts have been slowed down by the inability of the Spaniards to generate a spirit of enterprise, owing to the excessive ease with which they could acquire gold and silver, the superstition and ignorance of the clergy, and the oppressive ways of religion. The growth of towns shows this. Lima, founded in 1532, has, today, but 52,000 inhabitants; Philadelphia, which was founded in 1682, now has 92,000, and we can foresee that in 1960 the United States will have 462,752,896 citizens, living at ease and enjoying the fruits of happiness and liberty.

So runs the very beginning of the first American history book, intended for 'children and families'. It appeared in 1823, was published by John Prentiss and printed by Keane, of New Hampshire.

THE AMERICANS' PARALLEL OF HISTORY AND LEGEND

This opening passage already displays features that form the most widely-shared American heritage. That heritage was of course to alter, more than elsewhere, and did so dramatically at least twice – at the end of the nineteenth century, and in the 1970s. Still, the main features of this history emerge, even here. The tone is polemical, for Spain and the Catholic church are attacked as incompetent: they wrecked Latin America. Already, we have a myth, of a paradise to be built with sweat and blood: 'The spirit of enterprise requires great self-discipline; only thereby can men bathe in the gentle rays of liberty, and linked by the beneficent laws of a single government, a single constitution, and a single nation stretching from the Atlantic to the Pacific.'

The very first books – the anonymous author from Massachusetts, Ridpath, Anderson and others – divided the history of the United States into five great periods. First, there were 'natives' who descended from the Israelites, then came the Discovery, by Vikings or by Columbus; next, the colonial era, followed by the age of revolution and by the 'national' era. Appendices sometimes dealt with other nations past and present. The Massachusetts author is very succinct as to the history of Assyria and Syria, and devotes half a page to Egypt, Greece, Rome, Carthage, China, the 'Tartars', 'Hindostan', France, Spain, Germany, Russia and England. B. A. Hathaway gives a list of dates at the beginning of his book, and history – as in contemporary Europe – appears as a continuation of religious history, intermingled with legendery.

Creation of the world; Adam and Eve	4004
Birth of Cain	4003
The Flood destroys the old world	2348
Construction of the Tower of Babel	2247
Ninus, the son of Belus, founds the kingdom of Assyria	2059
Joseph dies in Egypt, thus concluding Genesis	1653
Cecrops leads a body of Egyptians to Attica and founds Athens	1556
Miracle of Moses; 600,000 Israelites, 'not counting children' leave Egypt	1491
Olympic Games at Olympia	1453
The Rape of Helen, and start of the Trojan War	1193
Carthage founded by Dido	869
Romulus, first king of the Romans	753
etc.	

In such works, the needs of teaching disrupt the exposition of history's great moments. Hathaway said in 1882 'You must not only know the names of the discoverers or the list of presidents of the United States; you should also know what the Monroe Doctrine stated, and the significance of events and individuals.' His book takes the form of endless questions and answers on the United States. Moral judgments abound.

> *Question:* Why should we admire the Pilgrim Fathers?
> *Answer:* Because they endured sufferings for their faith.
> *Question:* How widespread was religious liberty in Massachusetts?
> *Answer:* Only members of the church were citizens, and the colony was as rigid and intolerant as any sect in Great Britain.

Question: Why should we admire William Penn?

Answer: Because he was kind to the Indians. He was a Quaker, died in 1718 and was a benefactor of humanity.

Question: What led to the foundation of the United States?

Answer: Religious persecution. It brought the Puritans to Massachusetts, the Quakers to Pennsylvania and the Catholics to Maryland.

FROM THE IDEOLOGY OF THE CIVIL WAR TO THAT OF THE 'MELTING-POT'

Until around 1900, history emphasized what had divided the American nation – from the conflicts of the foundation to those between different Christian sects, the confrontation between Jefferson and Hamilton, the Civil War and the great social struggles before 1914.

The Great War revolutionized this situation. Millions of new Americans were integrated with the nation, and a new reality was given, in the trenches, to the ideology of the melting-pot. Past conflicts were relegated and buried, whether they involved ideology or nationality. In fact, people who questioned the American system were considered, after 1918, as 'un-American' – the communists, for instance, being hunted down and treated as outlaws.

Thereafter, the stress lay on things that united the Americans and helped forge the American nation. Past troubles were played down, even the Civil War, the disastrous consequences of which – the destruction of agrarian society in the South, or problems of employment in the North – received greater emphasis than its causes, whether these involved generous notions concerning slave-emancipation or the North's fear that the South, with its cheap labour, was becoming too strongly competitive for the industrial Yankees. The great strikes of 1890–1910, far from being seen as an expression of the class struggle (the general view before 1914), were regarded as the inevitable pangs of a difficult birth, that of the new American society. As Pierre Nora says, it all amounts to a 'history-less history'. But it did have a point: history recorded improvements in the human condition, in the sense of the Founding Fathers – equality, happiness and liberty. Whereas the history of Europe is built on wars, corpses, victors and vanquished, American history, at least from 1918 to the 1970s, is innocent of such ambivalence.

The natives, whether southerners or Indians, did have their eulogists, but not in history. The South found its voice in the novel, with Faulkner, Caldwell and others, and the Indians found theirs in film. The ordinary cinema also profited from this development. It was popular entertainment for people of different dialects, and was therefore simple and direct, meant to be seen and understood by all, Jews, Italians, Greeks, Irish, grandparents and grandchildren alike. It was a cinema of morality that followed a code which was written down and signed by the main Hollywood producers in the 1920s. Films clearly follow the trajectory described above. Any film made on the Civil War, after 1918, was a commercial failure. Birth of a Nation had success in 1915, and it had been preceded by other successes on the Civil War, such as Old Kentucky (1911), Barbara Frietchie (1911) and The Coward (1914), but the films that came after, such as Selig and Churchill's Crisis, failed even though they relied on tested dramatic formulae – a family torn apart, with a Federal father and a Rebel son (or vice versa), a love-affair where a – usually – southern woman falls in love, after initial hatred, with a handsome man from the North, or an old friendship destroyed by 'the worst of scourges', a divided nation.

It was not until 1939 that the theme of Civil War regained popularity, through Gone with the Wind, but this was transitory, since it was the only box-office success of its kind at this time. Even King Vidor's So Red the Rose, which expressed the resentment of southern whites, was a failure, as were Red Badge of Courage and

Shenandoah, although the latter featured James Stewart. What was the case over the Civil War was also true of other problems that divided Americans, particularly the question of the blacks. Most versions of Uncle Tom's Cabin, such as Edison's, of 1903, were made before 1914. Here, an old black servant rejoins his little mistress in heaven, having mourned her on earth; she has become an angel, witnessing the great moments of civil discord in American history – Jefferson and Hamilton, the struggle against the British, and Lincoln's declaration of black emancipation which, as the film shows, was hardly respected. After 1917 very few such films were made so incriminatingly: they occur largely as historical pieces.

Birth of a Nation, juxtaposed with Gone with the Wind, shows quite clearly how one ideology shades into another. The first is based on an evocation of great events and great men. There are many reenacted historic moments: Sherman's march through Georgia, Lee's surrender at Appomatox courthouse, Lincoln's murder, etc. Griffith, reproducing these events, acted as historian: he tried, so he said, to be impartial and objective. His script is, however, explicitly racialist and ideologically committed. For instance, evil is represented by Austin Stoneman, a shady deputy with a black mistress who 'wants to subject southern whites to the blacks.' His punishment comes when a mulatto, whom he has promoted to be lieutenant of Carolina, wants his daughter's hand in marriage: when the father refuses, the girl is raped. A young member of the Ku Klux Klan appears as the avenger of liberty. Twenty-five years later, in his adaptation of Margaret Mitchell's novel, Selznick offered another Civil War, although its focus was not on the events. The work turns less on politics than on personalities and individuals (although the film never risks becoming 'history seen from below'). The heroes, Scarlett O'Hara and Rhett Butler, are anti-heroes: neither Lee nor Lincoln comes into the film. The horrors of war are brilliantly done, as with the burning of Atlanta, but the work is one of national reconciliation, and the only thing it has in common with Griffith's film is that the good blacks are all servants.

History is thus emptied of political content, for its conflicts are made neutral, and a kind of anti-intellectual populism triumphs – disliking newly-acquired money (in view of the Crash of 1929) and preferring the American virtues of family, good neighbourliness, etc. In this sense, the work of John Ford, together with school textbooks, is a perfect representation of the popular American memory of the years 1930–60. It idealizes the armed forces (*Fort Apache*), the Indian wars (*Rio Grande*), the traditional family (*How Green Was My Valley*), the death of the Far West and the outlaws (*The Man Who Shot Liberty Valance*). *Young Mr Lincoln* was simply an ode to the great founder and avoided all political issues.

HISTORY AS ROMANCE

Such problem-less, disinfected and explicitly moral history comes up when Laura recalls the life of her pioneer-relatives, the Ingalls family. She wrote a best-seller with her serial *Town on the Prairie*, published in 1941 and several times reprinted since. Here is her description of the school fête around 1880:

> Suddenly Laura heard Mr Owen calling, 'Laura Ingalls!'. His little and very pale face showed his trouble. The crucial moment had come. Laura rose, and found herself on the dais without quite knowing how she had got there. Then Mr Owen announced, 'Now we shall hear a general account of our country's history, Over to you, Laura.' Laura faced the crowd and began:
> 'Christopher Columbus discovered America in 1492. He was born at Genoa, in Italy, and spent a long time in getting permission to try a new sea-route, travelling west to reach India. . . .' Her voice trembled slightly; but she relaxed, and

carried on in a more self-assured voice. She could not quite understand how she was there, on the dais, in her blue cashmere dress, with mummy's mother-of-pearl brooch pinned to her lace collar. She talked of the French and Spanish explorers, their first plantations, Raleigh's failure in founding the colony of Virginia, the Massachusetts trading companies that bought Manhattan Island and set up in the Hudson valley. To begin with, emotion had clouded Laura's sight. Then she began to pick out faces; her father's swam out of the crowd at her. He was gently nodding his head and his eyes met Laura's.

Then she embarked on the great history of the Americans. She mentioned the new idea of liberty and equality in the New World, recalled Europe's oppressed condition, the war against despotism and tyranny, the struggle for the independence of the Thirteen Colonies, the drawing-up of the Constitution; with the pointer she indicated George Washington's portrait. Her voice sounded out through an attentive silence while she told of his unhappy childhood, his defeat by the French at Fort Duquesne, and then his long and desperate war-years. She told of his unanimous election as first president of the United States, and how he was succeeded by John Adams and then by Jefferson. Jefferson, who had played an important part in the War of Independence, established religious liberty and the right to property in Virginia, and acquired land between the Mississippi and California. . . . She lost her breath somewhat once she had talked on the war of 1812, the burning of the Capitol and of the White House. . . . Some years later, President Monroe dared to challenge the most ancient and powerful nations and to tell their tyrants not to interfere henceforth in the affairs of the New World. Andrew Jackson and the Tennessee militia fought the Spaniards and took Florida, which the United States were honest enough to purchase from Spain. In 1820, the United States went through a difficult period. The banks went bankrupt, business stopped, everyone lost his job, and starvation reigned.

Laura then used the pointer to show John Quincy Adams and she told the story of his election. She mentioned the Mexicans' struggle for independence. Trade grew with Santa Fe; the first covered waggons soon reached Kansas . . .

Laura had done her share. She put down the pointer, and bowed towards the silent audience. A storm of applause caused her to jump and gave her the impulse to go back to her place . . .

The sister, Ida, told the rest of the story. Such history has been reproduced, time and time again, especially in the cinema, for it is the story of half of the American population. King Vidor recorded it, no doubt with verisimilitude, in his *An American Romance*. The film relates the story of a Croat or Slovene immigrant: he seeks work, learns to live in liberty, and appreciates that 'here, anyone can rise to become president.' He goes from job to job across the country, finds a girl, and marries (1899). He acquires a little house, settles into a welcoming community and becomes middle-class – he has a car, and his children have music-lessons. The day his son wins first prize, he praises the glories of American democracy, becomes a foreman and then a small entrepreneur; his son volunteers for the army in 1917 and is killed in the war. In *Fana*, Brian Donlevy, at Indianapolis, decides to build a racing-car, but the trusts turn down his prototype and so he resolves to construct it himself as a series. A full-scale strike breaks out at his factory, and he is appalled to find that it was started by his second son – 'We don't want your job, and we don't want control over you: we just want job security. Remember the past, Dad.' The father understands that his son is not really attacking the system, but really wants collaboration and the reconciliation of classes. When the Second World War comes, they fall into each other's arms.

LIVING MUSEUMS

As in South Africa, for reasons both similar and different, the American historical memory gives a special place to the cult of 'sacred sites'. This is a rather 'assumed' memory for the waves and waves of immigrants, who are taught to forget their real ancestors and to identify themselves with the old capital of the United States, Annapolis, to visit with reverence the tomb of John Paul Jones or to survey the battlefield at Gettysburg where Meade defeated Robert E. Lee. The United States (and Canada) are the only communities where 'living museums' exist: there, in a short visit, old men can rediscover their far-off youth, and reenact, for the benefit of future generations, how sheriffs, post-office clerks and primary-school teachers used to behave in the old days.

THE GREAT CHANGE

A revolution, even in historical writing, is never an isolated event. The great change which I believe occurred with the cata-lyst of the First World War had its origins in the reaction of the white, Anglo-Saxon Protestants (WASPs) to the mass arrival of immigrants, Irish, European, Mediterranean and Asiatic. In New York, for instance, the Catholics had already demanded, in the name of equality, their share of public funds. The outcome of a long battle, starting in 1840, had been the founding of public schools, controlled by elected school-boards, which, to begin with, no one had wanted. In the name of efficiency, professional training, modernization and centralization the WASPs managed to have education handed over to specialists. The immigrants could thus be assimilated, and Americanized according to the norms of business efficiency. The interests of the ruling classes coincided with hopes on the part of the immigrants, for they had come to America in search of a new life, and they were highly respectful towards a system that offered them fortune and openings. Rejection of the old culture, the relic of an out-dated civilization, was not difficult, so long as the ideology of the 'melting-pot' prevailed. The Second World War consolidated the dominant position of this ideology for it gave the Americans the feeling that, since they already had the greatest industry in the world, and the best and most efficient economy, they must also have the best political and cultural system as well.

The large-scale democratic change after the war brought an enormous increase in the intake of schools and universities. Blacks, Puerto Ricans and all non-WASPs were now in the major- ity, and they cared more about the training a school gave them than about its proper educational function. The schools became a means to social promotion. Moreover, the Russians' progress in science and technology had a somewhat traumatic effect and the USA took up the challenge of *Sputnik*. Money flowed into all areas of research, and specialization was, even more than before, the order of the day, even in the humanities and history. The student revolt of 1968 in America was linked with protest against the Vietnam War, but it also reflected the imbalance between egali- tarian talk of universities as institutions, and the profound social inequality that the system perpetuated, and even reproduced. Criticism shifted from the function of studies to the content of courses, especially history, for the dissenters asserted that schools developed a WASP cultural model that ignored the rich- ness of other cultures and perpetuated a legend of a self-satisfying kind about American society instead of exposing its defects, or listing the physical (Indian) or cultural (non-WASP) extinctions that had been perpetrated in freedom's name. Today, as Fitzger- ald has shown in a book that caused a great stir in America, the entire former view of the past has been reversed, so as to emphasize the cultural identity of each separate community. In her own words, America has gone from melting-pot to salad-bowl.

America has leapt, all of a sudden, into a questioning of both her own history and the way it is taught. Up to a short while ago, the country's rulers were only aware of good-fortune history, which recorded American progress and happiness; Americans were represented as tolerant, level-headed, lively and critical, and democratic. Anything running counter to this was seen as 'un-American.' Even in 1974 families in West Virginia protested because, in the school history-book of Kanawha County, passages written by black authors gave a less comforting view of America.

American democracy is very real at the grass roots, and so allows and encourages all kinds of pressure-groups. One such protested because children's books included a biblical satire by Mark Twain. Others criticized the printing of pacifist poems, and some even wanted the adventures of Robin Hood – 'a communist' – to be excised. Well-organized private interests were at hand, such as the American Advertising Federation, which managed to suppress Rugg's work in 1939 because it condemned the effects of advertising and showed how stupefying it was. The churches were well to the fore, as was the John Birch Society, in a vigilante role. History books, though selected democratically by the school-boards, were subject to all sorts of pressure, and publishers had to amend the author's original to ensure sales.

These pressures turned full circle in the 1960s with the democratization of education and the emergence of black civil-rights movements. In this change, black people were pioneers in dismantling the old version of history, with which they had never identified. True, even before the 1960s explosion, history books had already begun to 'decolonize' the writing and illustration of the past; even then, in picture-books, black people were shown not just as wretched plantation-hands in the 'Solid South' but also as skilled workers in the modern factories of the East Coast and centre. Several blacks, hitherto ignored, were now mentioned – Booker T. Washington, Carver, Ralph Bunche (US ambassador to the United Nations) and Martin Luther King, together with members of the civil-rights NAACP (National Association for the Advancement of Colored People); soon afterwards, three chapters on the blacks were added to the historical work on New York. Nowadays there are even schools in which black history is made the basis of all American history, for the blacks mean to assert their own history just as, when faced with the 'white' films of Hollywood, they set up their own firms and created their own black cinematic image.

These efforts were a failure: films such as The Right of Birth presented blacks as models of virtue, and bored everyone, though it was different with books that upgraded the place of blacks in American history. The black example extended to all non-white minorities, such as the Puerto Ricans and Mexicans, and thereafter all non-WASPs, who could see that their part in the traditional history had been insulting.

Now, each minority seeks a version of American history that will give it a privileged position, whereas other schools propose a version of history in which the balance is an object of contention between author and publisher. According to Fitzgerald, the various cultural groups do not all come off equally well. The place and role of non-WASP whites – Irish, Ukrainians, Jews etc. – are easier to upgrade and the revision of books in that respect is well under way. As regards the blacks, the change has been revolutionary, for their destiny and role was becoming a subject of central concern in the books, whether in the Civil War or over the Ku Klux Klan or the Black Panthers. Conversely, there has been some regression as regards the Indian problem. To begin with, as I have shown, the Indians were seen as having their own civilization. But when the West was won, after 1870, history in the early years of the twentieth century showed the Indians as cruel, savage and unassimilable: 'the massacres then committed had to be justified.' Now, history books are a long way behind film: the Vietnam War revealed much as to the Indian problem, and the Indians have been revalued in so far as America now rejects her nightmare experience in the Vietnamese adventure.

BLACK HISTORY

History as taught to blacks in the USA, or more exactly 'black history,' as written in books by blacks, is organized along lines quite different from those found in other textbooks. It is distinguished by the struggle for freedom and equality, and its periodization is very jagged. 'There was a black, it seems, in Columbus's crew and historians debate about this' – so begins this history, which fixes the start of blacks' past, dissociating it from slavery.

> The first blacks to arrive in America were not slaves, but servants who were freed after a few years' work; slavery was not recognized in English law. Only a century after the arrival of the first twenty blacks, in 1620, could slaves be legally owned. . . . Gradually, blacks lost their rights and slavery was allowed in the Thirteen Colonies.

They could not own weapons, hold meetings, marry whites, bear witness against whites or undertake contracts and deals. In some states they were legally forbidden to learn to read and write, and they could not move without their master's consent: they were seen as inferiors and able only to work for others.

Many of the Founding Fathers of the United States – Washington, Franklin, Jefferson, Adams, Madison – opposed slavery, but several southern states refused to enter the Union if it were abolished. Even so, on 1 January 1808 there was a law to prohibit importation of new slaves. The problem of slavery became the chief problem of American life, as the slave-owners tried to allow slavery in the new states of the Union, whereas the abolitionists wished to confine it to states where it already existed.

Already at the Declaration of Independence, there was a movement for abolition:

> The blacks' activities during the Revolution were not incidental to it. In the Boston massacre, one of the first to die for American liberty was a fugitive black slave, Crispus Attucks, in 1770. In the war with the British, there were almost 5,000 blacks in the army and navy.

The path of emancipation seemed open. 'But a single invention changed the course of history, and did much to perpetuate slavery. That machine was Eli Whitney's cotton-gin, which allowed the hitherto small plantations to expand and so furthered their demand for labour.' For the planters, slavery became a way of amassing vast riches, and northern abolitionists now had to make very great efforts through their newspaper, *Liberator*, to assert their cause. One of the outstanding champions was a young fugitive slave, Harriet Tubman, who

> smuggled over 300 fugitive slaves into the North. A price of $40,000 was set on her head, but she became a nurse and spy in the Civil War. The movement's leader was Frederick Douglas, who tried to free blacks with northern support. This was not easy, because many people feared black competition in the labour-market. The 'American Colonization Society' wished to return the blacks to Africa, and 12,000 of them left in 1820, to found, eventually, the state of Liberia. However, the journey was expensive, and most blacks wanted to stay in America. Their discontent and disappointment caused revolts – those of Denkey Denmark and Nat Turner, in which over sixty whites were killed. But lack of organization stopped such revolts from succeeding.

Thomas Waterman Wood's painting, *The Veteran*, reminds us

that 40,000 blacks were killed in the Civil War, and a further 2,000 crippled. Even so, the blacks faced an uncertain future. They were no longer slaves after Lincoln's Amendment, but they were not fully-fledged citizens. Southern planters had been ruined by the war, but the blacks had no money and the whites feared what they might do with their new liberty. Blacks hoped to remain in the South, and to have schools and land; for ten years, up to 1877, the South was under Federal control, and fourteen blacks were elected to the House of Representatives and the Senate. Much had been done to assist blacks, especially as regards education and acquisition of land, etc. but bribery and corruption discredited some of the activities allegedly designed to help blacks: the principle of white supremacy was speedily reaffirmed and the southern whites soon regained key positions in the administration. Secret societies were formed, such as Ku Klux Klan, to undo what 'Reconstruction' had meant to achieve; for instance, the southern states implemented 'Negro Codes' which restricted rights and imposed electoral taxes which eliminated the very poor or otherwise prevented blacks from voting because of various kinds of tests. Measures were taken to segregate blacks from whites in restaurants and railways; the Supreme Court laid down that such measures were not unconstitutional, so long as black and white were 'separate but equal.' Separate they were; but not equal.

THE EMERGENCE OF BLACK LEADERS

An innovation in the late nineteenth century was the emergence of black leaders who often had been born into slavery and now tried to achieve emancipation. They disagreed among themselves: all had the same goal, but they differed as to how it might be attained. Booker T. Washington, founder of the Tuskegee Institute in Alabama, was the most famous. He thought that blacks had first of all to equal the whites in school and at work before they could gain true citizenship. In the eyes of William E. Dubois, Washington was a weak compromiser; he felt blacks must be given all their proper rights, so that 10 per cent of them could be trained to exercise leadership. George Washington Carver, a botanist and scholar, with pioneering achievements in American agronomy to his name (e.g. the study of yam and peanut cultivation) believed in the force of example. Frederick Douglas encouraged blacks to develop self-confidence and show themselves the equals of whites. All of these men had tasted freedom and devoted their efforts to bringing it back to life.

The struggle for equality was all the more marked in the twentieth century as, following the participation in the Great War of 367,000 blacks, many of them emigrated to the North and East, to Chicago or St Louis and elsewhere, where they encountered the same measures of segregation as in the South and where trade unions were generally hostile. If sackings had to be carried out, it was always blacks who suffered first, and they always had the worst and lowest-paid jobs. Racial conflict and rioting gave rise to a climate of hatred that, hitherto, had been absent; and disillusion was greatest when black veterans returned from France where they had often been better treated and found that, once the parading had stopped, their place had already been allotted – the lowest. There was violence in 1919, fuelled by xenophobic propaganda against any critic of the American way of life.

The crisis of 1929 worsened the blacks' position, and they organized in various ways – through the NAACP and the 'Urban League' which tirelessly fought for legal defence of blacks' civil rights. The accession of Roosevelt brought another great change, since he took advice from a 'black cabinet' led by F. W. White, president of the NAACP. The administration called in leading figures of the black community, such as Ralph Bunche, American mediator with the United Nations, and R. C. Weaver, who was to hold a government office under President Johnson. In the army there was not much progress, and the Second World War changed little in this respect, despite the conscription of over 3,000,000 blacks. Benjamin O. Davies did become the first black American general, but true integration was not seriously advanced. The greatest victory occurred when K. Philip Randolph, president of the 'Brotherhood of Sleeping-Car Porters', convinced Roosevelt into making Order 8802, by which segregation in the war industries was stopped (in June 1941). The first measures to promote active desegregation were then taken, and were effected by Truman in the Korean War.

SEPARATE BUT EQUAL

When the war was over, blacks once more returned to the unequal status they knew so well. The only new decision of any importance had been the Supreme Court's decision, in 1944, to outlaw measures meant to stop blacks from voting in the primaries. Other measures were taken to grant and guarantee blacks' rights in these respects. The most important innovations encouraging further steps towards equality came in the field of civil rights.

In 1896, in the Plessy-Ferguson case, the principle of 'separate but equal' had been laid down, although in reality it meant separation without equality. In 1938 the state of Missouri had to accept a black student in its state university, since he had no 'equal' alternative. The battle against the 'separate but equal' law reached its peak in Brown v. the School Board of Topeka where segregation was clearly shown to be preventing equality, i.e. the operation of the law. The NAACP won this great judicial battle which initiated desegregation in schools; it gained support even from the Supreme Court and the Federal authorities at Little Rock. Black pupils were given armed protection to enter the high school, which had locked its doors against them in protest.

In Pastor Martin Luther King, the blacks' struggle became a

mass movement, though a non-violent one. It used the weapons of boycott such as the Washington March of 1963, at the height of the civil-rights movement. Some blacks became Muslims and 'the Black Muslims' of Elijah Mohammed and Malcolm X advocated both a separate black state and violent means to achieve it. It all caused Congress to adopt a set of measures at the initiative first of Kennedy and then of Johnson to outlaw any form of discrimination in restaurants, hotels and public places, and to prohibit discrimination in employment.

Martin Luther King received the Nobel Peace Prize for his pacific campaign for civil rights. The black problem would, however, never be solved until social inequality had ended; unrest continued to grow in the black ghettos. There came a flaring-up of violence in the later 1960s, which ended in bloody rioting, especially at Detroit, where there were over forty deaths from violence. Tanks and armoured cars were used to restore order. It was this social aspect of the black problem that gave the Black Panther organization a field for action. The Panthers saw themselves as revolutionaries, as much as blacks, and aimed to create an anti-government that would be both black and revolutionary. Stokely Carmichael's ideas were popular, but went against the overall wishes of the majority of blacks, who looked for integration into the American nation, not separation from it or continual combat against it.

IRISH-AMERICAN HISTORY

The version of history taught to Irish-Americans starts, naturally enough, with the difficulties of life in the old country up to the Great Famine of 1845, the miseries of the Irish lot, the exploiting landlords and especially the evictions of the weakest people, who were driven off their land because they could not pay the rent. The help sent from America during the Famine, it is said, had much to do with the desire of so many Irish to leave, at all costs, for such a generous land. The voyage and arrival in America could be hazardous, for the Irish were often ignorant, and fell victim to 'dream-merchants' and so found themselves frequently impoverished or in debt even before they reached American soil. Over there, they were often a prey to 'runners' or agents who, for a fee, would promise a job.

The life of 'Paddy', the Irish immigrant, was no idyll. To survive, he had to accept any form of work and mostly the worst forms, such as the digging of the Erie Canal which turned New York into the largest city in the world, or the construction of the North-Western and Union Pacific railways. 'Paddy' suffered all kinds of danger, and the newspapers would daily report that this or that Irishman had been drowned, burned or crushed in an accident at work. Circumstances were now turning the once-rural Irishman into a town-dweller, and they met for family occasions or St Patrick's Day; soon, they entered public services, such as the fire-brigades or the local police. Their fault was hard drinking, and it was this weakness that created the stereotype of the brawling, quarrelling Irishman.

AGAINST BLACKS AND CHINESE

The Irish opposed the abolitionist movement because they feared that the blacks, once freed, would become rivals in the job-market. They themselves found life difficult enough in the urban slums, without further being asked to pity the blacks. Still, when appeals were made to their loyalty, they did respond, and condemned the South for wishing to secede from the Union. The Irish Brigade fought in several battles, and it was a general of Irish origin, Meade, who undertook the defence of Gettysburg.

The Irish were certainly brave, but they were also difficult to control once they had received their pay. When conscription was introduced in 1863, the Irish regarded it as an injustice, and exploded at New York in rioting, in July, because the $300 which it cost to find a replacement conscript was too much for the low-paid Irish. In the first 1,200 names drawn (allegedly) by lot for the draft on 11 July, the Irish were in a large majority. This 'trick of fate', which occurred after two years' heavy losses in the fighting, was not alone. Lincoln's act of emancipation had clearly shown that the war was intended not just to keep the Confederate States in the Union, but to liberate the negroes. Tension between them and the Irish reached its most critical point when the government used blacks to break the Irish dockers' strike in the port of New York, and the ensuing riots lasted for four whole days, as the Irish attacked blacks, beating, and even lynching, them. It was a classic example of poor wretches taking revenge for their miserable condition on people more wretched than themselves.

After the Civil War, Irish energies were dispersed in various directions. Many Irish were integrated into American life, but not all for some of them protested at the arrival of Chinese immigrants as yet more competition in the job-market – the employers used them to break strikes. Dennis Kearney launched an 'America for the Americans' movement, which resulted in a Chinese Exclusion Act of 1882 against 'the yellow peril.' The Irish imposed on new immigrants procedures of whose unfairness they had themselves complained in the past.

THE FENIAN INVASION OF CANADA

The Irish were especially active in the Fenian movement, which set up an Irish Provisional Government and an army of liberation to deliver Ireland from the British. They hoped to attain their aim by seizing Canada. On 1 June 1866 an Irish Fenian army, led by John O'Neill (a former officer of the Civil War), invaded Canada and occupied Fort Erie. They called on Canada to declare independence. The Canadians resisted, however, so O'Neill recrossed the border, and his men were taken prisoner by

American soldiers. This marked the failure of an effort to provoke revolution simultaneously in Canada and Ireland, to involve
the USA in war with Great Britain and so obtain American
recognition of an Irish Republic.

A SECRET SOCIETY: THE MOLLY MAGUIRES AND PINKERTON

Harsh labour conditions in the coal mines caused many Irish to
form a secret society designed to improve things: such were the
Molly Maguires. Their members used terroristic methods against
those who caused the abuses to which they had been victim.
No one knew the identity of the Molly Maguires, except they
themselves, and it was ill-advised to try for further information.
A conspiratorial silence united those both for and against them.
The miners, who might be cheated over the weight of coal
extracted or the number of coal-lumps or even the shape of the
coal-waggons, became more and more angry, for their work was
even more dangerous than that of the old black slaves; even
children had been sent into these inhuman conditions.

The president of the Philadelphia and Reading Railway Company wished to be rid of the Molly Maguires, and he hired a
detective from the Pinkerton detective agency, one James McParland, himself a young Irishman. McParland had himself hired as
a miner and, though he was never able fully to unmask the
organization, succeeded in having many of its members arrested.
He was found out by a railway-worker, and had to leave town,
but took with him evidence sufficient to incriminate the organization. The Molly Maguires subsequently lost their influence,
and their overall effect was simply to associate trade-unionism
with terrorist practices. Nevertheless, Irishmen played a pioneering part in the development of American trade unions, as is
exemplified by the figure of George Meany, for many years
president of the American Federation of Labor.

IRISH INTEGRATION

From then on, Irish integration became obvious in all aspects of American life – Eugene O'Neill or Scott Fitzgerald in literature, James Cagney, John Wayne, Grace Kelly, Lionel Barrymore and Sean O'Fearna (alias John Ford) in the cinema, the famous cigar-smoking Cardinal James Gibbons in the church, and the same in architecture, or in business. The Irish were especially good at political activity and the Democratic Party machine which they controlled early on in New York, through Tammany Hall, acquired a grip on the vote of the very poor, to whom the machine gave aid and succour. The Irish lobby's power became evident for the first time in the election of President Cleveland in 1884; his opponent had used the unlucky slogan of 'Rum, Rome and Rebellion' in allusion to the Irish component of the Democratic Party. The 'Irish vote' was among the first to organize at municipal and then at federal level, and it swept the many towns where Irish people lived: thus J. Daley took Chicago and Ronald Reagan, California. Nationally, even though Al Smith, the governor of New York, lost the presidential election of 1928 to Herbert Hoover, the Kennedy family was to succeed, despite the eldest son's tragic death: he had been groomed by Joseph Kennedy since his breach with Roosevelt as presidential candidate, in place of his father. The young man died as a pilot in the war, but his brother John took over and in 1960 became the thirty-fifth president of the United States.

THE MAKING OF 'NEW HISTORY'

There are almost as many versions of the American past and present as there are schools and textbooks. In one case, the country will be marching forward, in progress, and in another, it will be courting disaster. There is a good variety of points of view, which are never compared and juxtaposed, and so they are inevitably perplexing to the reader. There is no fundamental truth to be revealed: is there then some truth in each one of the viewpoints?

That cannot really be said, for despite all the chaos, we at least have been building up a more positive and less ideologically-dominated body of knowledge, which owes much to the social sciences. In a Chicago high school, history-teaching is based on an essentially sociological approach. The class in which I participated studied the history of America since the Second World War, in both town and country. The term's twenty-five lessons examine town-life, crime, school-integration (blacks, etc.), electoral ratios between city and suburb, private and state education, health-organization, minority problems, marriage and divorce, professional and social mobility, urban and state finance, etc. The course that I have seen involves three short talks, lasting for twelve minutes each, separated by discussion. There were some fifteen black and white girls and boys, aged from fourteen to sixteen, and all clearly of working-class origin.

The analysis of marriage is most remarkable. It is based on a statistical graph that Earl Bell hands out to his class, which shows how, between 1918 and 1980, the curve of divorce suddenly rose between 1941 and 1945, fell during the 1950s, and gradually rose again during the 1960s and 1970s. The curve also shows that, since the 1970s, people, once divorced, are less and less likely to remarry. Lisa Cohen, aged fourteen, related the fall in the marriage rate to the crisis of 1929 and that of 1973; she showed the effects of feminism on the divorce rate and the development of legislation, comparing the states where divorce is easy with those where it is not, and examining the consequences of remarriage. Politics and economics criss-cross with ideology and chronology. This girl is not yet fifteen, and yet her logic and perception were compelling.

The two other talks, by Dan Spiegel on juvenile crime and by Mike Kaonhi on urban planning, were more technical, for they

had to deal with criminal law, definition of offences, age discrimination, comparison of reforms carried out in various parts
of society, political parties and churches, in the first talk, and, in
the second, with types of financing, the roles of different authorities in urban development, the various types of construction
systems, and the organization of buildings into groups, in the
interests of greater harmonization.

This form of introduction to social life is clearly a remarkable
way of entering upon maturity. It is based on the history of an
American town, its population and pressure-groups; the past is
not studied for its own sake, but to allow an understanding of
modern problems. The non-directed character of the teaching
resembles methods used in France and Belgium, except that in
the American case the pupils are three or four years older and
can construct coherent and skilful exposés. Unger's textbook,
These United States. The Questions of Our Past is used as an auxiliary
text. It expounds the problems of each period, and undertakes
analysis of them.

On Reconstruction after the Civil War, for instance, the question set is: Why did it fail? and the answer is: Industrialization
did not occur. Then again: was Big Business responsible for this?
On the First World War, the question set is: did it have to do with
idealism, national interest, or the rights of neutral states? On the
New Deal, pupils are asked whether it was too much, or not
enough. Earl P. Bell has suggested possible problems in the
whole history of American society: the various controversies are
to be analysed. He chooses some key problems which are
expounded according to various criteria, i.e. whether they
greatly mattered at the time; or allow us to understand today's
USA better, because they lie at the heart of other problems; or
stimulate debate among historians and others; or may provoke
an interest in the study of the past and the future.

As to the colonial era, for instance, between 1620 and 1763,
six questions are set:

1   Were the first colonial settlements democratically constituted societies?

2   Did policy towards the Indians undergo significant change?

3   Did the development of the colonies affect the power of religion?

4   Was the working of institutions related to the colonialists' origins?

5   Did the British control the colonial economy?

6   How far have computer studies altered the traditional views of the family in colonial times?

On foreign policy since 1945, the following questions appear:

1   Should Congress forbid unilateral US intervention in foreign countries?

2   Should nuclear arms be supervised by an international organization?

3   Should Congress limit and supervise foreign investments in the USA?

4   Should the defence industries be nationalized?

5   Should Congress limit the powers of the president in matters of peace and war?

6   Should America intervene in the Middle East to safeguard her oil supply?

For each question, there is a little dossier, containing the main points for debate – extracts from speeches, various parties' arguments, statistics.

This method is unquestionably quite different from traditional historical teaching. Stories and anecdotes have hardly even a decorative function. As at the school in St Germain-en-Laye, these new methods reduce narrative to a secondary level of information. Textbooks now do the same job as a dictionary, they give references and landmarks, not arguments or even, except rarely, analysis. It all amounts to a revolution in history-teaching. Earl P. Bell is of course *avant-garde*, for how many teachers have successfully attempted to restructure traditional historical knowledge, and how many of them use Unger's work? Not many of them, it would seem, for the majority prefer history as a decent, problemless, chronology.

PROVINCIALISM IN HISTORY

Still, uniformity of approach is not homogeneity of content, and there is enormous variety in teaching in the USA. History is matched with citizens' requirements and education, whether private or public, is dependent on funds from private, municipal or state sources. American society as a mass is more traditional than its academics, and the law of democracy is such that society can more or less impose its views, for better or worse. There is clearly a good variety of teaching, more so than in other countries, whether in the content of the historical material to be analysed or the methods of examination, but there is a common feature, the lack of interest in non-American history. It is of course studied at high school, but it is clearly not part of pupils' common stock of knowledge. This is even true of university students if they are not specialists.

The Americans lead the field in ignorance of the outside world. This can easily be seen in newspapers, which devote only a very small share of their news to foreign countries, unless they have some bearing on American life. The same is true of television, where the greater part of the news is taken up with the USA and even the state – Alabama, Michigan or whatever. This decentralization of interest is all the more striking to the European visitor as it runs counter to what takes place in older and more centralized countries. In Massachusetts, the Boston news matters more than the 'main' news, and in Illinois the same holds good for Chicago news; after that will come news of the

USA as a whole, and then foreign news. The share for this last is minimal, and often non-existent. Indeed, in each state there can be a comparison with some other state, say with Ohio, in Indiana, as if they were two foreign countries. The individual states of the USA have the status almost of veritable little nations. French or Spanish regionalists might be delighted at such treatment, but in the American case there is an almost insatiable desire to probe questions of urban life, desegregation, or whatever. You can sense this as an almost psychoanalytical need in an anxious society wondering as to its own instructions (since Watergate, especially) and as to the future.

This probing always comes in the same way, an analysis that amounts to a kind of social narcissism, together with a superiority complex towards the economic, political and cultural systems of other nations and societies. In history, it is obvious that the ignorance of the problems of Islam or the USSR is, except among academics, as uncomprehending as total. The American myth has led to a supposition that America took in people from the whole world, so the rest of the world is not worth serious attention. The relationship of America to other countries is wholly distorted. For instance, the idea that American imperialism can exist is dismissed as abhorrent, insulting and absurd; and there are few history books that even consider this problem, except perhaps to say that in the era of the 'Big Stick' in 1901, Theodore Roosevelt 'delivered the Cubans from Spanish oppression.'

A final characteristic is that there is no other country in the world where there is such a large gap between the sophisticated understanding of some professional historians and the basic education given by teachers. E. P. Bell is an exception. Is this perhaps the obverse of a democratic process which was originally designed to satisfy the various needs of each section of society, and therefore has to be protected against 'specialists' who, if allowed to use their knowledge too broadly, would thereby gain privilege?

14

'FORBIDDEN HISTORY': CHICANOS AND ABORIGINES

The 'losers' version' is now much better-known in history thanks to Nathan Wachtel and his pioneering work on the Peruvian Indians after their conquest and colonization. In Peru, the story of the Conquest was written down in the Apu Inca Atahuallpaman elegy, and comes through in folk-tales, but it has remained an anti-history that has been prohibited, lacks institutional support and leaves no trace in the Peruvian school-books. In Mexico, on the other hand, such anti-history has been 'established': it took power. Between these two poles is the history of the Chicanos or Mexican-Americans. In their case, the anti-history has indeed been institutionalized, but has not quite taken power.

The change-over in Mexico was complex. In the account of Josefina Vasquez de Knauth, Mexican history was reserved as the chief terrain of a struggle between Spaniards, uninterested in the pre-Conquest past, and Creoles, who emphasized that past in the light of independence, which was won in 1821. In the 'First

Educational Plan' of 1843, the (civic) aims of education were laid down, and teaching was systematized. History was compulsory in the first year, and Cortez is not even mentioned. Morellos, Mina and Iturbide were seen as the founder-heroes, and great men of the Mexican Pantheon. As the church and the conservatives resisted, Cortez soon reappeared, although his 'knightly character' was still eclipsed by the grandeurs of the Indian past. Throughout the nineteenth century, the historical terrain was disputed between conservatives and liberals; for instance, Iturbide was expelled from the Pantheon when the revolutionaries took over, to be replaced by Cuatemoc and Juarez, the heroes of resistance to Napoleon III. In fact, the battle with the – essentially American – foreign imperialists became an obsessional theme in history, to the point where, at the time of Pancho Villa and of Zapata, 'nativism' took over from the earlier prevailing Catholic and Eurocentric vision of the Mexican past.

Beyond the Rio Grande, there were also 'Mexican-Americans' after 1848 – also called Chicanos or Raza whose view of history was a mirror-image and who, this time against the USA, similarly contested the traditional version of the American past.

This historical mirror-image has been established in the Chicano movement. The interesting feature is a revision of the prevailing periodization, which had reflected east-coast concerns. The 'colonial period' is no longer dated between 1607 or 1620 (the Pilgrim Fathers) and 1776 (independence) but rather from 1536 (arrival of the Conquistadores in New Mexico) and 1821 (independence from the Spanish metropolis). The history of the Raza (a generic term for the Hispano-Indian population of the four states lost to the USA in 1848) thus falls into five periods: from 1536 to 1809 is an era of Spanish–Indian synthesis; after 1810 comes 'Anglo-Saxon' penetration and the 'Texan Revolution'; 1848 to 1910 is an era of American conquest and the integration of the four states, whose Mexican-American inhabitants became a 'forgotten people'; between

1910 and 1940 the influx of Mexican immigrants caused Chicanos to be seen as a foreign enclave in their own country; whereas the years since 1940 have seen a reawakening of the *Raza* and the emergence of a Chicano movement, claiming its own cultural identity, recognition of the *pocho* language and of popular traditions.

Throughout the world there are numerous 'minority' groups which, like the Chicanos, have created their own anti-history in reaction to their overlords. Some of them, however, have only just begun to articulate this anti-history, and no institution serves their purpose as yet. Still, efforts are being made. Such is the case with the Aborigines of Australia, whose initial and almost child-like vision of history is being formed. Here is how they see their distant and their more recent past.

THE AUSTRALIAN ABORIGINES: THE ACADEMIC ACCOUNT

> The Australia discovered by Cook in 1770 was only thinly populated, with a few thousand very primitive natives ... some 300,000 or 400,000 people, who were easily pushed back by the new arrivals. ... Today there are 40,000 Aborigines of pure blood and 30,000 half-castes.

These lines come from the authoritative *Encyclopaedia Universalis* and are as dry and anonymous as a medical statement. Neither the geographer nor the anthropologist who discuss the distribution of the Aborigines and their blood-types is concerned with why and how they disappeared. The outstanding scientific book on the Aborigines, that of Professor A. P. Elkin, devotes a mere paragraph to their population-growth since 1930. In its French edition, the book has 452 pages, but you look in vain for a single reference to the demographic collapse which took place in the nineteenth century. As to that, not a word is said. The disappearance of three-quarters of the population somehow seems to be of no interest to any scientist of whatever type and no work is done on it. In the end you learn more by reading Jules Vernes's *Les Enfants du Capitaine Grant*: for Verne was always keen to show the crimes committed by the English.

> The major argues that they are apes. The colonists regarded the blacks as wild animals, to be tracked down and shot. The great authorities of jurisprudence were called in to show that the Australian was beyond natural law: the Sydney press even suggested a good way of exterminating them by mass poisoning. . . . Murder was organized on a vast scale, and whole tribes disappeared.

According to academic classification, the Australian Aborigines are 'history-less' people. . . . Still, they remember. Oral tradition preserves this memory of the past, reproduces it and today is being transcribed by the children themselves.

THE CHILDREN'S VERSION

The document below is unique, and its existence is owing to Wandjuk Marika, who runs the department of native culture in Australia. He asked Aborigine children to reproduce either in writing or in drawings what they had been told of the past by their parents and grandparents. It is a transfigured memory, between myth and history, of genocide.

These passages were written by different children and they have the purity or poetry of freshness, for they come from boys and girls aged between eight and twelve; unlike other passages in this book, I shall offer no commentary on them.

They concern the creation of the world, the old days, the arrival of the Macassans, of the 'strangers' or 'whitefellas.'

THE CREATION: THE OLD DAYS

The sea moved up and touched the shore. . . . Here there were white hills: these hills are sacred, for it is here that our two creators disembarked. There were two of them and they came to catch fish. They were called Jankawn and Barama. They divided us, the Aborigines, into two groups called Dhuwa and Yirritija. . . .

In the beginning there was darkness. The spirits had created the people and the rivers, the caves, the rocks and everything that lives. Each clan had its land, its totems and its dreams. . . .

Neither people, birds nor animals could see, for there was no light and so each remained in his place, stationary. One day all the animals assembled and said: 'We must do something to create light.' They discussed and discussed, but nothing happened. Finally the frog said that the sun might come if they sang a magic chant. They sang and they sang and then suddenly, from behind the hills, the sun's rays appeared and lit everything up. All living creatures were happy, for they could now come and go as they pleased, and it was finally possible to see the trees, the grass, the hills and the rivers around them. . . .

We have many stories from the old days.

It was during this time that there was once a great Aborigine hunter who found an enormous brolga with a broken wing. The bird was so big that the hunter took fright and ran away. But he felt so sorry for the poor bird that he crept back and asked the bird politely what had happened to it. When the bird told the hunter his story, tears began to run from his large sad eyes. He sobbed and he sobbed and his tears became so great, that they formed a river which ran down the mountain.

As he told his story, the poor bird died from grief while the hunter ascended to the skies where he became the star of the morning . . . .

At this time the animals were creatures just like ourselves: then they were transformed and we took them as our totems. If we belong to the brolga totem, it is because we were brolgas during the old days. . . .

Long, long ago there lived a brolga who was very proud of his plumage and his dance. Every night, while the other brolgas were asleep, he left in secret and, far away, took off into the light of the moon. Today, as you go through our country, the country of the Moil, you will see that our people still dance by moonlight.

OUR LIFE IN THE OLD DAYS

In the olden days, long before the arrival of the white man, we wandered freely across the bush. My ancestors lived then and their only occupation was to make their axes and swords. The women looked for food, fetched water and looked after the children. Nobody worried about clothing, for they could cover themselves with whatever they found. They wore bracelets and necklaces made from coral and stones. They led a happy and sociable life. My father told me this. . . .

When people married, the man had to catch the woman in his arms, while the woman had to pretend that she did not want her man. But if she really was unwilling, her parents and friends would provide her with a hiding-place.

At this time, the eldest men would teach the young boys to kill emus and kangaroos and to scavenge in the bush.

THE ARRIVAL OF THE MACASSANS

There are tamarind-trees at the Cape of Drimmy. These trees are tall and powerful. We call them the Jambangs; they produce fruits like peanuts which have the taste of lemons; we make a drink out of them; the tree is thick with branches and leaves and gives a lot of shade. Forest people tell us that some of these trees are more than 500 years old.

The tamarinds arrived with the Macassans, who came from Indonesia. . . .

They had been surprised by the Aborigines, who lived close by with their families. The Macassans were looking for tripang, which is what we call dariba. This looks like a large, black cucumber and can be found when the tide is out. We helped them to cook tripang and then they constructed a sort of hut and lit a fire inside to smoke it. They left with the tide to sell tripang to the Chinese. They arrived with the largest ships we had ever seen, which looked like great birds floating on the sea. They gave us hammers, knives, pipes and tobacco; we taught them how to hunt tortoises. Our relations with them were largely friendly. They taught us to fly a flag when somebody dies so that people do not enter the house. They gave us many words: rupees (money), balanda (white men), ngarali (tobacco).

THE 'STRANGERS': 'WHITEFELLAS'

One day, when the Aborigines had gone to catch fish, they saw a boat full of strangers. The Aborigines took fright and hid behind the bushes; then they climbed to the top of the hill and rolled rocks down onto the strangers as they approached. The Aborigines thought they had killed them, but they hadn't and the strangers shot at them with their guns. The Aborigines hid once again and then threw their spears at the strangers, who managed to escape and climbed aboard their ship and disappeared. . . .

One day, one of the strangers came back; he was called Captain Cook. He moved into the Bush. A spear was thrown and narrowly missed him. He was very frightened, especially when the black Aborigines chased him with their sharpened spears. He climbed aboard his ship and disappeared. . . .

The English army arrived at Fort Dundas in 1824. We did not kill them because we were friends. There were fifty of them and two thousand of us and we were not afraid of their cannons: in the bush we were invincible. They had black boots which came up to the knee, white trousers and red tunics and faces. We called them Murumtawi, which means 'red-faces.' They knew how to fish but were totally incapable as hunters. They made bricks out of mud and suffered from fever in humid weather. They said they would stay for five years. They did not kill each other but they caught one of our men named Tambu, capsized his canoe and crushed his head with the paddles. . . .

When the Aborigines saw a white man on horseback for the first time they thought that this was a single creature and they did not realize their error until the man got down from his horse. Some said that the white men were their ancestors who had returned in a new form, others said that they were spirits, and others that they were animals, like kangaroos. Yagan, an Aborigine hero, went to see them and made friends with them, but they wanted war; then he said that he would kill a white man for every Aborigine that died. Then, Yagan's brother was shot when he passed by at that moment. Things got worse and worse and then Yagan and his old father were killed.

The widowed mother cried a great deal.

THE EXPLOITS OF JAPANANGKA

In 1928 a group of Aborigines were working for a white man. The white man slept with an Aborigine woman. He then took another one prisoner and said that he would kill her if he was not left alone.

The elders then got together to kill the white man. They told the woman to start screaming so that they could isolate the white man. They threw spears and boomerangs at him and the old Japanangka cut his throat with an axe. Then the old men cut the body up and buried it in a rabbit-hole.

Another white man discovered what had happened and went to the police. The white men formed a battalion, found the camping Aborigines and killed them all. The white man's assassins were now far away, but the white men continued to kill Aborigines. But Japanangka was not easily caught. With the help of an Aborigine, the white men followed his tracks, but they were unable to catch him. When they saw an encampment of Aborigines at one oasis, they killed them all.

'THE MISSION TAUGHT US TO LOVE GOD'

A long time ago, a mission came to the river. The five priests and seven brothers worked hard in the sun. They wore large hats to protect themselves from the heat. They grew rice, tobacco, yams and raised pigs. They wanted the Aborigine children to come and see them. The adults brought them fruit in exchange for tea, sugar and clothing. And so our children learnt their customs and language. The father of the community said: 'Let them stay with us. We will teach them to love God.' So they built a church and baptized the children and taught them to build houses and cultivate a kitchen-garden. The mission grew bigger, adding a hospital and a garden. They called their land 'Unia,' and the Aborigine children went to school.

When I was young, I would often cry. So my grandfather and grandmother took me to the missionaries who put me in their hospital. I thought that the lights were fire, such as belonged to my own people, the Walbiri. When I arrived at the hospital I was very frightened because everyone was white. When I saw the white men I began to cry.

THE GREAT TRIBAL WAR WITH THE JAPANESE

The Japanese and the Europeans fought a great tribal war. They killed practically all the inhabitants of Bathurst Island with a bomb. One day a Japanese plane came and the Australian planes were destroyed. But the Japanese pilots were also wounded. Mathias knew that they were hidden in the bush. He hid himself and watched them; they were holding a boy named Clarence whose parents were looking for him everywhere. They said to Mathias: 'Take us to them.' Mathias walked and walked until he found the Japanese. He sneaked up behind them and, pulling out a revolver, shouted: 'Hands Up.' The Japanese held their hands up and Clarence was saved.

'I WOULD LIKE TO WORK FOR THE COMPANY'

The people who went into the desert showed little respect for the Aborigines and their food. They destroyed all their land and their caves.

Now the mining companies have arrived in the Aurunkun region. People are in disagreement over these mines. Some are for them and others against. As for me, I would like to work for the company, to earn money, own a house and drive a tractor.

There are houses down there which are uninhabited. The water-tanks are empty. There are only dingoes, snakes and lizards there. . . .

This is our country; it has come a long, long way from the old days. It was us who settled here, but all that will remain of us will be the ashes and bones of animals which children have killed.

Soon, even our footprints will be erased by the wind. . . .

These memories express the vision of history as an immutable cycle in which the desert reconquers the land and the wind destroys the traces of the past. But there is also a myth of emergence which has much in common with the memories of other peoples 'without a history.'

Among the Pueblo Indians there is also a myth that in the beginning there was night, while two living beings, though without gender, are the creators. (L. Sebag).

Among Aborigine children there is a clear but frustrated desire for absorption; it emerges here and there and reduces the form of past truths by distorting or concealing them. At the end of this history the white man appears, as elsewhere, and starts the apocalypse. This can be seen in the oral tradition gathered by Haveaux and edited by Randles. It tells of the first contacts with the blacks of Angola experienced with the Portuguese around 1700. The similarities are striking.

Our forefathers lived happily in the Lubala plain. They had cows and cultivated gardens. They had salt-marshes and banana plantations.

Then one day they saw a large boat sail up on the seas;

This boat had white sails, shining like knives;

White men came off the boat and said a few words which no-one understood.

Our ancestors were frightened and said that they were Vumbis and other returning spirits.

They forced them back into the sea with a shower of arrows. But the Vumbis opened fire with a thunderous explosion. Many men were killed and our ancestors took flight.

The notables and augurs said that the Vumbis were the original owners of the land.

Our forefathers retreated, fearing the return of the Ulungu boat.

The boat returned and the white men asked for chickens and eggs in return for cloth and pearls.

From that day to this the whites have brought us nothing but war and misery.

15

ANALYSIS OF A CRISIS: 1939–1945 REVISITED*

Fifty years after the outbreak of the war, self-justifying history is still thriving; when you examine works written in Britain, in West Germany, in the German Democratic Republic, in France, in the Soviet Union, and even in the United States, you realize that the time is not yet ripe for a definitive diagnosis of the history of the Second World War. Furthermore, only the textbook published in Spain, a country that remained neutral during that period, openly refers to the divergences that separate the historians of different nations. This comparative exercise, however, is not without its interest, for it permits us to reveal more clearly the focal points of this history. Some of them are identified below: they concern the sense of guilt arising from massacres, whether organized or not; the problem of responsibility for the outbreak of war; and the

* This chapter first appeared in *Libération* (1 September 1989) and is here republished with the author's permission.

problem of its conduct and the secret intentions of the belligerents.

WAR CRIMES

Do the examples that illustrate the different texts give us a summary of the idea each nation has of this war, or is this opinion better and more discretely expressed by silences and absences? Each nation, each institution has its family secrets which it would be shameful to disclose. But your old enemy will always do it for you.

In American works, for instance, there is not a single illustration of the bombing of Hiroshima. The manufacture of the A bomb is referred to, but nothing is said about its terrible effects. On the other hand, in the West German textbook, we are shown, next to each other, the living dead of Hiroshima, the living and the dead in the Jewish concentration camps, the tragic exodus of the Germans fleeing from the Russian invasion in 1944, and Cologne razed by the Allies – a way of making the crimes committed by each of them seem commonplace.

And conversely, in the American book, the text clearly indicates 'the number of 80 000 dead, at Hiroshima . . . and an even higher number of victims at Nagasaki', but this figure is given after the 6 million victims of the Nazi concentration camps, and without mentioning the later effects of the bombs on the people they fell on. There is a remark added: 'numerous foreign scientists collaborated on developing the bomb, particularly the anti-fascist Enrico Fermi' (Einstein is not mentioned), and the Americans also note that between the dropping of the first bomb and that of the second, the USSR declared war on Japan, a way of reminding us that, at the time, nobody condemned the Americans. The Americans skip over the reason given at the time for the dropping of the atomic bomb: that in this way, High Command would save a million American lives, the number that would have been killed if Japan had been invaded. But the West German works remind us: 'why did the United Nations not tackle this problem, any more than it did the origins of the bombing of Dresden (which caused 250 000 dead)?' – 'Did the Americans want to compare the effects of the A bomb with those of the bombs dropped on Dresden?', the Germans ask. Indeed, the bombing of Dresden in 1945 was carried out on the initiative of the British, as a reprisal for the total destruction of Coventry by the Luftwaffe in 1940: *Koventrieren* had even become the verb invented by Hermann Goering to refer to the ultimate destruction of other British cities. But those bombings are not mentioned by the German works.

Drawing up a list of war victims, the (West) Germans distinguish four categories:

1   soldiers;
2   civilian deaths caused by bombings;
3   collective (unspecified) deaths and partisans;
4   displaced persons.

Thanks to this mode of classification, in column 2, Germany and Japan appear as the countries most affected by the war and, in column 4, the Germans are the principal victims, indeed, practically the only ones. . . . In Italy, the mode of classification is different. Victims of war and victims of racial discrimination are shown next to each other. This lay-out enables one to see that it is the Italians (together with the Danes and the Bulgarians) who best protected the Jews from the Nazi terror.

The Germans do not seek to hide their responsibility in the extermination of the Jews and the Gypsies. Nonetheless, it is noteworthy that they insist on the 'secret, carefully concealed nature' of the crimes committed in the camps; whereas in fact, the British observe, at least 200 000 persons were directly concerned by this massacre and witnessed it at first hand. In fact, the

German procedure has the aim of whitewashing its society of the crime most directly associated with the Nazi rulers – that regime which German society continued to applaud, at least until defeat loomed. Only the textbook from East Germany dares, in its own way, to reject simultaneously the regime and those who supported it: adopting an internationalist point of view, *Kominternien*, it puts itself squarely in the 'anti-imperialist' camp, reduced in Germany to a handful of oppositional figures whose combats it follows against the trend. The survival of German communists, the action of anti-Nazi resistance groups such as *Rote Kapelle*, *Weisse Rose*, the role of Geman prisoners in Russia, etc., are dwelt on at length: the photographs of those unknown militants, of Sorge and Thaelmann, are shown – while the traditional images of the Germans' joyful acclaim of Hitler, which after all marked the tragic failure of the Communist Party, are ignored.

The joy of the French at the advent of Pétain is barely more evident in history books in France: there is definitely a blind spot in our official memory on this issue. To be sure, in French works, the genocide is dwelt on at length nowadays, and the role of the Vichy leaders is willingly and severely criticized; but little is said about the reactions of society at large. Another blind spot is the hostility that the Resistance sometimes encountered; those 'terrorists' were suspect, at a time when a considerable part of the population was favourable to the Americans and hostile to the Germans: but above all, people were afraid, afraid of the reprisals that the action of the Resistance could occasion. Of the Germans' acts of terror, little or nothing is said – except in France – and this fear is quite ignored: Pétain had nourished and fostered it, and for many it served as an alibi for their cowardice. This is barely spoken of in France: people prefer to discuss the collaboration, or the Resistance – De Gaulle, the communists, the French fascists, etc.

The (West) Germans also abstain from mentioning the terror

they unleashed, which left its traces throughout occupied Europe. They acknowledge, completely, the martyrdom inflicted on the Jews and say, as it were: yes, we are ashamed, but it's essentially all Hitler's fault; whereas you – who destroyed Dresden and Cologne – didn't even have our excuse, as you were living under a democracy. This is why the Germans mention neither Coventry nor the reign of terror they unleashed with the help of the Wehrmacht, the administration, the civilians – everyone.

THE ORIGINS OF THE WAR

On the origins and causes of the war, there are multiple interpretations; but only Antonio Fernandez, the author of the Spanish textbook, says and acknowledges as much. He observes that if there is a 'consensus' on Hitler's responsibility, on his expansionist militarism (we are reminded that the invasion of Poland had been decided on before the Danzig crisis and independently of it, as part of the policy of 'Lebensraum'), on the other points linked to the responsibility of the military powers there is no longer any such 'consensus'.

In West Germany (but also among certain historians in Britain), the conclusion is easily reached that the Allies' desire for peace came down to not acknowledging the iniquities of the Versailles Treaty: in particular the violation of the principle which was deemed to legitimate it, the right of peoples to self-determination. Neither in Austria (where the Parliament had wanted an *Anschluss* as early as the end of 1918) nor among the Sudetes, joined against their will to Czechoslovakia, nor in Danzig which was three-quarters German, had this right been respected. Works written in the German Federal Republic account for this iniquity by showing the Austrians who were happy, at Klagenfurt, to welcome the Wehrmacht; but they also show the very different situation in Prague, where the Czechs shook their fists as they watched the same soldiers marching in.

To account for the mechanism which led to war, the Spanish take up the model of the 'four shifts' developed by Jesus Pabon in 1946 which explains the period from the Locarno Pact (between France, Britain, Italy and Germany in 1925) to the state of war declared in 1939. The first shift was that of the French, with their attempt to form a rapprochement with the USSR; this rapprochement made Germany hostile and Poland mistrustful towards everything emerging from Paris; the second shift was the Anglo-Italian quarrel caused by the Ethiopian affair, when Britain put an end to its policy of a European balance of power and adopted the principle of 'collective security'. This led to the third shift, that of Italy, which sacrificed Austria to its rapprochement with Hitler. This was the Rome–Berlin axis. The Czech crisis was a continuation of it. The fourth shift was that of the Germans, who formed a rapprochement with the USSR in August 1939: Poland and the Baltic states were the reward for this volte-face, and war too was the result, since Britain had given its guarantee to the Polish frontiers.

This itinerary does not explain the ideological or psychological factors, even though these are essential. In Britain and the United States, people 'cling' to the vision of Churchill and Roosevelt (not that of Chamberlain and the American isolationists): it was the violations of the Versailles Treaty which were at the origin of the crisis. 'What strategy should we adopt faced with that fanatic, Hitler?' asked the Englishman Josh Brooman. In this way, an indictment is drawn up of the way France and Britain abandoned their duty; in Britain, this cowardly policy was due, according to the British, to the absence of an army, the weakness of aviation, the absolute certainty that nothing could be done to save Czechoslovakia. To be sure, there was a later change of tack, in France as well according to the British, but there was no confidence that the USSR was capable of intervening, and Poland could not be forced to accept that the Soviet army would cross its borders to ensure a second front against Hitler. The words of the Polish Prime Minister are repeated endlessly: if Poland were occupied by Germany, she would lose her freedom; if she were occupied by the Russians, she would lose her soul. 'Our negotiators with the USSR were in no hurry to finish', explains the English text: 'they travelled to the negotiations by sea . . . '. But the English textbook is not really taken in: it suggests that at bottom, the French and the British were dreaming of turning Hitler's forces against the Soviet regime. So the book publishes a Russian caricature of 1938 in which, seeing Hitler's car appear at a crossroads, two traffic agents, Daladier and Chamberlain, show him, with a smile but a certain embarrassment too, which way to go; not west but east: in the direction of Moscow.

Naturally, it is on this aspect of the French and British policy of appeasement that the Soviets insist: they show that, basically, the entire policy of Georges Bonnet and Daladier aimed at turning the aggression of German power against the USSR. That there is a certain truth in this assertion is obvious, and the French Right judged that 'alliance with the USSR means war' – and a war against the only power which could protect the West from Bolshevism. This implicit view was later clearly shown at the time of the Finland campaign of 1939: the French newspapers of the time were more anti-Soviet than anti-Nazi – to the surprise of the British themselves: 'We have declared war on Germany and not on the USSR', the British reminded the French at a council of the Allies, to such an extent was the Senate showering its congratulations on Finland. Having adopted a wait-and-see policy towards Germany, the French leaders were seized by impetuosity towards the USSR; part of this attitude resurfaced in France after the defeat.

The East Germans go much further. They conclude that the capitulation at Munich and the abandoning of Czechoslovakia were aimed at giving Hitler a chance to expand eastwards and that the negotiations with the USSR, later on, were merely a lure, a pretence. The USSR had to put an end to them for its own security, for it was threatened twice over in the summer of 1939, by Germany and by Japan – the Japanese being halted by Mongol and Soviet troops at the battle of Chalchyn Gol, which took place precisely between 20 and 31 August 1939. Hence the pact with Hitler, as Russia could not fight on two fronts. So the German-Soviet pact is here presented with purely defensive arguments, the East German textbook adopting an internationalist perspective: the pact thwarted the plan to set up a powerful anti-Soviet front and it limited the aggression to the revision of the borders of eastern Europe.

THE CONDUCT OF THE WAR

Whilst the problem of war crimes sets the German view against that of the Allies, and the problem of the origins of the war makes the Russian, Allied and German explanations irreconcilable, when it comes to the problems of strategy, the Soviet version – even more radical in the German Democratic Republic – is quite different from the western view.

The Russians have no lack of arguments to show that at every turn of the hostilities the 'imperialist camp', first led by Churchill, then by Truman and Foster Dulles, did everything to ensure that its victory over Germany and Japan would also be a victory over the USSR, with certain circles not hesitating to give priority to the struggle against Bolshevism over the struggle against Nazism. The delay in establishing a second front constitutes the cornerstone of the demonstration. The East Germans go so far as to conclude that the Normandy landings took place only to prevent the Soviets from 'liberating' the whole of Europe. The demonstration would have been more convincing if the Italian campaign, which began in July 1943, did not occupy a mere three lines of the seventy pages devoted to the Second World War. . . .

The presentation of Anglo-American policies in the Soviet textbooks is certainly more securely based than the allegations of the East Germans. They clearly show that, during the first phase of the war, just after the 'surprise' invasion of the USSR, Churchill hoped to conquer Germany by more and more intensive bombings, to bleed it white. This strategy, revealed, they claim, at the Moscow Conference of October 1941, consisted in supporting the USSR only insofar as its defeat had to be prevented. The Soviets conclude that Roosevelt and Hopkins did not show the same reluctance as the British, but they were so sceptical about the capacity of the USSR to win that they did not want to 'waste' equipment by sending it to the Russians. Or else, they tried to take advantage of the weakness of the USSR by attempting to have bases in Siberia conceded to them, should war with Japan break out.

The Russians make no bones about claiming that the battle of Moscow won during the winter of 1941–2 had the effect of stimulating, in Britain, the supporters of a second front, and encouraging and fostering the action of the resistants in occupied Europe; above all, 'the battle saved Great Britain from a German landing, if not in the British Isles, at least in Africa'.

If we refer to the decisions made at the Washington Conference, Churchill's defensive conceptions, focused on the Mediterranean, prevailed in the second half of the war over those aimed at giving effective help to the USSR. Despite a promise affirmed on 26 May 1942, arguments of a technical order led to a constant deferral of the landings in the west. According to the Soviets, the Dieppe landings, the result of the pressure of public opinion, had as sole effect (or 'sole object'?) to reassure the Germans on the inability of the Anglo-Americans to land, at least for the time being.

The Russians write that Japan was dreaming at the time of intervening against them (end of 1941), 'afraid of missing the bus when the time was already ripe'; but the resistance of the

Red Army, which did not have to move troops west during the battle for Moscow, discouraged the Japanese – already trounced a year earlier. So as to get the Japanese to intervene against the USSR, Hitler 'had to treat on equal terms with a coloured race': by the convention of 18 January 1942, Germans and Japanese mutually undertook not to sign any separate peace and they divided up their zones of operation throughout the world; Japan saw itself allocated all the lands to the east of the 70th degree of longitude east, including America; Germany and Italy, everything to the west, including America. The fleets would pass from one ocean to another as the need arose. It is highly possible that the advance of General Rommel in North Africa in spring 1942 was not unrelated to this treaty. Whether this was so or not, Japan did not make up its mind to send its forces against the USSR and, after Stalingrad, it no longer felt strong enough. This is an exaggerated interpretation, no doubt, since we know that in Japan, the circles in the navy and the business world, aware of how Japanese troops had got bogged down in China, preferred 'a strategy of profit' – towards the southern seas – to 'a strategy of loss'. But it is true that it would have lost even more now that the USSR was demonstrating its capacity for resistance.

Then came Stalingrad, the decisive turning point which forced Germany to launch almost all of its air force against the Soviet front, which, in the Russian view, explains both the British victory at El-Alamein and the easy landings in North Africa. It was also Stalingrad which triggered a crisis in the fascist clan, in Italy above all, then in the satellites of Germany, which were emboldened to make their first peace overtures; the tactic of Romania, Hungary and Finland was the same: demonstrate to the Anglo-Americans, whom they desired to negotiate with, that having fought against the USSR, the states of central Europe had basically helped to safeguard the fundamental interests of the West.

This would explain Churchill's repeated efforts, which were

in fact crowned by success, to turn the Americans away from a landing in the west and to strike in the south so as more effectively to cut off the advance of Soviet troops towards Austria and Germany. And this is where we again encounter the extreme thesis defended by the East Germans.

This version, certain details of which are reminiscent of the way the French credited themselves with victory in the 1914–18 war, is a useful corrective to the view, born during the cold war, according to which the USSR had been able to hold out, from 1941 to 1943, only thanks to Anglo-American equipment. But it still ignores essential points: the importance of Yugoslavian resistance; the ambiguous role of Stalinist policies in China, supporting Chiang Kai-Shek and not Mao Tse-Tung; and there is not a word about the hostility of the USSR towards France obtaining a zone of occupation in Germany; nor is there any mention of the times when Stalin was favourable to the partitioning of Germany. And there is nothing, of course, on the Katyn massacres, on the voluntary halt of the Soviet troops outside Warsaw so that the Germans could tranquilly massacre the inhabitants of the city who had risen in revolt. In *Kanal*, defying the censors, Wajda had admirably described this criminal duplicity: when the Poles, hidden in the sewers, try to break out so as to survive, the cannonade that has previously been heard in the distance – that of the Russians – falls silent. This silence – which cannot be censored – signifies that the Russian advance has voluntarily halted; it's a sentence of death.

For their part, western textbooks do not account, at least not enough, for a fact which was nonetheless perfectly evident to the inhabitants of occupied Europe: it was the Soviet army which broke German military power; if they mention the greatest tank battle in history, that of Kursk, won by the Russians over the Wehrmacht, the Germans omit to remind the reader of this sign of their technical inferiority. Above all, neither the West Germans nor the Allies really do justice to the two Polish resistance movements, that of the Norwegians, the Dutch, etc. Except in Italian books and those written in East Germany, insufficient appreciation is given to the sacrifice made by anti-fascists in the Italian resistance: more of them died than did Italian soldiers in North Africa or Russia.

The British, insisting on fair play, are happy to admit that they gave hardly any help to the Allies in May 1940, even if we now know that they lost more than 900 planes during the Battle of France. They emphasize the crucial importance of Dunkirk: without dwelling on the fact that, contrary to the legend that they saved 'the British first and a handful of French afterwards', they in fact rescued 123 000 French and 215 000 British, they see in this episode above all the ordeal which enabled them to 'test out' successfully their combined air-sea operations, which acted to some degree as a prelude to the victorious defence against the Germans during the Battle of Britain. As for the rest of the war, they do not exaggerate their role excessively – and they are the only ones who do not; but they too completely ignore the forces of interior resistance (in Poland, in Czechoslovakia, in Belgium, in France, etc.), confining themselves to alluding to those resistance forces abroad (de Gaulle, Sikorksi, etc.). They also ignore the Nazi terror, limiting it to the tragic example of the Jews. Nothing is said about the effect of this terror in Czechoslovakia, Poland, Russia, etc.

Is it a coincidence if the counter-history, the unofficial version, the one established by cinema directors, has been the only one to account – brilliantly – for the tragic fate of those who died obscurely, in Italy (*Paisa*), in Poland (*Kanal*) or elsewhere?

Conclusion

THE BROKEN MIRROR

The mirror has been shattered. Universal history is dead; it died from being a European mirage, which reflected Europe's own illusions as to her own destiny. The other peoples who figured in this history did so only in a transitory way when Europe chanced in their direction: Egypt, for instance, before the birth of Europe, then under Rome, and next with the Crusades or Bonaparte, Mehmet-Ali or Nasser. What is true of Egypt applies equally well to India, Armenia and the rest. Their history only counted when it crossed the path of ours.

There is a Marxist variant of this history, one which, because of its self-proclaimed scientific nature, also claimed to be universal: it was Marxian before becoming Marxist, or Marxist-Leninist, or Marxist-Leninist-Maoist. It dealt, not in eras, but in modes of production and it divided history into periods based on these lines, which were unshakably laid down, much like the statistics of regimes that patronized this kind of history, Russian and Chinese variants of which I have discussed. An extreme illustration of this position is a recent history of France published in Moscow: significantly, its third volume opens with 1917–18, as if this were somehow a new era in French history: the illusion of a single autumn, when Lenin seized power.

With such reductionist enterprises around, it is no surprise that various groups have tried to make their own history for themselves, even if it means adopting camouflage towards the victors. Consequently, victors and vanquished alike speak in the name of their own faith, church, party, trade union or homeland: Arabs, Armenians, Europeans and Indians have all constituted middle empires. The stereotypes of western history have therefore been transplanted: the Japanese sing the praises of their beautiful nature, just as does 'gentle France'; India, like Greece, claims always to have seduced her fierce conquerors. In places, the stereotype itself is altered or reversed: for instance, the Algerians and Turks glorify nomadic civilization, in contrast to the European view, and rehabilitate the Tuaregs or even Attila the Hun. India and Black Africa reject the myth of progress, and praise the equilibrium said to have existed before the European conquests.

|

Through all these epochs and cultures, history clearly stems from many different centres with their own ways of doing, forms, norms and demands. There is, first of all, 'institutional history' which dominates, because it expresses or promotes a policy, an ideology or a government. Whether it serves Christ, sultan, republic, church or even party, it is based on history in the making; like all history, it therefore evolves and constantly changes its referential system. It undergoes all kinds of metamorphosis and can accommodate all manner of writing.

Such history is based on a hierarchy of sources. At its head in all their glory come the words of the great, royal autographs and other holy texts, whether Marxist or Maoist; then, though less imposingly, come commentaries, laws, treaties, *hadith*, or statistics; and at the tail of the procession, like some humble third estate in black, march public and private documents, anonymous or named witnesses whose role is at most to confirm the miraculous doings of the rulers. Such history-from-above is embodied in institutions and, since it essentially deals with acts and decisions of a particular power, whether by official right or indirectly, it perishes when its supporting institution collapses. Armenian historians, for instance, disappeared when Armenia herself did and reappeared in the eighteenth century when an organization was born that carried the seeds of the later rebirth. Jewish historiography underwent the same silence when history treated the Jews badly, and it degenerated into mere rabbinical chronicles or predictions: it came to life again with Zionism. The same phenomenon of impoverishment existed in Shiite countries for, as B. Lewis has shown, the only element nourishing history was the list of signs announcing the Mahdi.

Still, an anti-history that is also institutional may exist parallel to that of the victors, whether church, nation, party or state. It could not of course have the same support, and survived sometimes only in oral form, or otherwise if a written culture prevailed. This buried history, the history of the defeated side, was first stated forcefully by the colonial peoples, but it appears or reappears wherever a formerly independent social group feels threatened, exploited, degraded in its identity and banished from history – thus it revives its own traditions. Chicanos, Bretons, Québécois, League of Women and all the outcasts have resurrected their daily lives and doings of the past. Or perhaps, instead, a parallel history can be constructed. One of the most fundamental characteristics of this institutional history or antihistory is that it looks to its own community's outer borders and defines itself in terms of others, whether centres of power, beliefs, nations or whatever. A further characteristic, mentioned above, is changeability, for, like history itself, it is subject to variation.

II

Societies' memories, whether individual or collective, are a second centre of history. At some times and in some particular places, this centre can be confused with the first, especially with institutional anti-history, when the group can only preserve its identity through traditions, whether oral, cultural or even alimentary. However, this centre itself is quite different in several respects from the first one.

History of this kind does not have specialist servants at its beck and call, i.e. historians. Hence it does not have to observe the customs and rules of the guild, which vary across time and place, but are at least identifiable, regulated and defined in all cases. A singularity in such history is that it is not subject to criticism; another feature is that it often confuses time, e.g. with myth and reality, especially as regards matters of origins, as with Berber tribes, the Japanese nation, or whatever group. History like this survives as autonomous and intact or perhaps incorporated elsewhere, and it has flourished despite all the denigration it may have to face in official, scholarly history. It is not transmitted in the same way as anti-history but lives side-by-side with the institutional history, which it may have been itself, in the distant past, though it has long vanished as such.

In this case, it is not the historical content that changed, but rather its status. Some of the Spanish festivals, such as *Moros y Cristianos*, some trade-fairs such as the memories of the Alsatian Jews (analysed by Raphaël) and even the celebrations of Bouvines studied by Duby all embody elements of a particular history which has a feature all its own: it is unchanging, after a certain time, but then proceeds to inexorable dissolution as the centuries go by. It is turned in on itself, not towards the outside, and is bound to crumble with time, though it stands up to the last moment, when it becomes meaningless rubble.

III

These two centres of history prevail: they mix certainty and illusion, and cannot produce a single universally-trusted scientific truth, for the versions of the past suggested, imposed or copied are different and contradictory. In these circumstances, to 'grind out' some 'universal history' from a single centre, and even more, a single institution, is an act of imposture or tyranny. It is the heart of liberty to allow several historical traditions to co-exist and even to fight it out. To ignore these histories would, however, also be illusory and absurd, because they have a reality as do all beliefs, faiths and power. To construct a history on the basis of such histories would be wrong, if that were all that was attempted. This was appreciated by the founders of the *Annales* School, Bloch, Febvre and in particular Fernand Braudel, who saw the two-fold necessity of knowing history and of putting it on new, generally experimental foundations. I myself know practitioners of such experimental history who take as their starting-point documents, figures or pictures to undertake analysis of the past. This kind of history is still incomplete and fragmentary, and cannot claim to offer a universal explanation of societies' development as a whole. It tries to be comprehensive, and even total, but it is not totalitarian. It is the future of history.

HISTORY: WHAT TEACHING METHODS FOR THE FUTURE?

For over a generation the western world has successively debated the nature and function of history as a discipline. This debate is a result of several phenomena:

1 The bankruptcy of ideology has had the effect of making

historical discourse less authoritative; quite suddenly, historical writing has appeared to be suspect in its approach, perhaps excessively indulgent towards one or another style of thinking: liberal, conservative, Marxist. Such questioning affects not only the interpretation of events ('Who caused the war of 1914–18?' or 'Was the revolution of 1917 inevitable?'), but also the very choice of 'facts' to be discussed and regarded as significant (is it more important to study wars or taxation during the reign of Louis XIV? Is it more important to study family history or international relations?, etc.).

2 The changes that the world has seen since 1945, especially decolonization, have had the effect of multiplying the various centres of historical production. Besides 'white history', which itself varies according to ideology, other perceptions and interpretations have emerged which are not Eurocentric, for example, in the Islamo-Arab world, and in the Far East, in China. Parallel to this, and in contrast to the nation-state vision of the past, many societies have also claimed their right to a place in history, and have contested the official version (Corsicans and Bretons in France, blacks in the USA). The idea that there might be a single and universally acceptable vision of history has become increasingly illusory.

3 The multiplication of forms of history, which is seen by the appearance of films, television programmes, novels or even cartoon-strips, has relativized the traditional discussion of history, previously the domain of schools and scholars alone. In the consciousness of today's societies, there is a certain telescoping of historical knowledge, the verdicts emanating from these various sources. Their multiplication has also caused some confusion in chronological structuring, in that the reader or viewer is successively assailed by Napoleon, the Vikings, and the First World War.

4 The questioning and this relativization of historical discourse have become all the more confusing because historians

themselves have for many years been attacking traditional history. This history, described as 'chronological' (i.e. based on events), is no longer seen as a final product. Rather, the narration itself must be 'deconstructed' and used as a starting-point for historical analysis. To achieve this, historians have recommended a method of defining questions, objects, objectives and problems to be solved. This implies a divorce from the old chronological history: such narratives, being a synthesis of a single society's various individual memories, are said no longer to represent the culminating point of historical work, but only a stage of this work.

Besides, it has become clear that the division of history into chronological parts, though useful for the reconstruction of what has been experienced, none the less ignores long-term historical processes such as social and economic trends, the transformations of customs and beliefs, etc.

5 Furthermore, some teachers have become conscious of these kinds of problem and have sought to understand the mechanisms of the society in which they teach history. They have been struck by the fact that their students want to understand the connections between the present and the past, and they have felt that their discipline needs to help make comprehensible the origins of our own times, i.e. to create aware and self-conscious citizens. Without such efforts, the very discipline of history would lose its significance. Such teachers have thus analysed the status and the positions of those to whom their teaching is addressed, so as to adapt their teaching to the needs and capacities of each one, according to age, social and ethnic origins, etc. A debate over the ways of teaching history has to a certain extent taken over from the acquisition of knowledge pure and simple; and in the classroom sociological enquiry has taken over from general historical knowledge. In some cases, in France, for instance, single-street histories of schoolchildren's neighbourhoods have become widespread as an extreme

response to the questioning of 'historical facts'. Consequently, students learn how to approach documents – even contemporary ones – rather than merely memorize dates and events. The result, however, is that sometimes 'children no longer know any history'.

Given this situation, the aims and objectives of the teaching of history at the end of the twentieth century should be as follows: 1 A chronological sense of the national past must be taught in any case, but so must a knowledge of the differing visions and interpretations of that past; 2 Pupils must be introduced to an understanding of other societies in order both to understand those societies and to confront those societies' visions of history with our own; 3 Historical teaching should also be aimed at an overall understanding of historical phenomena and at an evaluation of the relationship between particular problems (towns, regions, countries) and the overall course of history; 4 The teaching of history must also provide students with the capability of distinguishing between those historical vestiges which have completely died, those which have survived over the long term and those which have perhaps even survived to our day; 5 History must also give everyone the possibility of making his or her own assessment of historical and contemporary problems and of learning how to formulate questions. (For a discussion of these problems, see pp. 327ff.) A practical knowledge of social science methods – economics, demography, etc. – must thus be taught in conjunction with history. (On the use of films, see my book, *Analyse de films, analyse de sociétés*, Paris, Hachette, 1975.) In this way, progress in historical knowledge will come about not through the accumulation of knowledge of more events, but through the acquisition of a better methodology of comprehension.

BIBLIOGRAPHY

GENERAL WORKS AND WESTERN HISTORIES

Roy Preiswerk and Dominique Perrot, *Ethnocentrisme et histoire*, Paris, Anthropos, 1975.

Dominique Maingueaneau, *Les Livres d'école de la République, 1870–1914*, Paris, Sycomore, 1979.

Pierre Nora, 'Ernest Lavisse, son rôle dans la formation du sentiment national', in *Revue historique*, 1962.

Jacques Ozouf, 'Le thème du patriotisme dans les manuels scolaires', in *Le Mouvement social*, 1964.

Christian Amalvi, *Les Héros de l'histoire de France*, Paris, Phot'oeil, 1979.

Bernard Guénée, *Histoire et culture historique dans l'occident médiéval*, Paris, Ambier-Montaigne, 1980.

G. Huppert, *L'Idée de l'histoire parfaite*, Paris, Flammarion, 1973.

Historiographie de la réforme, ed. Ph. Joutard, Neuchatel, Delachaux, 1977.

Alice Gérard, *La Révolution française, mythes et interprétations*, Paris.

See also, the *Bouvines* of G. Duby (Paris, Gallimard); the study on the 'bataille de Poitiers' by E. Caprentier, *Revue historique*, 1980.

On England, see Suzanne Baudemont, *L'Histoire et sa légende dans l'école élémentaire victorienne (1862–1901)*, Paris, Klincksieck, 1980, for a comprehensive bibliography.

As for general histories see:

F. Braudel, *Ecrits sur l'histoire*, Paris, Flammarion, 1972.

P. Nora and J. Le Goff, *Faire de l'histoire*, 3 vols, Paris, Gallimard.

Aujourd'hui, l'histoire, Paris, Editions Sociales, 1972.

Dialectiques, nos 10–11 and 30; *Recherches*, no. 23.

Paul Veyne, *Comment on écrit l'histoire*, Paris, Le Seuil, 1971.

Claude Lefort, *Les formes de l'histoire*, Paris, Gallimard, 1979.

François Chatelet, *Naissance de l'histoire*, Paris, Editions de Minuit, 1962.

François Hartog, *Le miroir d'Hérodote*, Paris, Gallimard, 1980.

On cartoons: *Histoire et bandes dessinées*, Colloque international, 13640 La
     Roque.

ON NAZI GERMANY

Rainer Riemenschneider, 'L'Enseignement de l'histoire en Allemagne sous
     le IIIe Reich', *Francia, Forschungen zur westeuropaischen Geschichte*,
     1979, 7, pp. 401–28.

F. Selmeier, *Das nationalsocialistische Geschichtsbild und der Geschichtsun-
     terricht, 1935–45*, Munich, 1969.

J. Altmann, 'Movies' Role in Hitler's Conquest of German Youth',
     Hollywood Quarterly, III, 4.

Harlam Veit, *Im Schatten meiner Filme*, Siegbert Mohn V., 1966.

S. Kracauer, *From Caligari to Hitler*, Princeton, Princeton University Press,
     1948.

F. Courtade and P. Cadars, *Histoire du cinéma nazi*, Eric Losfeld, 1974.

D. S. Hull, *Film in the Third Reich*, Berkeley, University of California Press,
     1969.

R. Taylor, *Film Propaganda: Soviet Russia and Nazi Germany*, London,
     Croom Helm, 1979.

On *Kolberg* and *Unkle Kruger*, see R. Taylor; on *Le Juif Süss*, F. Garçon, 'Les
     Trois Discours du Juif Süss, *Annales*, 1979, pp. 694–721.

M.-I. Christadler, *Kriegerziehung in Jugendbuch, Literarische Mobilmachung
     in Frankreich und Deutschland vor 1914*, Dissertation, Frankfurt 1977.

See also, P. Ory, *Le petit nazi illustré*, Paris, Alabtros, 1979.

Textbooks

Grunwald-Lukes, *Von der Urzeit zur Gegenwart*, Frankfurt, 1936.

Um Volk und Reich, Erster Band, für die erste Klasse der Hauptschule,
     1944.

Volk und Führer, Deutsche Geschichtbilde für Schulen, herausgegeben von Dietrich Klagges, 1942.

Klasse 1. Erzählungen zur deutschen Geschichte.

Klasse 4. Preussen gestaltet das Reich.

Klasse 6. Von der Vorgeschichte bis zum Ende der Stauf enzeit.

BLACK AFRICA AND THE 'WHITES'' HISTORY

Textbooks

A. M. M'bow, J. Ki-zerbo, J. Devisse, *Du VIIe au XVIe siècle*, Paris, Hatier, 1978.

L'Afrique et le reste du monde du XVIIIe au début du XIXe siècle, La traite négrière, Paris, Hatier, 1978.

Legacy of the Past, a History for Transvaal Schools, STD III, by A. N. Boyce and W. A. Harrison, Johannesburg, 1967.

Other works

Histoire générale de l'Afrique Noire, de Madagascar et des archipels, Paris, Presses Universitaires de France, 2 vols, 1970.

Claude Perrot, 'Le temps dans la société agni', *Annales*, 1972.

Denise Bouche, *L'Enseignement dans les territoires française de l'Afrique Noire, 1817–1920*, Dissertation, Lille, 1975.

Denise Bouche, 'Autrefois notre pays s'appelait la Gaule', *C.E.A.*, 290, 1968.

Afrika Zamani, African Historical Review, Yaoundé.

L'Esclavage en Afrique précoloniale, seventeen studies presented by Claude Meillassoux, Paris, Maspero, 1975.

Conversion to Islam, ed. N. Levtzion, New York, Holmes & Meier, 1975. See the five articles on Black Africa by J. Knappert, O. Fahey, M. Last, N. Levtzion, H. F. Fischer.

J. Afan, *Le Mythe de Chaka dans la littérature négro-africaine*, thèse de 3e cycle, Paris III, 1974.

Guy Hennebelle and C. Ruelle, *Cinéastes d'Afrique Noire*, Cinem-Action, Paris.

Camara Laye, *Le Maître de parole*, Paris, Plon, 1978.

Jacques Chevrier, *Littérature nègre*, Paris, A. Colin.

Georges Balandier, *Afrique ambiguë*, Paris, 1963.

W. R. Randles, *Le Royaume du Congo*, Paris, 1974.

Godo-Godo, review of the University of Abidjan.

M. S. Bamba, *Bas-Bandama précolonial*, thèse de 3e cycle, Paris I, 1978.

Documents in South African Education, ed B. Rose and R. Turner, Johannesburg, A. Donker, 1975.

Marianne Cornevin, *L'Apartheid: pouvoir et falsification historique*, Unesco, Paris, 1979.

Credo Mutwa, *My People*, London, Blond, 1969.

See also the article by J. Devisse, 'Comment enseigner l'histoire en Afrique?' in *Recherche-Pédagogie-Culture*, 46, 1980, pp. 34–44; I. B. Kaké and E. M'bokolo, *Histoire générale de l'Afrique*, Paris, ABC, 1979.

INDIA

On teaching methods

Education and Politics in India, Studies in Organization, Society and Policy, ed. S. Hoeber Rudolph and L. I. Rudolph, Harvard, Harvard University Press, 1972.

G. Gautam, *Crisis in the Temples of Learning*, New Delhi, 1972.

N. Khagendra, *Education and the Nation, an Indian Perspective*, Calcutta, University of Calcutta, 1970.

Monographs and textbooks

Childrens' History of India, Delhi, Publications Division, 1960.

Modern India, a Textbook of History for Secondary Schools, Delhi, National Council for Secondary Schools, 1971.

In Memory of Gandhiji, Delhi, Indian Illustrated Classics (cartoon).

On historiography

Historians of India, Pakistan and India, ed. C. H. Philips, London, Oxford University Press, 1961.

H. Mukhia, *Historians and Historiography During the Reign of Akbar*, New Delhi, Vikas Publishing House, 1976.

C. Markovits, 'Le nationalisme indien', *Annales*, 1979, pp. 512–25.

Works referred to

L. Dumont, *Homo hierarchicus, essai sur le système des castes*, Paris, Gallimard, 1966.

D. Dubuisson, 'Trois thèses sur le Ramayana', *Annales*, 1979, pp. 464–90.

J. Pouchepadass, *L'Inde au XXe siècle*, Paris, Presses Universitaires de France, 1975.

J. Pouchepadass, 'Terre, pouvoir et marché, la naissance du marché foncier dans la plaine du Gange', *Annales*, 1979, pp. 490–12.

K. Panikkar, *Histoire de l'Inde*, Paris, Fayard, 1958.

A. and D. Thorner, 'Le monde indien', *Le monde depuis 1945*, vol. 2, Paris, Presses Universitaires de France, 1973.

A. Ahmad, *Studies in Islam in the Indian Environment*, Oxford, Clarendon Press, 1964.

W. Brown, 'La vache sacrée dans la religion indoue', *Annales*, 1964, pp. 643–65.

M. Brown, *The United States and India, Bangladesh, Pakistan*, Cambridge, Cambridge University Press, 1972.

K. S. Shelvankar, 'Le sous-développement outre-mer, le cas de l'Inde', *Annales*, 1962, pp. 517–33.

On the English view of India

A. J. Greenberger, *The British Image of India*, London, Oxford University Press, 1969.

J. Richards, *Visions of Yesterday*, London, Routledge & Kegan Paul, 1973 (on cinema).

ISLAMIC COUNTRIES

Historians of the Middle East, ed. B. Lewis and P. Holt, London, Oxford University Press, 1962.

P. Fargues, *Aspects idéologiques de l'enseigenent de l'histoire en egypte*, EPHE 6e section, 1973.

J. Szyliowicz, *Education and Modernization in the Middle East*, New York, Cornell University Press, 1973.

A. Miquel, *Géographie humaine du monde musulman*, Paris, Mourton, 1975.

C. Cahen, *L'Islam des origines au début de l'empire ottoman*, Paris, Bordas, 1970.

D. and J. Sourdel, *La Civilisation de l'Islam classique*, Paris, Arthaud, 1968.

F. Rosenthal, *A History of Moslem Historiography*, Leiden, E. J. Brill, 1968.

W. Fishchel, 'Ibd Khaldun: on the Bible, Judaism and the Jews', *Ignace Goldziher Memorial Volume*, part II, pp. 147–71, Jerusalem, 1958.

Abdallah Laroui, *L'Histoire du Maghreb*, Paris, Maspero, 1970.

L. Valensi, *Fellahs tunisiens, l'économie rurale et la vie des campagnes aux XVIIIe et XIXe siècles*, Paris, Mouton, 1977.

Ahmed Abdesselem, *Les Historiens tunisiens des XVIIe, XVIIIe, XIXe siècles, essai d'histoire culturelle*, Paris, Klincksieck, 1973.

O. Carré, *La Légitimation islamique des socialismes arabes*, Paris, 1979.

M. Rodinson, *Mahomet*, Paris, Club Français du Wure, 1962; see also his *Les Arabes*, Paris, 1979.

J. Berque and J. P. Charnay, *De l'imperialisme à la décolonisation*, Paris, 1965.

B. Lewis, *Race and Colour in Islamic Countries*, London, Harper & Row, 1971.

A. Abdel-malek, *Idéologie et renaissance nationale, l'Egypte moderne*, Paris.

P. Holt, A. Lampton and B. Lewis, *The Cambridge History of Islam*, vol. 1, Cambridge, 1970. See especially the articles by B. Spuler, H. Inalcik, R. Savory.

'Islamic Education in the Traditional and State Systems in Northern Nigeria', *Conflict and Harmony in Education in Tropical Africa*, ed. G. Brown and M. Hiskett, London, 1975.

A. Tibawi, *Islamic Education: Its Tradition and Modernization into the Arab National Systems*, London, Luzac, 1972.

B. Lewis, *History Remembered, Recovered, Invented*, Princeton, Princeton University Press, 1975.

H. Inalcik, 'Some Remarks on the Study of History in Islamic Countries', *Middle East Journal*, 6, 1953, pp. 551–55.

E. Sivan, 'Modern Arab Historiography of the Crusades', *Asian and African Studies*, 8, 1972, pp. 109–49.

S. Shafak, 'Patriotic Poetry in Modern Iran', *Middle East Journal*, 6, 1952.

Mohammed El Nowaiki, 'Al-sh'ir al-jadid', *Texas Quarterly*, 1966, pp. 148–57.

W. Barthold, *Histoire des Turcs d'Asie centrale*, Paris, 1945.

Textbooks

Al Tarikh Al Arabi Al Islami, Al Saff Al Khames Al Abtiday, Baghdad, 2 vols (in Arabic).

Al Mawad Elegtemaeia, Cairo, 1976, 2 vols (in Arabic).

Noamen Zakari and J. Riviou, *Nasser*, Paris, Publications de la Presse Africaine Associée, 1973 (in Arabic).

F. Talberg, *From Cyrus to the Pahlavi*; approved by the Pahlavi University, Tehran, 1976 (in Persian).

I. Kafesoglu and A. Delorman, *Tarih, Lise I, II, III*, Istanbul, 1976 (in Turkish).

USSR AND ARMENIA

School textbooks

M. Mel'nikov and A. Kalasnikova, *Novyi put'*, Moscow, 1930.

S. Alekseev and V. Karcov, *Istoria SSSR*, Moscow, 1956.

M. Neckina and P. Leibengrub, *Istoria SSSR*, Moscow, 1972.

A. V. Efimov, *Novaya Istoria*, Moscow, 1977.

I. Berxin and I. Fedosov, *Istoria SSSR*, Moscow, 1975.

Histoire de l'URSS, Éditions en Langues Etrangères, Moscow, 1962.

See also the children's publication on Lenin by A. Kononov, I. Grinstein, S. Mikalkov, N. Krupskaya, etc.

Historiography

A. Mazour, *Modern Russian Historiography*, New York, 1958.

A. Mazour, *The Writing of History in the Soviet Union*, Stamford, 1971.

C. Black (ed.), *Rewriting Russian History*, New York, 1956, in essential, particularly the studies by Cyril Black and Yaresh.

J. Keep (ed.), *Contemporary History in the Soviet Mirror*, London, 1964; see especially the essays by M. Fainsod, B. Wolfe and L. Schapiro.

J. Keep, 'The Rehabilitation of M. Pokrovsky', *Revolution and Politics in Russia*, ed. A. and J. Rabinowitch, Indiana Press, 1972.

G. Enteen, *The Soviet Scholar-Bureaucrat, M. N. Pokrovskii and The Society of Marxist Historians*, Pennsylvania State University Press, 1978.

Further works referred to

B. Delmaire, 'L'historiographie soviétique et le problème des origines russes', *Annales*, 1974, pp. 151–66.

R. Portal, *Russes et Ukrainiens*, Paris, Flammarion, 1970.

S. Blanc, *Pierre le Grand*, Paris, Presses Universitaires de France, 1974.

G. Enteen, T. Gorm and C. Kern, *Soviet Historians and the Study of Russian Imperialism*, Pennsylvania State University Press, 1979.

M. Ferro, *La Révolution de 1917*, Paris, Aubier, 1976; English translation, *October 1917, A Social History of the Russian Revolution*, translated by N. Stone, London, Routledge & Kegan Paul, 1980.

Armenia

V. Parsamjan, S. Pogosjan and S. Arjutunjan, *Istorija Armjanskogo Naroda*, Erivan, 1967.

Histoire de mes ancêtres, ed. the Mekhitarist Fathers, Venice, 1979.

A. Aharonian, *Les Anciennes croyances arméniennes*, Dissertation, Lausanne, Editions, paranthèses, 1912.

Contes et légendes arméniennes, adapted by C. Dar Melkonian, Beirut, 1964.

Contes, légendes et épopées populaires d'Arménie, presented and translated by F. Maclaire, Paris, 1928.

H. Toumanian, *Oeuvres choisies*, translated by J. Champenois, Moscow, 1969.

M. Arlem, *Embarquement pour l'Ararat*, Paris, Gallimard, 1977.

See also the histories of Islam and the Caucasus referred to elsewhere in this bibliography, as well as the histories of Armenia, especially:

H. Pasdermadjian, *Histoire de l'Arménie, depuis les origines jusqu'au traité de Lausanne*, Paris, Librairie Samuelian, 1949.

G. Dédéyan, 'Les Arméniens dans l'empire byzantin', *Histoire de l'Arménie*, Toulouse, Privat, 1981.

A. Ter Minassian, 'Le mouvement révolutionnaire arménien', *Cahiers du monde russe et soviétique*, 3 and 4, 1974.

M. Matossian, *The Impact of Soviet Policies in Armenia*, Leiden, 1962.

G. Mouradian, 'L'Arménie soviétique et la diaspora arménienne après la 2e guerre mondiale', *Cahiers du monde russe et soviétique*, 1978.

V. N. Dadrian, 'Nationalism in Soviet Armenia: A Case-Study of Ethno-centrism', *Nationalism in the USSR and Eastern Europe in the Era of Brezhnev and Kosygin*, ed. G. W. Simmonds, Detroit, University of Detroit Press, 1977, pp. 202–59.

On Greece, see:

S. Mappa, *Conscience et idéologie de la nation chez les Grecs*, Paris, EH ESS, 1981.

POLAND

School textbooks and pedagogical works

G. Markowski, *Historia, dla Klasy V*, Warsaw, 1975.

M. Rosman, *Historia, dla Klasy VI*, Warsaw, 1976.

A. Kersten and T. Lefkowski, *Historia, dla Klasy II*, PZWS, 1968.

M. Siuchninski, *An Illustrated History of Poland*, Warsaw, Interpress, 1979.

A. Bornholtzowa and W. Moszczenska, *Nauczanie historii w szkole a nauka historyczna*, Warsaw, 1964.

A. Rogowska, 'Okres przygotowawsczy w nauczaniu histoii w klasie V'.

A. Rogowska, 'Jak zaznajamialam uczniov z przeszloscia wlanego regionu na lekcjach historii w klasie V'.

J. Olszewski, 'Realizacja zadan wychowawczyck na lekcjach histoii w szkole podstawowej'.

In *O Lepsze winiki w pracy nauczyciela historii*, Zbior odczytow pedgagogicznich, pod redakcja Krystyny Kuligowskiej, Warsaw, 1968.

Works referred to

A. Gieysztor et al. *History of Poland*, Warsaw, 1968.

R. F. Leslie (ed.), *The History of Poland since 1863*, Cambridge, Cambridge University Press, 1980.

M. K. Dziewanowski, *The Communist Party of Poland*, Cambridge, 1959.

M. Malowist, 'Un essai d'histoire comparée, les mouvements d'expansion en Europe aux XVe et XVIe siècles', *Annales*, 1962, pp. 923–30.

M. Serejski, 'Les origines et le sort des mots civilisation et culture en Pologne', *Annales*, 1962, pp. 1107–17.

A. Wyczanski, 'L'économie du domaine nobiliaire moyem en Pologne 1500–1580', *Annales*, 1963, pp. 81–88.

I. Gieysztorowa, 'Guerre et répression en Masovie aux XVIe et XVIIe siècles', *Annales*, 1958, pp. 651–69.

C. Bobinska, 'L'action sociale des paysans polonais', *Annales*, 1965, pp. 528–37.

K. Pomian, 'Religion et identité culturelle, le cas polonais', *Groupe de travail sur l'Europe centrale et orientale, Bulletin d'information*, 3, 1980, pp. 77–89.

CHINA AND JAPAN

W. G. Beasley and E. G. Pulleybank, *Historians of China and Japan*, Oxford, Oxford University Press, 1961.

Etienne Balazs, *Chinese Bureaucracy and Civilization: Variations On a Theme*, New Haven, Conn., Yale University Press, 1964.

R. J. Smith and R. K. Beardsley, *Japanese Culture: Its Characteristics and Developments*, London, Methuen, 1963. See in particular the studies of E. Ishida, I. Yawata, N. Egami, S. Ono.

Cyrus H. Peake, *Nationalism and Education in Modern China*, Columbia University Press, 1932. Comprehensive appendices.

Roberta Martin, 'The Socialization of Children in China and in Taiwan: An Analysis of Elementary Textbooks', *China Quarterly*, 62, 1975.

Ridley Charles, Paul Godwin and Dennis Doolin, *The Making of a Model Citizen in Communist China*, Stanford, Calif., Stanford University Press, 1971.

Albert Feuerwerker (ed.), *History in Communist China*, Massachusetts Institute of Technology Press, 1968. Essential reading, particularly the studies of J. R. Levenson, H. Willhelm, James P. Harrison, H. L. Boorman.

J. A. Cuadrado, *The Socialization Goals of the Two Chinas as Manifested in the Editorial Content of Children's Primers*, under the direction of S. Levinson, 1978.

A Textbook for Secondary-School History Teachers, Shanghai, Shanghai Education Centre, 1958–59 (in Chinese).

Zhingguo Lishi, for secondary schools, vol. 1, Peking, Institute for Popular Education, 1956 (in Chinese).

Lishi, vol. 1, National Institute for Education, Taiwan, 1972 (in Chinese). See also the cartoons, in Chinese, on *Lenin, The Underground War*.

Pierre-François Souyri, *Comment enseignait-on l'histoire aux jeunes japonnais avant la guerre*, Mémoire de maîtrise, Paris X, 1977 (under the supervision of M. Vie).

Harold Wray, *Changes and Continuity in the Japanese Image of the Kokutai and Attitudes and Roles Towards the Outside World*, Dissertation, University of Manoa, Hawaii, 1971.

P. A. Narasimba Murthy, *The Rise of Modern Nationalism in Japan: A Historical Study of the Role of Education in the Making of Modern Japan*, New Delhi, 1973.

Ivan Morris, *The Nobility of Failure: Tragic Heroes in the Liberty of Japan*, London, 1975.

John Caiger, 'Ienage Saburo and the First Post-War Japanese History Textbook', *Modern Asian Studies*, 3, Jan. 1969.

Tanaka Hajime, 'Les contradictions de l'enseignement au Japan', *Recherches internationales*, 28, 1961.

Delphine Baudry-Weulersse, *Récits de l'histoire du Japan*, Paris, Fernand Nathan, 1975.

Keenleyside, H. Llewellyn and A. F. Thomas, *History of Japanese Education and the Present Education System*, Tokyo, 1937.

Alan Silver, *The Samurai Film*, South Brunswick and New York, Cranbury, 1977.

Histoire nationale élémentaire, re-edited 1903–43 with several additions and alterations, translated into French by Pierre Souryi from the original of 1938.

The Illustrated Encyclopedia: The History of Japan, under the supervision of Professor Kodama at the University of Gakushin, Shogakukan, 1973 (in Japanese).

USA

Frances Fitzgerald, *America Revised: History Schoolbooks in the Twentieth Century*, Atlantic, Little-Brown, 1979; has a comprehensive bibliography of school textbooks.

Diane Ravitch, *The Great School Wars, New York City, 1805–1973, A History of Public Schools as Battle-Field of Social Change*, New York, Basic Books, 1974.

Pierre Nora, 'Le fardeau de l'histoire aux Etats-Unis', *Mélanges Pierre Renouvin*, Paris, Presses Universitaires de France, 1966, pp. 51–74.

Marcus Cunliffe and Robin Winks (eds.), *Pastmasters, Some Essays in American History*, Harper Torchers, 1975.

R. A. Stockheim (ed.), *The Historian and the Climate of Opinion*, Reading, Mass., Addison-Wesley, 1969.

Robert L. Belknap and Richard Kuhns, *Tradition and Innovation: A General Education and the Reintegration of the University*, A Columbia Report, Columbia, 1977.

Jack Spears, *The Civil War on the Screen*, South Brunswick and New York, 1977.

Randall M. Miller (ed.), *Ethnic Images in American Film and Television*, Philadelphia, The Balch Institute, 1978.

Thomas Cripps, *Black Films on Genre*, Bloomington, Indiana University Press, 1978.

Jeffrey Richards, *Visons of Yesterday*, London, Routledge & Kegan Paul, 1973.

History of the United States of America, with a brief account of some of the principal empires and states of ancient and modern times for the use of schools and families, by a citizen of Massachusetts, Keene, New Hampshire, published by John Prentiss, 1823.

John Clark, *History of the United States, Prepared especially for schools*, J. Brothers, 1869.

B. A. Hathaway, *1001 Questions and Answers on U.S. History*, Cleveland, 1882.

F. Friedl and H. N. Drewry, *America Is*, Columbia, Ohio, C. E. Merrill, 1978.

MEXICO AND THE CARIBBEAN

Apart from the classical studies of J. Soustelle, N. Wachtel, etc., on Mexico, Indian America and the viewpoint of the defeated, see:

Josefina Vasquez de Knauth, *Nacionalismo y educación en México*, Colegio de México, 1970.

Giorgio Bini et al., *Los libros de texto en América Latina*, Mexico, Editorial Nueva Imagen, 1977.

W. Moquin and C. Van Doren, *A Documentary History of the Mexican Americans*, Praeger, Bantam Books, 1971.

Ciencias Sociales, tercer grado, Mexico, 1973.

Ciencias Sociales, quinto grado, Mexico, 1972.

I. Appendini y S. Zavala, *Historia Universal Moderna y Contemporanea*, 1968.

J. M. Siso Martinez and H. Bartoli, *Historia de mi patria*, tercer grado, Caracas, 1968.

Sheila Duncker, *A Visual History of the West Indies*, London, Evans Brothers 1965–75.

E. H. Carter, G. W. Digby and R. N. Murray, *Our Heritage: History of the West Indian Peoples*, London, Nelson & Sons (18 further editions up to 1975).

AUSTRALIAN ABORIGINES AND THE PACIFIC*

A. P. Elkin, *Les Aborigènes australiens*, Paris, Gallimard, 1962.

The Aboriginal Children's History of Australia, written and illustrated by Australia's Aboriginal children, Melbourne, 1977.

C. M. Tatz, 'Education for Aborigines: Present Facilities and Needs', *Critical Writings on Australian Education*, ed. S. D. Urso, Sydney, J. Wyley.

A Child's History of Hawaii, written and illustrated by Hawaiian children, originated and directed by E. J. Mcgrath jr, Honolulu, 1973.

Gavan Daws, *Shoal of Time: A History of the Hawaian Islands*, London, Macmillan, 1968.

David Maclagan, *La création et ses mythes*, Paris, Le Seuil.

* Since this work was written in 1979, the situation has changed in Australia, at least in the way history is taught: the sense of guilt towards the Aborigines has replaced the ignorance that had reigned hitherto. There are now innumerable works on this theme, all published over the past few years. Among the best is: Robert Hughes, *The Fatal Shore: a History of the Transportation of Convicts to Australia, 1788–1868*, London, Pan Books and Collins, 1987. Its content goes far beyond what the title suggests.

INDEX

Routledge Classics
Get inside a great mind

The French Revolution
From its origins to 1793
Georges Lefebvre

'This is more than a history of the French Revolution. . . . in its class, whether synthesis or textbook, this is one of the best ever produced.'
A. J. P. Taylor

Internationally renowned as the greatest authority on the French Revolution, Georges Lefebvre combined impeccable scholarship with a lively writing style. His masterly overview of the history of the French Revolution has taken its rightful place as the definitive account. In tracing the web of intrigues and influences that transpired as the French Revolution, Lefebvre illuminates the fundamentals of historical interpretation and, at the same time, tells a story that will compel every reader.

Hb: 0–415–25547–3   Pb: 0–415–25393–4

The Century of Revolution
1603–1714
Christopher Hill

'This is a book we have all been waiting for – a history of the political and religious conflicts of the seventeenth century that is rooted in reality; and it will be a long, long time before this brilliantly lucid and forcefully argued book is bettered.'
J. H. Plumb, The Spectator

This is an extraordinary book by *the* historian of the English Civil War. In a revolutionary history of a revolutionary time Christopher Hill succeeds magnificently in showing what these dramatic events felt like to those who lived through them. Provocatively argued, this essential history gives a picture of events that had a colossal impact throughout the world and which continue to resonate today.

Hb: 0–415–26738–2   Pb: 0–415–26739–0

For these and other classic titles from Routledge, visit
www.routledgeclassics.com